BROADCASTING &

COMMUNICATIONS

ARCO PUBLISHING COMPANY, INC. New York

Edited by Linda Fox

Published in 1978 by Arco Publishing Company, Inc.,
219 Park Avenue South, New York, NY 10003.

© Marshall Cavendish Limited 1978
All rights reserved

Printed in Great Britain

Library of Congress Cataloging in Publication Data

Main entry under title:

Broadcasting and communications.

"This material has previously appeared in the publication 'How it works'."
SUMMARY: Describes the inner workings of the equipment used in telecommunications and broadcasting.
1. Telecommunication – Juvenile literature.
2. Broadcasting – Juvenile literature. [1. Telecommunication. 2. Broadcasting] I. Fox, Linda.
II. How it works.
TK5102.4.B76   384   77-28273
ISBN 0-668-04557-4

This publication is not to be sold outside of the United States of America.

INTRODUCTION

When Morse perfected his first crude telegraph apparatus he did not imagine that his invention would rapidly revolutionize communications for the public, governments, newspapers and shipping throughout the world. Passing messages by electricity was at first an exciting novelty; indeed, none of the early pioneers could have envisaged the day when not only speech but moving pictures would be transmitted by electricity and without wires. They would certainly have been incredulous at the idea that information might one day be passed through outer space to and from space probes, across distances measured in millions rather than hundreds of miles.

It is fair to say that the vast majority of switchboard and telex operators, as well as telephone and television engineers, have very little idea of how the apparatus really works beyond the basic knowledge needed to operate or repair it. We tend to be awed by the sheer complexity of modern communications technology, an understandable attitude in view of the mystique and jargon that surrounds much of it.

Broadcasting and Communications not only elucidates the technical aspects of communications technology; it also sets the inventions in their historical context and examines the exciting and challenging prospects that the future holds in store. It is for everyone who is interested in the exciting developments which have already changed our daily lives for the better or for worse, and which will undoubtedly impinge on every aspect of our lives more and more. We are living in an era of rapid change, and if we do not examine the implications of the new communications technology closely we will only have ourselves to blame if the 'wired society' of the future is not to our liking.

CONTENTS

COMMUNICATIONS IN WAR, COMMERCE AND EDUCATION

NEW FRONTIERS

INDEX

EARLY COMMUNICATIONS SYSTEMS

BEFORE THE TELEGRAPH

Communications today is a complex and sophisticated subject. And we tend to take so much of our modern communications network for granted: we can pick up the phone and dial a friend across the Atlantic direct, or watch a television programme transmitted live from the other side of the world via a communications satellite. The advances in technology of the past 100 years particularly have been staggering, and it is no exaggeration to say that the world has 'shrunk' as a result, nor can it be denied that the mass media of radio and television have contributed to higher levels of general education and an awareness of political events throughout the world never before possible. Yet the basic principles of telecommunications systems are not hard to understand, and the story of the inventors and the development of their first crude apparatus to the standards we know today is fascinating and often surprising.

Over many centuries men have practised the art of passing messages without having to carry them by hand or word of mouth, by means of signal fires, tom-toms, heliographs (mirrors reflecting light from the sun in a series of flashes) and church bells. These, of course, are primitive signalling methods, limited in their range and not able to carry complex messages. Yet some were surprisingly effective. In 1558, for example, chains of warning beacons were set up all over England, and most of the country knew of the arrival of the Spanish Armada within a day or two of its appearance in the English Channel. Mail services of one kind or another have existed since the birth of civilization, the most famous perhaps being America's Pony Express, which was put out of business in 1861 by the advent of the telegraph. The printed word—in the form of ballads and broadsheets, or newspapers in more modern times—remained the mainstay of information and the general dissemination of news and ideas until the age of broadcasting. Newspapers remain vital in the communications network, since a newspaper can provide a wide selection of national or local news items and information, far more than any news bulletin. But the development of industrialized modern societies demanded better communications, able to pass messages quickly and accurately over great distances.

Semaphore
About the beginning of the nineteenth century it seemed that semaphore was the best system available. The brothers Ignace and Claude Chappe developed a line of semaphore stations between Paris and Lille in 1794 for passing official information. Their system was based on a semaphore machine with a beam about 12 ft (3.5 m) long with pivoted arms or extensions at both ends. This beam was itself centrally pivoted at the top of a mast and by means of ropes, pulleys and counterweights could indicate 36 different signs. The crew consisted of three men: one with a telescope announced the signs from the sending station and observed that the next station was repeating them correctly, the second manned the winches to make the signs and the

third man wrote down the message and told the second man what to send. Each sign took 20 seconds: 4 seconds to make and 16 seconds to allow it to be read and understood. A contemporary British system was the shutter telegraph developed by the Admiralty in 1795 which used six separately controlled discs pivoted on a frame instead of arms. This proved less clear than the French semaphore—the system was in any case much dependent on dry weather and good visibility. A new system consisting of two arms pivoted on the top of a post was adopted by the Admiralty and introduced into the Fleet in 1816. Lines of semaphore signalling stations were built in strategic positions. A time signal was passed daily from the Royal Observatory in Greenwich to Whitehall and on down the Portsmouth

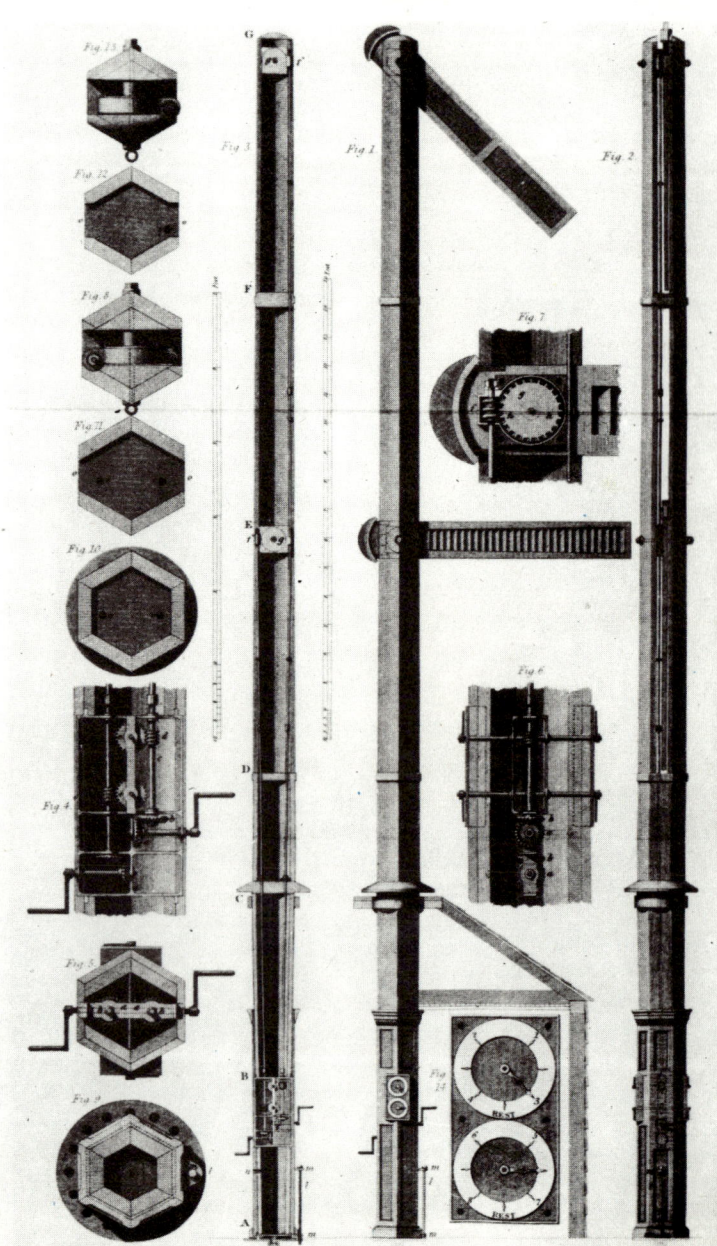

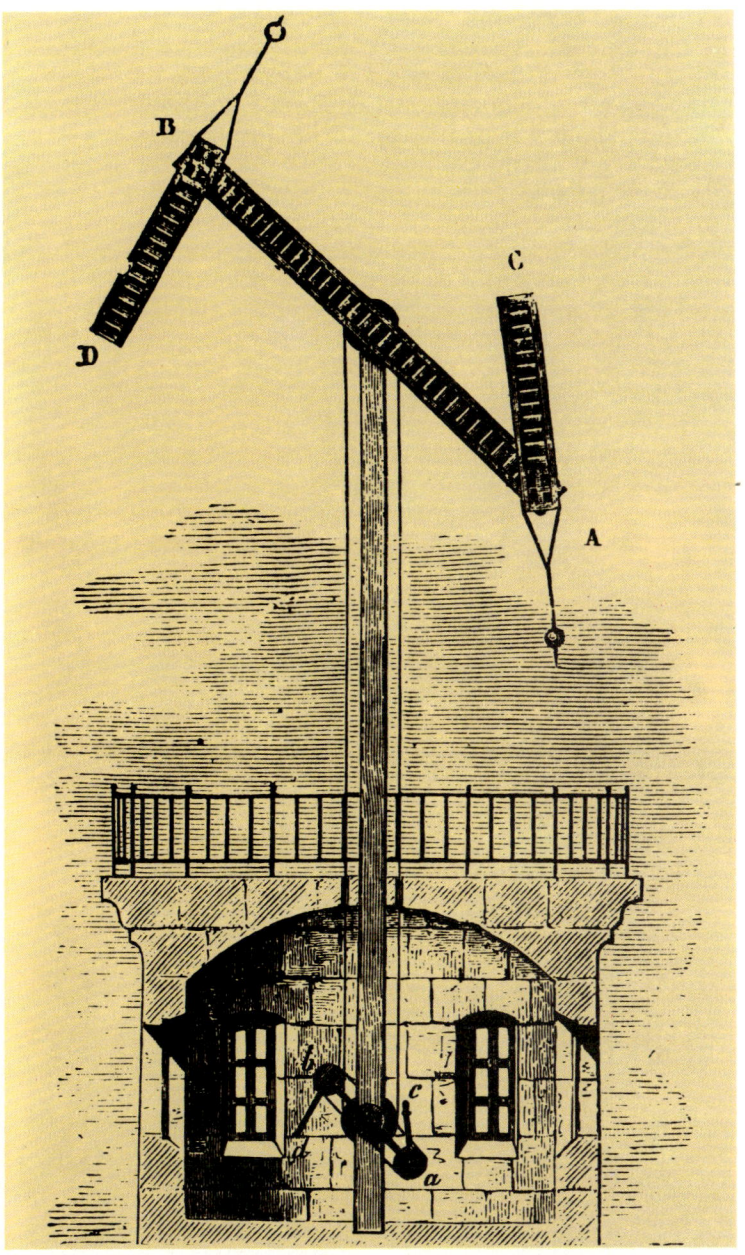

line—this was a distance of 68 miles (109 km) and went through fifteen stations in a time of 45 seconds. The last message on this line was sent on 31 December 1847. The advent of the electric telegraph had rendered the semaphore stations obsolete.

One or two of the buildings remain today and many points of high land on maps marked 'Telegraph Hill' are in fact semaphore sites. Nevertheless, the semaphore system continued to be used by both Army and Navy, and naval signal ratings had to be proficient in sending and reading semaphore messages by hand flags at the rate of 15 to 20 words a minute. Nowadays semaphore has been replaced by morse code signalled with flags.

Far left: Sir Home Popham's semaphore machine, 1816. The two arms were controlled by gears and rods. A separate display showed the operator the arm positions on connected dials. Left: sectional view of a telegraph tower using Chappe's semaphore system. The signs were operated by means of ropes, pulleys and counterweights. Top: the British army using a captive balloon fitted with a semaphore system. This was used as an observation post from which information was signalled to the ground. Above: a semaphore tower at the Battery at the entrance to Portsmouth harbour (about 1830). This was at the end of the Whitehall to Portsmouth line. Semaphore was the most highly developed system for passing official information, military information and time signals.

9

ELECTRIC MESSENGERS

Even while the lines of sempahore stations were being built, the early 19th century experimenters were showing that electricity could travel along a wire, apparently instantaneously. The French Abbé Nollet, a monk and physicist, demonstrated this most convincingly as far back as the early eighteenth century. Two hundred Carthusian monks, holding lengths of iron wire, formed a circle 1.5 km (about a mile) in diameter, and all felt the shock simultaneously when the good Abbé connected them up to an electrostatic generator. We are not told what happened to the monks, but the speed of an electrical transmission had been clearly demonstrated. So while the semaphore systems, the mail coaches and the messengers on horseback continued to carry the growing volume of military and commercial messages, experiments continued in an effort to find a practical means of using electricity to carry information along a wire—the search for an electric telegraph.

When human beings communicate by speech or writing they use an auditory or visual *code:* the information is transformed into sounds or written words, which are 'de-coded' by the recipient. With the discovery of electricity it had occurred to many people that an electric current could be varied so as to convey a signal from one person to another along a wire.

Some of the early schemes were certainly ingenious. In 1795, Don Francisco Salva of Barcelona proposed using the discharge of Leyden jars, which store electrostatic charges, to give electric shocks to the operator on the receiving end! Development of a more practical system had to await the invention of the electric battery by Luigi Galvani and Alessandro Volta to free the system from the caprices of electrostatic charges. Soon the growth of the railway systems (the first public railway was opened in England in 1830) was to stimulate the demand for an electric telegraph. In other countries, particularly the United States where the distances involved were so much vaster, some such system became imperative. This was the only way to signal ahead of a train, which travelled in any weather and at night faster than a rider could gallop to warn of its approach. It is important to remember that the necessary knowledge was accumulated over a long period of time by the scientists of many countries: the battery, for instance, to generate a continuous electric current, use of copper in place of iron wire, and the development of electromagnets to detect a current by deflecting a compass needle. By 1830 the essential elements of telegraphy were all there, awaiting the innovative genius of the pioneers to pull the threads together and construct a viable communication system—the electric telegraph.

Cooke and Wheatstone

Above all it was the work of two Englishmen and two Americans who formed partnerships in their respective countries which led to the two major telegraph systems. In England, William Cooke and Charles Wheatstone designed first a five-needle telegraph (1837) then a two-needle telegraph (1839) for use on the railways. The five-needle system worked by using two needles at a time (out of five) to point to letters of the alphabet arranged on a diamond-shaped lattice. Although this did not demand a great deal of operating skill, it required five wires to connect it to the other end of the circuit (plus one wire as the return conductor). The two needle system reduced this to two wires at the cost of a more complicated operating procedure, but with trained operators this system could achieve a rate of working of up to 22 words per minute. This system was adopted extensively by the railways and by 1852 there were some 4000 miles of telegraph lines in use in the United Kingdom.

It was soon appreciated that electrical telegraphy could be usefully applied to other matters than simple railways. Public interest and excitement in this rapid means of communication were aroused by the capture of a murderer in 1845. John Tawell had killed a woman

Bottom left: Bright's Bell telegraph receiver. The bells are powered by a battery at the receiver but controlled via a solenoid by the signal voltage. The two bells, of different pitch, provide a binary code like the Morse system of dots and dashes, and which bell is sounded depends on the voltage polarity of the signal. Left: the two-needle telegraph. The handles turn a barrel switch which connects the battery either way round to the line. The number and direction of the needle deflections indicates the character. Below: a Morse telegraph receiver.

Samuel Morse

Samuel Finley Breese Morse invented a telegraph apparatus, sent the first telegraph signal in the United States, and devised the Morse code, still used for certain kinds of cable transmission. Like Thomas Edison, he had an intuitive mind rather than great scientific originality; like Robert Fulton, he was a painter as well as an inventor.

Morse was born in Charlestown, Massachusetts. His father was a controversial clergyman who wrote some of the first American books on geography. After graduating from Yale in 1810, Morse received his parents' reluctant permission to pursue a career as an artist, and sailed for England to study painting. Encouraged by his success there, he returned to Boston to set up a studio, hoping to make a living painting historical scenes. The only kind of paintings Americans wanted to buy, however, were portraits, and there were not many commissions even for those. For some years Morse made a precarious living at portraiture.

Between 1825 and 1828, Morse's wife, his mother and his father died. Together with his difficulty making a living as an artist, this was the beginning of a difficult period in his life. In 1829 he sailed for Europe, where he was influenced by some of the stranger political currents of the time in France and Italy. On his return trip in 1832, one of his fellow passengers demonstrated some electrical apparatus, and Morse suddenly became consumed with the idea of transmitting intelligence instantaneously by means of electricity. He outlined in his notebook the three basic elements of a telegraphy system: a sending apparatus to transmit by opening and closing a circuit; a receiving device operated by an electromagnet to record signals as dots and spaces on a strip of paper moved by clockwork; and a code. As he developed his idea, he realized that the code could be read by ear as well as recorded; he added dashes to the dots and spaces and his initial clumsy sending device became a simple sounding key. He did not consider his invention as a means of sending news and personal messages around the world, but as a means of transmitting important and secret government messages; accordingly he spent some time devising a secret code which required the use of a large decoding book.

In 1836 Morse showed his telegraph to his colleague Leonard Dunnell Gale. Morse's difficulty was that his knowledge of electromagnetics was several years out of date; he could not make his apparatus work more than 40 feet (12m) from his battery. Morse and Gale experimented with wire wound around Gale's lecture room until they could send messages as far as ten miles (16km). Morse then worked out a system of electromagnetic relays which would enable messages to be sent as far as desired. Cooke and Wheatstone were developing similar ideas in England, but a document filed in 1837 shows that the American research was original. In that year Morse reluctantly gave up painting and sailed for Europe again. He was honoured by scientists in France, but he could not obtain patents there or in England.

In 1843, a busy US Congress in a hurry to adjourn voted money for a telegraph experiment. A line was set up between Washington DC and nearby Baltimore; on 24 May 1844, Morse sent the famous message 'What hath God wrought' from the Supreme Court Room; it was returned accurately and a short conversation followed. Morse wanted to sell the invention outright to the government and go back to painting, but the postmaster general at the time thought that the telegraph would never pay.

Morse finally became a wealthy man because of his American patents. He was lucky in his choice of financial advisor, despite litigation with his enemies and his own capacity for being swindled. European governments showered him with honours, but continued to deny him patents. He was married twice and had eight children; his youngest son graduated from Yale more than sixty years after he died. When Morse died in 1872, the Congress paid tribute to his technical achievement but ignored his painting; since an exhibition of his painting in New York in 1932, he has been given credit for his influence on American art as well as his achievement in communications.

Left: receiver of Morse printing telegraph, c 1890.

THE WONDER of the AGE !!
INSTANTANEOUS COMMUNICATION.

Under the special Patronage of Her Majesty & H.R.H. Prince Albert.

THE GALVANIC AND ELECTRO-MAGNETIC
TELEGRAPHS,
ON THE
GT. WESTERN RAILWAY.

May be seen in constant operation, daily, (Sundays excepted) from 9 till 8, at the
TELEGRAPH OFFICE, LONDON TERMINUS, PADDINGTON
AND TELEGRAPH COTTAGE, SLOUGH STATION.

An Exhibition admitted by its numerous Visitors to be the most interesting and ATTRACTIVE of any in this great Metropolis. In the list of visitors are the illustrious names of several of the Crowned Heads of Europe, and nearly the whole of the Nobility of England.

"This Exhibition, which has so much excited Public attention of late, is well worthy a visit from all who love to see the wonders of science."—MORNING POST.

The Electric Telegraph is unlimited in the nature and extent of its communications; by its extraordinary agency a person in London could converse with another at New York, or at any other place however distant, as easily and nearly as rapidly as if both parties were in the same room. Questions proposed by Visitors will be asked by means of this Apparatus, and answers thereto will instantaneously be returned by a person 20 Miles off, who will also, at their request, ring a bell or fire a cannon, in an incredibly short space of time, after the signal for his doing so has been given.

The Electric Fluid travels at the rate of 280,000 Miles per Second.

By its powerful agency Murderers have been apprehended, (as in the late case of Tawell,)—Thieves detected; and lastly, which is of no little importance, the timely assistance of Medical aid has been procured in cases which otherwise would have proved fatal.

The great national importance of this wonderful invention is so well known that any further allusion here to its merits would be superfluous.

N.B. Despatches sent to and fro with the most confiding secrecy. Messengers in constant attendance, so that communications received by Telegraph, would be forwarded, if required, to any part of London, Windsor, Eton, &c.
ADMISSION ONE SHILLING.
T. HOME, *Licensee.*

Nurton, Printer, 48, Church St. Portman Market.

---

in her cottage in Slough, but was seen boarding a train for London. The information was telegraphed ahead of the train and the murderer was arrested, and subsequently tried and hanged. The public awareness of the great speed of the telegraph, stimulated by this sensation, soon led to the establishment of public telegram services and extensive press networks.

Wheatstone continued to design new forms of telegraph instrument. He favoured the letter-indicating form of device which did not require the operator to learn a pre-arranged code. In 1848 he built what he called the 'ABC' telegraph. This required only a single wire (with earth return), which energized an electromagnet to release a clockwork escapement. The clockwork rotated a disc to display the letters of the alphabet behind a small window, the disc pausing briefly at the required letters. In 1841 Wheatstone modified this design to directly print the characters on a paper strip by replacing the letter disc with a typewheel. Strangely, though, there was no demand for a printing telegraph at that time and the idea lay dormant for more than half a century. Wheatstone's final ABC telegraph design of 1858 was a beautifully executed 'repeater' which used an early form of servomechanism to position a pointer on the repeater dial (on top of the instrument). This design was in use for many years, even as late as 1920.

Morse Code

By 1835 Samuel Morse in America had constructed his first model telegraph, which used an electromagnet to deflect a pendulum carrying a pen, thus marking a strip of paper. He is said to have used part of an artist's easel to construct the frame, but the device did not work well. The famous Joseph Henry helped to improve Morse's knowledge of electromagnetism and, with the help of a young mechanic Alfred Vail who joined him in partnership, Morse developed an improved design which could receive signals at a distance of three miles (about 5 km).

This and the following developments of Morse and Vail moved the pen towards or away from the paper, and in place of Morse's original zig-zag recording drew *dots* and *dashes* on the paper tape.

Obviously an essential element in the use of such a system is the prearranged code by which the combinations of dots and dashes were assigned to letters and numerals. Just as Vail had helped redesign the original Morse recorder, he similarly improved the original Morse proposals for coding the messages. Visiting a local printer he noted the ratios of the numbers of different typefaces. He found 12,000 Es, 9000 Ts, 8000 As and so on down to 200 Zs—the least frequently used letter in the English alphabet. The famous Morse code allocated the simplest patterns of dots and dashes to the most frequently used characters to simplify its application.

As in Europe, once the benefits of electric telegraphy were appreciated by government, railways and newspapers, there was an explosive growth in its use. By 1866 the Western Union Telegraph Company had

some 75,000 miles of telegraph line in use.

In time it became appreciated that skilled operators could 'read' morse receptions by listening to the sound of the electromagnets without having to see the dots and dashes inked on paper tape. This led to the simplest of all electric telegraph systems which needed only a morse key, battery, line and *sounder*. The sounder is simply an electromagnet of which the *armature*, when it is attracted to the electromagnet, hits a stop and thus makes a click. Speeds of about 20 words per minute were usually obtained with morse equipment (one word is taken as having an average of five characters) and speeds of 30 to 35 words a minute could be achieved by experts.

Since it used simple equipment and only one wire to carry the signal, the morse system became the most widely used telegraph system in the world. It crossed the Atlantic and gradually ousted the Wheatstone ABC system. Wheatstone himself designed a system of

machines to increase the speed of operation.

The paper tape system

The Wheatstone automatic morse system introduced the idea of punched paper tape. This provided a means by which a message could be stored, then transmitted by a high speed transmitter which read the holes in the tape. The system designed by Wheatstone could transmit at speeds up to 600 words per minute, though the transmission line usually limited operation to much lower speeds. The punched tape was originally produced on a small machine called a 'stick perforator' which perforated the dots, dashes and spaces when the operator struck one of three plungers with rubber-tipped mallets. The tape (or 'slip' as it was generally known) was then transferred to a transmitter. Obviously several operators were needed to keep one high speed transmitter busy.

At the receiving end, the electromagnet moved an inked roller against the tape to produce the dots and

dashes. Later, by about 1915, a further range of machines designed by Creed in England and Kleinschmidt in America allowed typewriter style keyboard operation for perforating the tape and the reperforator machine, which punched a tape on reception instead of inking it. The latter development was especially useful since the reperforated tape could be used to retransmit the message on another circuit for onward transmission.

The reperforated tape could also be used by a morse printing machine which read the perforations and printed plain language characters on to a gummed paper tape. This was then stuck down on to the message forms for final delivery and the laborious manual transcription of telegrams was thus avoided.

This type of system, with a typewriter keyboard perforator, an automatic transmitter, and at the receiving end a reperforator and a tape printer, represented the highest point of development of the morse telegraph system for general message work. The morse coded equipment was rapidly overtaken from the 1930s by teleprinter equipment which had the advantage of the five unit teleprinter code and could be made much more compact while providing a direct keyboard input and page printout. But this was not the end of morse telegraphy.

Electric telegraphy, and more especially radio telegraphy using morse code, is still in use today and will probably still be in use for the foreseeable future. It still has the advantage of using the simplest possible equipment and, owing to the remarkable perception of the human ear, it has the advantage of being able to pass messages over transmission channels which are too noisy or faint to carry speech or even teleprinter signals. If you switch on a radio, the chatter of hand morse or the warble of automatic morse all across the dial can still be heard. Radio telegraphy remains invaluable to shipping, and the simple portable equipment makes it of use in many other situations even today.

TELEPRINTER AND TELEX

Teleprinters are the modern descendants of the early Wheatstone and Morse telegraph systems, and of the pioneering work of such men as Frederick G. Creed. As we have seen, it was Creed who developed the reperforator and tape printer which accepted the received message tape and decoded it into plain language printed characters on paper tape.

Creed's system formed the embryo teleprinter system of today, but the first teleprinter, as we know it, came from the United States—the Morkrum Teletype machine. This machine operated on a five unit start-stop signalling code and was a direct printer. It recorded messages directly from the incoming line signals, instead of from tape. The morse code cycle length was variable, whereas the length of the five unit code was fixed, making it much easier to handle the machine.

To enable an increasing world-wide population of teleprinters to contact each other, *telex*, a separate public exchange network, was introduced to provide standard communications facilities on a circuit switching basis. At the end of 1974 the telex network had over 700,000 subscribers world wide, and was growing at the rate of 14.7% per annum.

Telex operates in much the same way as the telephone network. Subscribers rent teleprinters from the Post Office and pay call charges dependent on the distance concerned and the duration of the call, as with the telephone. It is similar to the automatic telephone network in that the operator can dial directly the number of the subscriber to whom the message is addressed. Since there is no audible response from the switching equipment, a call button illuminates, indicating when to dial, and because there is no necessity for the operator to be present at the other end, the exchange equipment automatically generates a signal known as 'Who are You' in the addressed machine. This results in a responding signal, the 'Answer-back' of the called machine, being printed on the calling teleprinter, thus confirming the correct connection

The operator now transmits the message from the keyboard which normally follows the standard QWERTYUIOP typewriter layouts and may have three or four rows of keys. In the latter case, the numerals and punctuation marks are separated on to individual keys.

Coding

Each key depression is encoded into a five level binary code which is transmitted as a series of negative and positive electrical signals referred to as 'marks' and 'spaces' respectively. The cost has been internationally agreed by the CCITT (International Consultative Committee on Telegraphs and Telephones) to permit international working even with machines made by different manufacturers. It is known as the CCITT No. 2 alphabet, and is used by all national administrations for their internal teleprinter networks as well as for international working.

The five units create $2^5 = 32$ combinations, which is

insufficient for all requirements, so six of the combinations are used as function controls (such as the shift control) and the capacity of the code is thereby extended to 52 useful characters by allocating two interpretations to each of the remaining 26 combinations. For example, all combinations following a *letter shift* character will be printed as letters until the shift is changed by the transmission of a *figure shift*, and so the combination representing an 'E' following a letter shift will represent a '3' when it follows a figure shift. The receiving teleprinter decodes the signals and activates the printing mechanism, which can take several forms such as a type basket, like a typewriter, or a dot matrix printing head.

The message is normally printed on a continuous roll of paper by both transmitting and receiving teleprinters almost simultaneously. Six copies may be obtained by using interleaved carbons or by one of the several carbonless processes available. The transmitted message is often printed in red to differentiate it from the message received.

There are two standard speeds of transmission—50 bauds or $66\frac{2}{3}$ words per minute (six characters being the average per word), and 75 bauds or 100 words per minute. The baud rate is the maximum number of one-unit elements (marks or spaces) transmitted per second. Higher speeds are possible on suitable circuits; on these, transmission is usually made from pre-recorded paper tapes.

On completion of the message the operator gives an 'end of message' sign. If a reply is required an 'invitation to reply' sign is also sent. At the completion of the dialogue, line-feed and run-out keys are depressed to clear the message by about 10 line feeds (line spaces) beyond the paper tear-off position. The operator then disconnects from the line by holding down the 'clear' button until the lamp goes out, and then tears off the

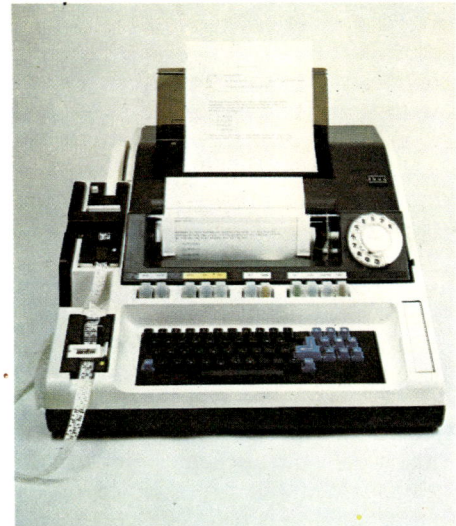

Far left: the punched tape reader from a modern teleprinter. Left: an early automatic printing telegraph. This is an illustration from 'Electricity in the Service of Man' by R. Wormell, 1896.

message for the recipient.

Punched tape

Many teleprinters are equipped with paper tape punches and readers. The tape is $\frac{11}{16}$ inch (1.75 cm) wide and is usually made of parchmentized paper, which is a special type of paper treated with sulphuric acid to make the fibres swell and containing short fibres which enable it to be cut cleanly.

When the tape is punched the same five unit code is used. A hole is punched for each mark element of a character, so a letter-shift (in which all the elements are marks) appears as a row of five holes across the tape with a sprocket hole between the numbers two and three. The sprocket holes are used to feed the tape through the tape reader.

The operator can prepare punched messages, again from the keyboard, for transmission at high speed later, either individually or as a stored collection. There are several advantages for the operator, as the message can be prepared without transmitting anything on the exchange circuit (the machine is said to be operating on 'local'), any mistakes that may have been introduced can be corrected, and then the tape reader can be used to transmit the tape at the most opportune time. On the later generation of teleprinters a tape can even be prepared while the machine is transmitting a message on-line, thus giving the skilled operator even more flexibility in the handling of messages.

combination numbers		5	4	channels 3	2	1	letters
1	–				●	●	A
2	?	●	●			●	B
3	:		●	●	●		C
4	who are you		●			●	D
5	3					●	E
6			●	●		●	F
7	optionals	●	●		●		G
8		●		●			H
9	8			●	●		I
10	bell		●		●	●	J
11	(		●	●	●	●	K
12	)	●			●		L
13	.	●	●	●			M
14	,		●	●			N
15	9	●	●				O
16	0	●		●	●		P
17	1	●		●	●	●	Q
18	4		●		●		R
19	'			●		●	S
20	5	●					T
21	7			●	●	●	U
22	=	●	●	●	●		V
23	2	●			●	●	W
24	/	●	●	●		●	X
25	6	●		●		●	Y
26	+	●				●	Z
27	carriage return		●				
28	line feed				●		
29	letters	●	●	●	●	●	
30	figures	●	●		●	●	
31	space			●			
32	all space						

feed holes

Top: a modern teleprinter. Above: the international 5-unit CCITT-2 teleprinter code showing the holes which are punched in paper tape to represent alphabetical and numeric characters, symbols and machine control codes such as carriage return and line feed.

THE TELEPHONE

Alexander Graham Bell himself gave the following definition of the principle of telephone transmission: 'If I could make a current of electricity vary in intensity precisely as the air varies in density during the production of sound, I should be able to transmit speech telegraphically'. Bell transmitted the sound of a twanging clock spring by wire in 1875, and it was from these early experiments that today's world-wide network of over 300 million telephones grew up.

Early telephoning was done over a single iron wire connecting two telephones, with an earthed grounded return circuit (that is, using the earth as the return conductor). In the USA and in the UK development was bedevilled by a plethora of private telephone companies rushing to set up non-interconnecting systems, often using incompatible equipment. In Britain the Postmaster General, in 1880, won a lawsuit giving him rights to 'acquire, maintain and operate' telephones, while private companies were allowed to operate under licence from the Government, the licences expiring in 1911. Thus the companies, which were largely American owned, held the patents needed to build up a good service, but lacked the incentive to develop services under the threat of a Post Office takeover. Growth was slow until 1912, when the Post Office took over the National Telephone Company and began working towards a compatible national network.

Engineering developments had not been standing still. Edison invented the carbon granule transmitter (or microphone), which is still used in most telephones today, and Ericsson combined the receiver and handset in the same instrument.

The UK public telephone system today consists basically of a large number of single telephones unevenly distributed throughout the country, each one connected to a switching centre, called a telephone exchange. Each exchange has lines to other exchanges and also a suitably positioned main switching centre—which has access to all other main switching centres in the system.

Although the shape of the telephone instrument has varied greatly over the years, the principles involved have remained constant. It contains a device to change sound waves into electrical waves, and also devices to reverse the process, to call the exchange, to indicate the required number, and to attract the subscriber's attention.

Transmitter and receiver

Sound waves are changed into electrical waves by a carbon granule transmitter. This consists of a thin metal disc—the diaphragm—and a box containing particles of carbon which are in light contact with the centre of the diaphragm. Sound waves cause the diaphragm to vibrate, which produces changes of pressure on the carbon granules with a corresponding change in the overall resistance through the granules. An electric current is passed through the carbon, and each change in pressure produces a similar change in

the flow of current.

The receiver, which reverses the process, is a metal diaphragm held tightly around its circumference very close to the two poles of an electromagnet. When a changing current passes through the electromagnet coils, the pull on the diaphragm varies accordingly. The diaphragm thus vibrates, and completes the process of converting the current changes back into sound waves.

The problem inherent in Bell's early telephones was that the changes in resistance of the carbon granule transmitter with changes in sound pressure were significantly smaller than the overall resistance of the wires connecting it to the exchange. Consequently ,the varying 'signal' current component was inherently small—a problem which was exacerbated the longer the connecting wires. Edison overcame this using a matching network consisting essentially of a transformer. The

Below left: a typical telephone handset. The two wires connecting this to the exchange handle both the speech signals and the pulses necessary to control the exchange switching equipment.

Below right: a modern pushbutton telephone. The caller keys in the required number as fast as he likes. Integrated circuits can store an 18 digit number and transmit it at a suitable speed.

circuit permits direct (DC) current to flow through the transmitter (necessary for its operation) while boosting the signal component, which is superimposed on this. This essential device is used in all modern telephones.

Signalling the exchange

Direct electrical current, supplied from a battery at the exchange, is used for signalling between the subscriber and the exchange. A circuit is completed between caller and exchange when the receiver is lifted, which closes a small set of contacts. In early manual systems, before the advent of automatic exchanges, the operator's attention was obtained by turning the handle of a hand generator which lit a lamp, rang a bell or operated an indicator at the exchange. The hand generator was also used to indicate the end of the conversation, this being achieved in modern telephones by simply replacing the receiver and separating the circuit contacts.

A dial is used to send the required number of signal pulses to the automatic processing equipment. The function of the dial is to interrupt the subscriber-exchange circuit a number of times corresponding to the figure dialled. As the dial spins back from the finger stop a toothed pulse wheel—attached to a common spindle—operates a pulse contact unit. There are 10 interruptions when 'O' is dialled. The return speed of the figure plate—and consequently the rate at which the pulses occur—is controlled by a centifrugal type of governor which is incorporated in to the dial mechanism.

In many countries, a variety of push button telephones have been developed to replace dial phones. Different approaches are used, but in general, tiny electronic circuits, oscillators and—in some types—silicon chip number storage units (needed to retain the numbers while an electromechanical exchange—which

Alexander Graham Bell

Alexander Bell was born in Edinburgh, into a family that was keenly interested in the study of sound. His grandfather, also Alexander Bell (1790-1865), was an actor who became concerned with clear pronunciation, so that his words could be plainly distinguished by all his audience. After perfecting his own speech, he went to teach elocution in London. His son Alexander Melville Bell (1819-1905) studied how the lips, tongue, mouth, throat and breath work together to form words. He drew pictures of how the mouth formed different sounds, and from this devised a pictorial code called *visible speech* which was used to teach the deaf and dumb to speak.

The third Alexander in the family, who called himself Graham to avoid confusion, was educated by his mother, who was an artist and musician, before he went to high school. It was said that he could manipulate his pet dog's throat to turn its growls into speech-like sounds. From the age of 16, Graham taught elocution, and in 1865 he conceived the idea of transmitting speech electrically. This idea came after reading Herman Helmholtz's book *The Sensations of Tone*, which taught him the principles and theory of sound.

In 1867 Graham Bell went to assist his father in his school of elocution in London, and in his spare time studied anatomy and physiology at University College, London. His brothers both died of tuberculosis and Graham was also showing signs of the disease. In 1870 his father decided to move what remained of the family to the cold, dry climate of Canada. Graham's health quickly improved after they set up home in Ontario, and the immediate acceptance of the visible speech system by North American instructors of the deaf ensured the family's success. Before the Bells arrived, few people had attempted to teach the deaf how to speak.

Graham went to Boston to set up a speech training school, where his patience and kindness with children became as renowned as the visible speech system. In 1873, he was appointed professor of vocal physiology at Boston University. While at Boston he met a wealthy American lawyer whose daughter had become deaf in childhood. He taught the girl, and the two became so attached that they married. The girl's father became one of Graham's financial backers.

Graham Bell had seen queues of people waiting at telegraph offices in Boston for a free line, and he devised a method for sending as many as six or eight telegraph messages along the same line. This method, called the harmonic telegraph, was patented in 1874. It worked by sending several different tones along the same wire, each of which could be interrupted by a morse key. But there were problems in the system, largely due to the difficulty of accurately tuning each receiver, and while solving these Bell realized how sound waves in the air could be made to vary the strength of an electric current in a wire. This was the breakthrough he needed for the telephone.

At the Massachusetts Institute of Technology, Graham Bell had found a device called a phonautograph. This had a mouthpiece in front of a stretched membrane, which had a bristle attached. Sound waves from speech made the membrane vibrate, and the bristle drew a pattern of the sound on smoked glass. From a study of how the human ear used the same

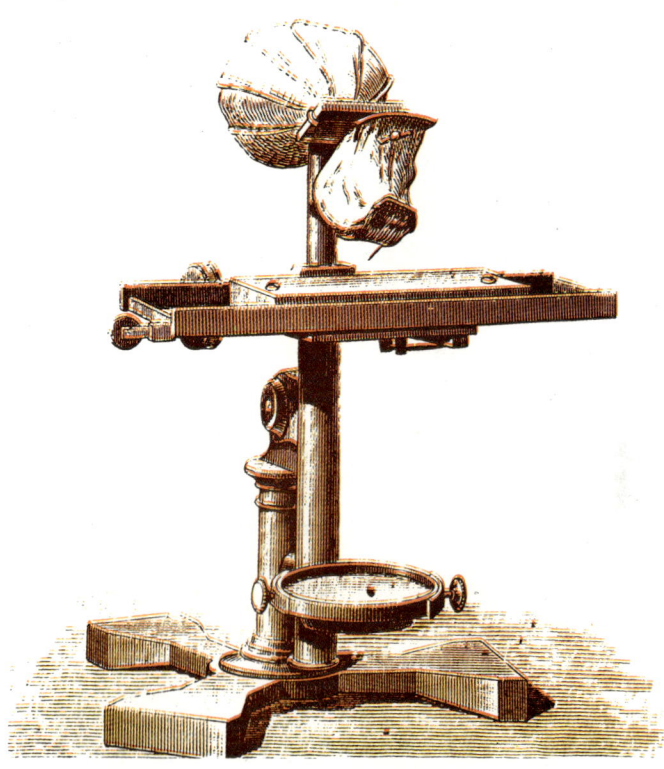

Top: when the telephone was invented, many people disbelieved Bell's claim that men in different cities would one day be able to converse as if face to face. But in 1892 he proved his point by making the first telephone call from New York to Chicago. He was a prolific inventor, but it is for the telephone that he is best remembered today.

Above: the phonautograph, which used a membrane and stylus to produce patterns of sound on smoked glass. The membrane's action was modelled on that of the human ear. This device, in the Massachusetts Institute of Technology, was one of Bell's inspirations for the microphone which is an essential component of the telephone apparatus.

*Below: Bell's liquid
transmitter which, on
10 March 1876, first
transmitted speech over
wires. Sound vibrations
changed the depth of a rod
on water, so varying the
electrical resistance.*

*Bottom: Graham Bell's
lectures, like this one at
Salem, Mass., in 1877,
were illustrated with
lantern slides and practical
demonstrations. The
blackboard illustrations
depict sound waves.*

principle, Bell learned how to make a microphone and a simple receiver that would translate a varying current back into sound. Bell's patent for the telephone was granted in 1876, while he was still experimenting to perfect the system.

On March 10 that year, while setting up his equipment, he accidentally spilled battery acid on his trousers and automatically called out to his assistant: 'Mr. Watson, come here—I want you'. Watson was waiting at the other end of the telephone circuit on another floor of the same building—but he heard the message the first words transmitted by telephone.

The telephone was exhibited in Philadelphia that same year, and impressed many leading scientists. The Brazilian emperor picked up the telephone and said in amazement: 'It talks!' Bell's fame was from then on ensured, and he set up the Bell Telephone Company to exploit his invention. By the end of 1876, telephone conversations between New York and Boston were possible. Despite legal battles over his patent, which was contested by Elisha Gray among others, the courts upheld Bell's claim to priority every time.

In 1880, Bell was awarded the Volta prize of 50,000 francs by the French government, and he used this to set up a laboratory in Washington, DC. There he made the staggering advance of using selenium crystals to transmit sound waves by means of a beam of light. This was the first true 'wireless' transmission, and anticipated many later developments in electronics.

At his new laboratory, Bell and his assistants produced the graphophone, an improvement on Edison's phonograph, which used wax records, both cylindrical and disc-shaped. With money from these patents, Bell set up the Volta Bureau for research into deafness. He never forgot his original calling of teaching the deaf.

In 1881, as President James A Garfield lay mortally wounded by an assassin's bullet, Bell invented a locator to detect metal objects in the body. But it was unable to save the President, because the metal of his bedsprings spoiled the readings. The next yeat Bell became an American citizen and set up a laboratory on Cape Breton island, Nova Scotia. His fertile mind was fascinated by the idea of flight, and he designed and built man-carrying kites as

well as a vertical take off propeller, which anticipated the helicopter rotor. Bell supported the aviation work of Samuel Langley, and formed the Aerial Experimental Association, whose members included the aviation pioneer Glenn Curtiss.

Bell's ingenuity and range of interest knew no bounds. When his study in Washington became too hot, he rigged up an air cooling system—the forerunner of air conditioning. Bell worked on sheep breeding for 30 years in an attempt to produce more lambs each season, and his work is continued to this day. He was a founder of the National Geographic Society, and also set up the learned journal *Science*.

Bell's interest in flight led him to examine the possibility of getting a flying machine airborne from water. He began to investigate hydrofoil boats, whose underwater foils provide lift in the same way as an aircraft's wings. Although he never succeeded in making a seaplane, Bell saw how the speed of a boat could be improved by lifting its hull out of the water, and with his assistant Casey Baldwin produced the HD-4, then the fastest boat in the world—in 1918 it reached a top speed of over 70 miles per hour (112 km/h).

But many of Bell's ideas were too advanced for the available technology. In his lifetime, the one invention that did have radical social consequences was the telephone. Bell participated in the opening of the first transcontinental telephone line in 1915. From the east coast he again commanded his old assistant, who was on the west coast: 'Mr. Watson, come here—I want you'. His invention, which at first had linked two rooms, now linked a nation—and before long it was to link the world.

is much slower—goes through its line selection processes) replace the dial and pulse contact units.

The final main component of a telephone is the bell or tone-caller. Both are operated by an alternating current from the exchange. A bell is operated by a pivoted armature with a hammer-end rocking in sympathy with the alternating current passing through two adjacent electromagnet coils. The 'warbler' type of telephone uses an oscillator circuit with amplifier and small speaker.

Distribution systems

Originally all telephones were connected to the exchange by bare copper, bronze, or galvanized iron wires carried on insulators fixed to poles. Overhead wires have numerous disadvantages: the effects of the weather necessitate using strong wires many times larger than is needed just to carry the current, and overhead wires are exposed to inductive action from nearby high voltage equipment and from atmospheric electricity. They are also unsightly and expensive.

Nowadays little overhead wiring is installed. Current practice is to use large, multi-pair cables running underground from the exchange. The cables have either paper or polyethylene insulation around aluminium or cadmium copper conductors. The cables may be sheathed in lead or polyethylene covered, and may have from one to 4800 pairs of wires in them.

The large cables split into successively smaller cables, culminating in distribution points. From these, single pair cables run to the subscribers' telephones. In areas where the telephone density is high, the distribution points are poles fed by an underground cable carrying, usually, 10 to 15 pairs of wires; overhead wires radiate from the top of the pole. These wires may be either a bare cadmium-copper alloy or drop wires, that is, a pair of copper-plated steel conductors insulated with PVC. In other areas each telephone is served directly by a one-pair underground cable from the distribution point.

Exchanges

The major cables run underground into exchanges and are terminated on distribution frames which split the cables into their component pairs of wires, for connection to the exchange equipment. Each national telephone system varies in its details, though most exchanges in developed countries are now automatic—Britain, for example, has no manual exchanges. At manual exchanges the telephone wires are connected to switchboards. By means of cords with plugs at each end, the operator can link any two telephone circuits together. She is alerted by a warning light, illuminated when the circuit is completed by the caller lifting his receiver.

The first important step in replacing the operator was the invention in 1889 of an electromechanical selector switch by Almon B. Strowger, a Kansas City undertaker. He conceived the idea of a many-position switch at the exchange, operated by pulses produced

Above: the cross connection frames in the Bahrain telephone exchange. Every telephone has its own pair of wires into the exchange and can be connected to any other telephone or exchange. Right: telephones are connected either directly to a local exchange or via a private exchange. Local exchanges are designed to suit local conditions and may vary in size from 600 to 20,000 subscribers. Long distance telephone links combine up to 2700 conversations in one coaxial cable using multiplexing equipment or can be transmitted over a microwave system. When a caller lifts his handset in a Strowger system, a uniselector finds a free first selector. The first digit dialled connects this to a free second selector, and so on until the required telephone number is obtained. Far right: the telephone microphone and speakers are of a simple and sturdy construction which has changed little in essence since Bell perfected the carbon granule transmitter and learned to convert electrical signals back into sound waves.

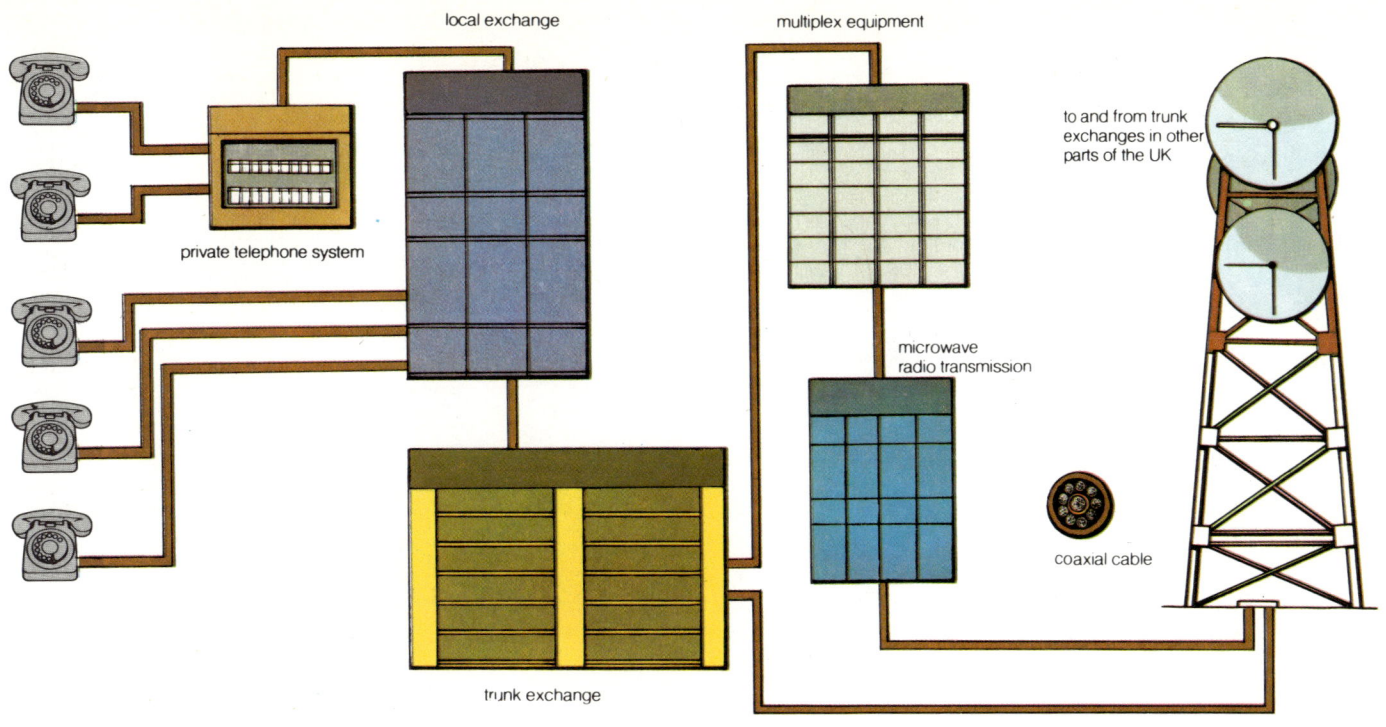

local exchange

multiplex equipment

private telephone system

microwave
radio transmission

to and from trunk
exchanges in other
parts of the UK

coaxial cable

trunk exchange

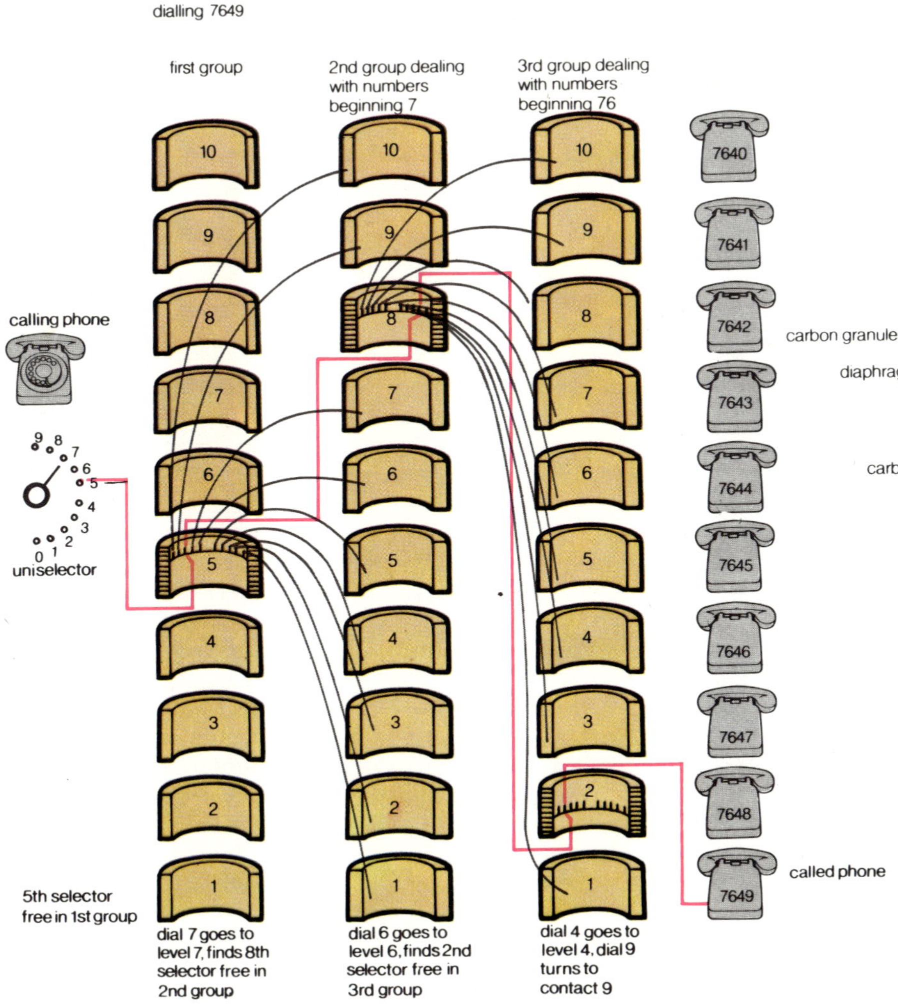

dialling 7649

first group

2nd group dealing
with numbers
beginning 7

3rd group dealing
with numbers
beginning 76

calling phone

uniselector

5th selector
free in 1st group

dial 7 goes to
level 7, finds 8th
selector free in
2nd group

dial 6 goes to
level 6, finds 2nd
selector free in
3rd group

dial 4 goes to
level 4, dial 9
turns to
contact 9

7640
7641
7642
7643
7644
7645
7646
7647
7648
7649 called phone

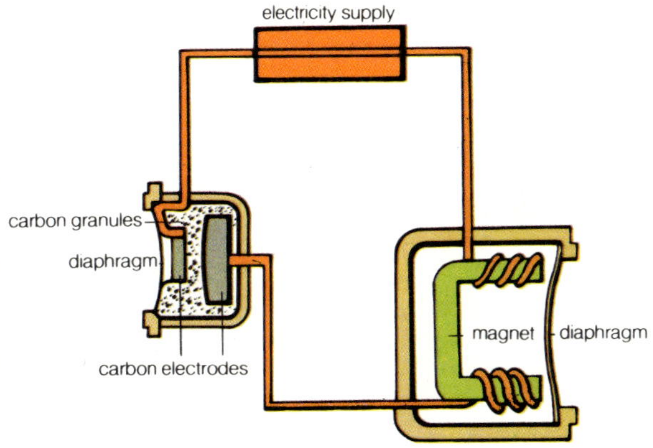

electricity supply

carbon granules
diaphragm

carbon electrodes

magnet   diaphragm

remotely by the subscriber's telephone dial. Switches using Strowger's principles, known as selectors, are used in the vast majority of the UK's 6000 exchanges, and Strowger-type exchanges formed the basis of automatic systems in other countries for many years. The following description refers particularly to the British system.

A selector in its simplest form consists of a movable set of contacting arms, known as a wiper assembly, associated with a fixed set of contacts known as a contact bank. The next step was the invention of *trunk-hunting switches*, a modification of the Strowger switch. When assigned to a particular call it automatically steps along a bank of trunk terminations until it finds a free one; that trunk line is then included in the call path until the end of the conversation.

When a subscriber lifts his receiver, completing the subscriber-exchange circuit, a rotating switch, called a uniselector, associated with that line starts searching for an unoccupied Strowger switch, the first selector. When a free first selector is found, the uniselector stops and a dialling tone is connected automatically to the caller's telephone. After the uniselector, two-motion selectors are used. The wipers of this type of selector can be moved in two planes. The selectors can have more than one contact bank, each of which is composed of 10 horizontal arc-shaped layers, known as levels, with 10 equally spaced sets of contacts on each level. The banks are positioned so that the levels are concentric with the shaft which carries the wipers, so the sets of wipers can be positioned on any set of contacts by two movements of the wiper-shaft—a vertical stepping motion and a rotary stepping motion. The shaft is motivated by a ratchet and pawl system. If, say, 3487 is

the number to be called, the first digit dialled—3—lifts the contact arm of the first selector switch to the third row of contacts. The contacts in this row are connected, by trunk lines (these refer to lines within the exchange and not those between main exchanges), to the second selectors. The first selector moves along the row until it reaches a contact point that is linked to an available second selector. If no contact is made, an 'engaged' tone is sent to the caller. If a free trunk is found, control passes to the wiper of the second selector, and it rises to the fourth row (4 was the second number dialled) and goes through the same process as in the first selector.

The process moves on to the final selector, which carries the connections to the subscribers' lines. The third number dialled lifts the wiper by the dialled number of steps (8) and the fourth turns it clockwise (by 7) to reach the contact corresponding to the number 3487. The final selector control circuit is arranged to test the called subscriber's line. If the line is not engaged, an alternating ringing current is sent to work the bell, and a ringing tone is returned to the caller. If the line is engaged, a busy tone is returned to the caller and the call is not recorded on the meter. When the caller replaces his receiver at the end of the call, the selectors restore to normal.

In theory an exchange like this should give a subscriber direct access to 9999 other lines (10 on the first selector, times 10 on the second, times 100 on the final, less the caller's own line), but in practice the capacity is reduced. The top level of the first selectors is connected to equipment allowing subscribers to dial their own long distance calls (subscriber trunk dialling, or STD). The code '100' is reserved for calls to the

Far left: a typical multi-pair cable may contain up to 4800 pairs. This is laid underground. It is terminated on a distribution frame in the exchange and split into smaller cables en route which terminate at distribution points. From here single pairs connect private telephones. Left: testing uniselectors in Strowger exchange equipment. Above: a reed relay/electronic exchange. Electronic techniques are used to control the reed relay function. Such systems are reliable, fast, and flexible.

operator, and the necessary equipment to route the call is connected to level one of the first selectors.

Another level (eight) of the first selectors is connected to second selectors giving access to nearby exchanges, while level nine of the first selectors leads to second selectors with access to exchanges, a little further away than those off level eight. Sometimes third selectors, connected to levels of second selectors, are required to give extra outgoing routes if there are a lot of surrounding exchanges. Further levels are reserved for information service final selectors and the emergency service. The provision of these direct dialling and service facilities means that at least four levels of the first selectors cannot be used for subscribers' line switching, so the capacity is reduced to around 6000 lines.

The circuits coming in from other exchanges and from the operator's switchboard terminate directly on first selectors which have access to both the subscribers on that exchange and certain of the outgoing routes to other exchanges. Access to the outgoing routes is provided to allow the exchange to act as a switch on calls between other exchanges, thus removing the need to have direct circuits between every exchange. The dialling code for such a connection will then consist of a code to route the caller through his nearby exchange to the intermediate exchange to the final one he needs.

The country is divided into groups of exchanges with one exchange nominated as the main exchange (switching centre) of the group. There are at present two group numbering schemes in use. The older one involves dialling a different code for the same exchange from different points in the group, but in the newer scheme, the same five or six digit number is dialled from anywhere in the group. Unwanted digits are absorbed within the equipment. The exchange 'close to the main exchange are usually called *satellite exchanges* and may be fully interconnected, as well as with the main exchange. To obtain subscribers on other exchanges with which there is no direct connection, the call is routed via the main exchange (it is used as a *tandem exchange*). A tandem exchange can be considered as a collecting point for small amounts of traffic from other exchanges which do not justify a direct route to a particular distant exchange. Exchanges further away from the main exchange—minor exchanges—have junction to the main exchange and to nearby exchanges, but are not fully interconnected. Each main exchange will be, or will have access to, a group switching centre (GSC) which is part of the STD network. Each GSC is fully interconnected with all adjacent GSCs and either directly or via another GSC to almost all GSCs.

Common control systems

Although the majority of British exchanges work on the Strowger principle, there are two other types in use elsewhere, and which are replacing Strowger exchanges in the UK. They use common control systems, whereby information about the call is first passed to a central control point which processes it and selects the path through the exchange the call will take. Not until the control equipment has found and reserved a free path do any of the switches operate.

One form of common control is the crossbar system. The crossbar switch consists of a matrix of relays, each having several springsets which are actuated when the relay armature operates. Each caller has access to a number of outlets, and wired logic ensures that no two callers can be connected to the same outlet. The springsets form a network of fixed precious metal contacts from which a path is selected electrically. Crossbar has fewer working parts than Strowger, is faster and operates more quietly. It is widely used in Europe and the USA, but another, even more advanced, system is being developed which uses reed relays and in the long term this is likely to replace both Strowger and crossbar.

A reed relay consists of reed inserts operated by an electromagnet; each reed insert consists of two flat springs—the reeds—made of ferromagnetic material and sealed in the ends of a glass tube. The glass tube is filled with an inert atmosphere to prevent contamination of the contact surfaces. When current flows through the electromagnet, the reed ends attract each other and

25

Above: an electromechanical switching matrix for a crossbar telephone exchange. The matrix has 10 inlets and 28 outlets. Like the reed relay system, this uses a common control system. Crossbar systems are widely used in Europe and the USA.

an electrical path is made through them.

When a subscriber originates a call, the calling loop is detected by the subscriber's line unit, which signals to the control equipment that a call is being originated. The control equipment then sets up a path from the line unit through the reed relay switching network and a selected supervisory relay set to one of a number of registers. When the caller dials, the number is kept in storage reed relays which stay open in the register while the control equipment checks that the required line is not busy or out of order. If the line is free, the control equipment selects and switches a path from the called subscriber to the supervisory relay set and checks that the connection is properly established. The supervisory set applies ringing current to the called subscriber's line and returns a ring tone to the caller.

The register and control equipment are released to deal with other calls, the control of the connection being left to the supervisory relay set. The control equipment can deal with only one connection at a time, but it works so fast that this is no handicap. From tests carried out to the present day, reed relays also seem to produce fewer faults than Strowger or crossbar.

Other developments

Whatever type of exchange is used, there are problems in sending electrical currents over long distances between them. In the early days of the telephone very thick—and unwieldy and expensive—cables were used, which created less resistance and allowed the current to flow more freely. Now long distance telephone circuits are passed through a series of repeaters, which contain amplifiers for each direction of conversation. By using amplitude modulation many different calls can be transmitted on different carrier frequencies within the same cable (which can be multipair or co-axial). The current is generally amplified by transistors. In ordinary land cables, separate amplifiers are used to avoid leakage of signals between wires, but on submarine cables a more complex two-way amplifier is used.

For short distances, a new system which can carry up to 30 telephone circuits simultaneously on two pairs of wires uses pulse code modulation (see page 98). The principle of this system lies in converting the analog (continuously varying) signal into a series of pulses. The pulses represent a binary code of the amplitude of the original signal, sampled (that is, inspected) at a frequency twice the maximum frequency of the signal that needs be transmitted. Because intelligible speech does not require high fidelity, the maximum frequency that needs to be transmitted. Because intelligible speech per second). Coaxial cables, however, have been designed which will handle frequencies in the megahertz (Mhz) region and so handle many PCM signals simultaneously. At the receiver a PCM decoder converts the pulses back into an analog signal.

A further alternative today is radio. A radio microwave network, in which high frequency radio waves are beamed between line-of-sight directional dish or horn shaped aerials, links major centres. Microwaves are also used for long distance telephone calls which travel via communications satellites (see page 105). Subscribers are able to contact almost every country in the world via satellites strategically sited over the Indian, Pacific and Atlantic Oceans.

SUBMARINE COMMUNICATIONS CABLES

Telegraph, telephone and telex operates through wires, and when a link is established between two continents this wire has to be carried along the ocean bed in a heavily insulated cable. The cost of laying and maintaining cables is a major factor in the economy of international telegraph and telephone communications systems.

Both land and submarine communications cables are coaxial—they have a copper wire held centrally inside a copper tube, by a layer of insulation, a design which is particularly suited to handling high frequency signals.

When air is used as the insulator between the inner wire and the surrounding copper tube, land cables can be designed to handle frequencies up to 60 MHz. Employing modern electronic techniques this permits up to 10,800 high quality one-way telephone channels or 259,200 modern telegraph channels to be transmitted along the cable simultaneously. With submarine cables, however, such high frequency handling characteristics are not possible because of the special construction technique required to protect them in the conditions encountered in the sea. To date the most that can be expected from submarine cables is an upper frequency limit of about 14 MHz.

The first successful transatlantic cable was laid by the *Great Eastern* in 1866. It was insulated with gutta-percha, a natural resin, and was protected and strengthened with galvanized iron armour wires, even in the deepest laid sections where protection was unnecessary, a practice which was continued in all submarine cables for almost a century. The early cables were telegraph cables with a bandwidth of only a few Hz (cycles per second); they were not coaxial since they only had a single conductor. The direct or very low frequency currents of a telegraph signal return via the sea which has negligible electrical resistance. At higher frequencies, the return currents tend to crowd closer to the centre conductor and to travel in the high resistance armour wires. A new type of cable was therefore required which could handle higher frequencies.

In 1921 Carson and Gilbert, in a paper presented to the US Franklin Institute, pointed out that for efficient transmission of high frequency currents a submarine cable should have a return conductor of low resistance material closely surrounding the insulation; that is, they proposed the submarine coaxial cable. Other important events in the development of submarine cables include the discovery of the plastic polyethylene in 1933 with its excellent insulating and pressure resisting qualities, the disclosure of the principle of negative feedback in amplifiers in 1934 and, more recently, the development of highly reliable electronic valves and transistors. These are discussed more fully on page 45.

Repeaters

No matter how good the design and materials, any practical cable will attenuate (reduce) high frequency signals more than low frequency ones. Unless the cable is very short these high frequency signals will become so feeble when received as to be indistinguishable from the electronic background 'noise'. The remedy is to insert amplifiers or repeaters at regular intervals to ensure that the signal-to-noise ratio is kept high. Such amplifiers must be very efficient and stable and use the principle of negative feedback, by which any distortion or change in amplification cancels itself out. Power for operating the repeaters is provided from the land terminals in the form of direct current at several thousand volts. The DC current through the cable is about 0.5 amp.

A number of non-repeatered armoured coaxial telephone cables were laid between 1921 and 1942. The first submerged telephone repeater was inserted in the Anglesey–Isle of Man cable in 1943, increasing the circuit capacity from 24 to 48 two way 4 kHz telephone circuits.

In 1951 a new sea cable was invented in which the strength member was placed in the centre. The first experimental sample was built on a neutral, that is, a non-twisting, steel wire rope with the centre conductor, a thin copper strip, folded around it. Its edges were locked in a 'box seam', like the seam used to make an ordinary tin can. The insulator was a polyethylene tube with 0.8 inch (20 mm) outside diameter, and the outer conductor consisted of six helical aluminium tapes. In order to guard against the risk of corrosion by the sea water in the unlikely event of the outer sheath being punctured, the tapes were bound with a cotton tape impregnated with a corrosion inhibitor (barium chromate). A low density polyethylene oversheath was extruded over the cotton tape.

This cable, known as lightweight cable, was more efficient, though it weighed little more than one third the weight of the armoured cable used for TAT 1, the first transatlantic telephone cable. The new cable was used for CANTAT 1, the first Anglo-Canadian transatlantic cable; and also for the New York–Bermuda cable laid in 1961, and the COMPAC and SEACOM networks linking Vancouver, Hawaii, Fiji,

Above: a modern rigid repeater shown in transit through a linear cable engine.

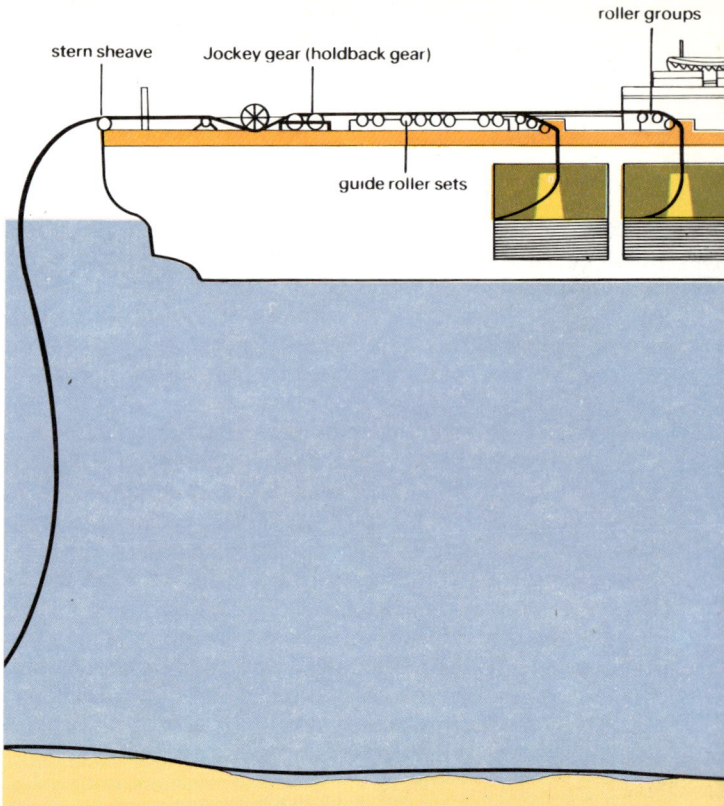

New Zealand, Australia, New Guinea, and South East Asia in the following years. With repeaters spaced every 26 nautical miles, a bandwidth of nearly 600 kHz or eighty 4 kHz two-way telephone circuits was provided.

Since 1961 there have been changes in design to meet new requirements, and there have been improvements in the materials available and methods of manufacture. Two important improvements have been the elimination of the box seam on the centre conductor and the substitution of a single longitudinal seam conductor for the six helical tapes.

The laying of the first successful transatlantic submarine cable in 1866, after several earlier failures, was rightly hailed throughout the world as a great achievement. Nevertheless, in comparison with the laying of modern high capacity submarine telephone cable it was a relatively simple operation. One reason for the increased complexity is that nowadays repeaters have to be spliced into the cables at regular intervals, which may be as little as five miles (8 km).

The very earliest repeaters (1943) were spliced into cable laid previously, a cable ship having to grapple for it and bring it on board to carry out the jointing operation. Each repeater was subsequently lowered to the bottom on a rope. This method could only be used in shallow water. For deeper water a design was needed which could be jointed into the cable on the ship and laid over the stern in a continuous operation.

In the early 1950s, when consideration was being given to a transatlantic telephone cable, the cable laying machinery on cable ships differed little in principle from that of the *Great Eastern*. The only repeaters which such machines could handle were flexible ones and the first transatlantic telephone cable, TAT 1, laid in 1956, used flexible repeaters of American design and manufacture. Of necessity they had to be electrically simple and could only amplify in one direction. Two cables, each with 51 repeaters, were required to provide 36 two way telephone circuits.

Meanwhile, in Britain a different approach to the problem had been made: that of developing the most efficient repeater possible together with suitable means for laying it. The design adopted could amplify in both directions and provide 60 two way circuits over a single cable. It was sealed in a cylindrical steel case 10.5 inches (26.7 cm) in diameter, 10 ft (3 m) in length and weighing 15 cwt (762 kg) with the cable entering at one end and leaving at the other. It could easily withstand deep ocean pressures of over 5 tons per sq in (772 bar). Sixteen of these repeaters were laid by HMTS (Her Majesty's Telegraph Ship) *Monarch* for the Newfoundland–Nova Scotia section of TAT 1. They were handled over the bows laboriously by a method which involved removing several turns of cable from the drum to allow the repeater to pass, then replacing them afterwards. Clearly a better system was badly needed.

Top: arrangement of the equipment above a cable laying ship. The cable is paid out over the overhanging bow and stern sheaves at speeds of from 3 to 8 knots. Above: the No.1 cable tank aboard CS Mercury with a lightweight transatlantic telephone cable for TAT 2 (laid in 1958). For the main section of TAT 2 flexible repeaters were used, but between Newfoundland and Nova Scotia rigid repeaters were used. Right: a British designed rigid repeater passing along groups of rollers to the stern chute of CS Mercury.

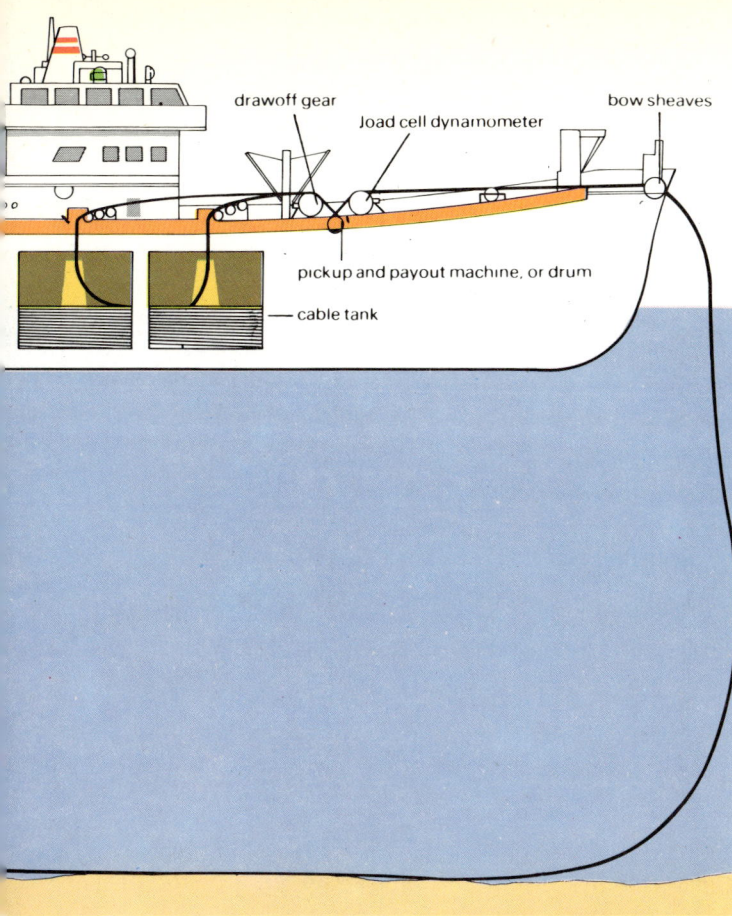

drawoff gear
Joad cell dynamometer
bow sheaves
pickup and payout machine, or drum
cable tank

Post Office Five Sheave Gear

Several interesting ideas were put forward and the one adopted became known as the 'Post Office Five Sheave Gear'. It involved a fairly simple modification of the existing stern cable engine on HMTS *Monarch* to enable a repeater to bypass it. The single drum was replaced by four 6 ft (1.8 m) diameter vee grooved sheaves (pulley wheels) and one plain sheave, all mounted in a fore and aft line, three of the vee sheaves being coupled directly to the drum shaft. The cable

passed alternately under and over the sheaves so that it was gripped firmly, but did not actually go right around any of them. A flexible steel rope called the by-pass rope was spliced to the cable ahead of and behind the repeater, which was mounted on a light trolley. As the trolley neared the first sheave the cable and repeater were diverted to one side but the rope continued to pass under and over the sheaves. After rope and repeater had passed, the cable was led back into the sheaves, rope and repeater being laid over the stern together, generally at a speed of 1.5 to 2 knots.

This machine was first used in 1958 to lay repeaters and the experimental lightweight cable, there being no alternative available at the time. It proved very successful and a total of nine cable ships, including five Russian ones, were subsequently equipped with it. Between 1959 and 1970 all British and Commonwealth, and some American deep water cables were laid by this method.

TAT 2, like TAT 1, used flexible repeaters for the main Atlantic crossing, but thereafter the USA changed over to lightweight cable and rigid repeaters, shorter and fatter than the British ones. They also designed a new cable ship equipped with a new caterpillar type cable engine to lay them. This machine was a very large and advanced one weighing about 80 tons and was capable of laying cable and repeaters at 8 knots. Cable was gripped by two vee-grooved caterpillar tracks which were pressed together by inflated airbags. These allowed the tracks to open up to accept the 13 inch (33 cm) diameter repeater.

The machine also had 'shear-limiting' facilities to permit the safe handling of lightweight cable at high tensions. Since virtually all the strength of such a cable lies in its steel heart, when it is gripped the outside layers will be subjected to shear stresses, that is, forces tending to make one layer slide over the one inside it. This could cause serious damage. The remedy is to spread the gripping force over a long length of cable. This was done in the caterpillar cable engine by allowing each individual gripping segment of caterpillar track to move longitudinally relative to the others against a spring. A tension of 7 tons could by these means be spread over a length of 30 ft (9 m) of cable. CS (Cable Ship) *Long Lines*, the AT & T ship equipped with the caterpillar machine, or linear cable engine as it is now called, laid TAT 3 in 1963 and has since laid a number of other cables in the Atlantic and Pacific Oceans.

The latest development in cable engines is the British Post Office linear machine, also capable of laying cable and repeaters at 8 knots.

Whilst tremendous advances have been made in the technique of laying submarine communications cables more cheaply, quickly and efficiently, it is interesting to contemplate the fact that the Atlantic was not bridged by telephone cable until 1956. Only four years later the first communications satellite was launched.

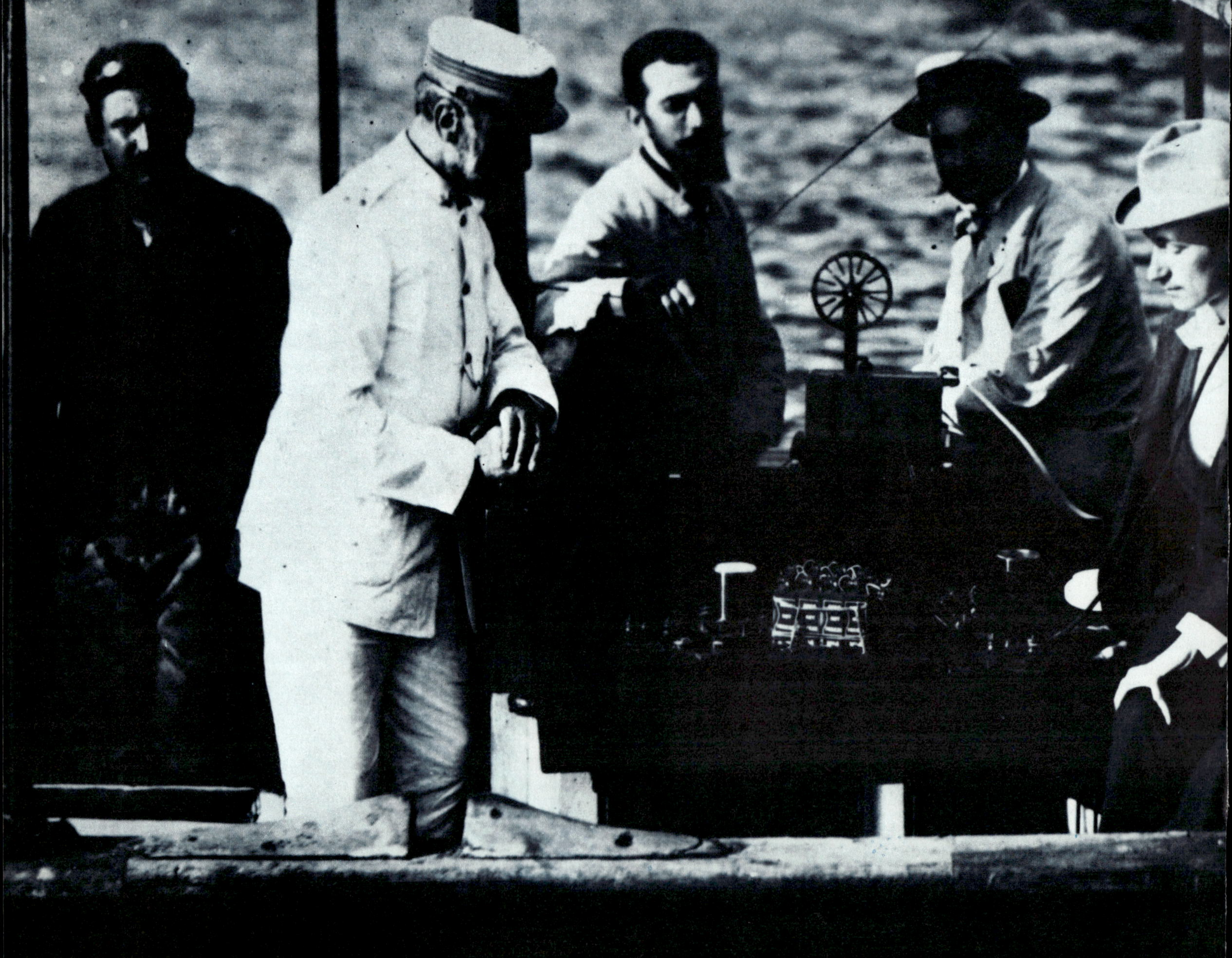

MESSAGES ON THE AIR

RADIO IS BORN

The date was 12 December 1901. The location, Signal Hill, St John's, Newfoundland. Guglielmo Marconi and two assistants could hardly believe the evidence of their ears. Ever so faintly, but unmistakably, they heard on their primitive receiver *dit-dit-dit*—the letter 'S' of the Morse Code—transmitted at a pre-arranged time from Poldhu in Cornwall, some 1700 miles to the east. The Atlantic Ocean had been bridged for the first time by wireless telegraphy!

Marconi was jubilant. He was no great scientist but he had faith in wireless communication. The best scientific opinion of the day was that transmission of signals without wires was a novelty suitable only for short ranges. Marconi had shown his critics they were wrong and by a single practical demonstration he accelerated the development of one of the most potent forces for good, and for evil, of the twentieth century.

The Atlantic had been bridged by a submerged telegraph cable as early as 1866. By the time Marconi made his historic experiment most important centres in the world were linked by the electric telegraph. But to be able to transmit information without wires over vast distances—this was really something new. It seemed as if it might prove profitable too. To lay a transatlantic cable cost a lot of money. The cable itself was expensive and its annual upkeep cost even more, spread over the years. Figures of £1 million for first cost and £100,000 a year for maintenance were quoted. In contrast a wireless transmitter would cost, perhaps, £50,000 and its maintenance only £12,000 a year.

Marconi's genius lay not in his inventive capacity but in his ability as a practical innovator. The German physicist Heinrich Hertz is credited with being the first man to demonstrate that electromagnetic waves could be generated at one point and received at another. This was in 1888 and what Hertz did supplied experimental proof of a theory propounded by James Clerk Maxwell some years earlier.

Marconi had heard of Hertz's work. So had the Russian scientist Popoff and the British scientist Oliver Lodge. All three had achieved wireless transmission by 1895 but it was Marconi alone who had the vision to see the new science in practical terms.

His family had money and connections in England, and in 1896 Marconi sailed from his native Italy armed with letters of introduction and unbounded enthusiasm. He was granted the first patent for telegraphic communications without wires and in the following year formed the Wireless Telegraph and Signal Company. Marconi was then only 23 years old. Three years later the company, based at Chelmsford, changed its name to Marconi's Wireless Telegraphy Company.

Wealthy backers of the new company, greedy for the rich dividends that had accompanied the growth of wire telegraphy, were in for a shock. Wireless was slow to catch on and no dividend was paid during the years 1897 to 1910. But if there were no dividends there was technical progress. The first wireless station in the world was set up at Alum Bay on the Isle of Wight in 1897. It handled its first paid message in 1898. In that year, too, the new-fangled wireless received royal patronage, with Queen Victoria using it to keep in touch with the Prince of Wales who was abroad the royal yacht. In 1899 radio signals from Chelmsford were received in Boulogne—a distance of 85 miles.

Then came the great triumph of 12 December 1901 with the Atlantic bridged for the first time. Marconi achieved this by using a very much longer wavelength than had previously been used. It had been supposed, up to that time, that wireless waves travelled only in straight lines in the same way as light. This would mean that to overcome the curvature of the Earth the transmitting and receiving aerials would need to be immensely high so that they could 'see' each other. Marconi demonstrated that long waves (he used a wavelength of 1,500 metres) must, in some way, be reflected from the sky to get round the bulge of the Earth.

The ionosphere

The following year the theory was propounded independently by Oliver Heaviside in England and A. E. Kennelly in the United States that there was, in fact, a layer in the sky which reflected wireless waves of suitable wavelength. In 1925 Appleton was able to demonstrate experimentally that such a layer existed about 60 miles above the Earth's surface. It was also found that other layers existed at heights varying from 55 to more than 200 miles high in a belt we now call the ionosphere.

The behaviour of the ionosphere is important. It consists of positively charged ions and free electrons and is completely transparent to light and to very short wireless waves. Long waves are heavily reflected and medium waves less so. The layers and their composition vary in a complex manner according to time of day, season and the degree of radiation from the sun. The number of sun spots, for example, has an intense effect on the ionosphere. The ionosphere can be distributed so fiercely at times by abnormal solar radiation that communication is completely obliterated. At other times, changes in the height of the ionized layers give rise to fading and distortion.

Despite Marconi's success with transatlantic trials he was unable to capture commercial traffic between land stations from the cable companies and he turned to the use of wireless for communication with shipping as a profitable alternative. It was here that he succeeded. By the outbreak of the First World War, wireless equipment was becoming commonplace on ships. Its usefulness was demonstrated dramatically by the sinking of the *Titanic* in 1912. The *Carpathia* picked up the distress signals from the sinking ship and 700 lives were saved. It was shortly after this that most maritime nations passed legislation to oblige all ships over a certain tonnage to fit wireless. From this moment on the success of the Marconi companies was assured.

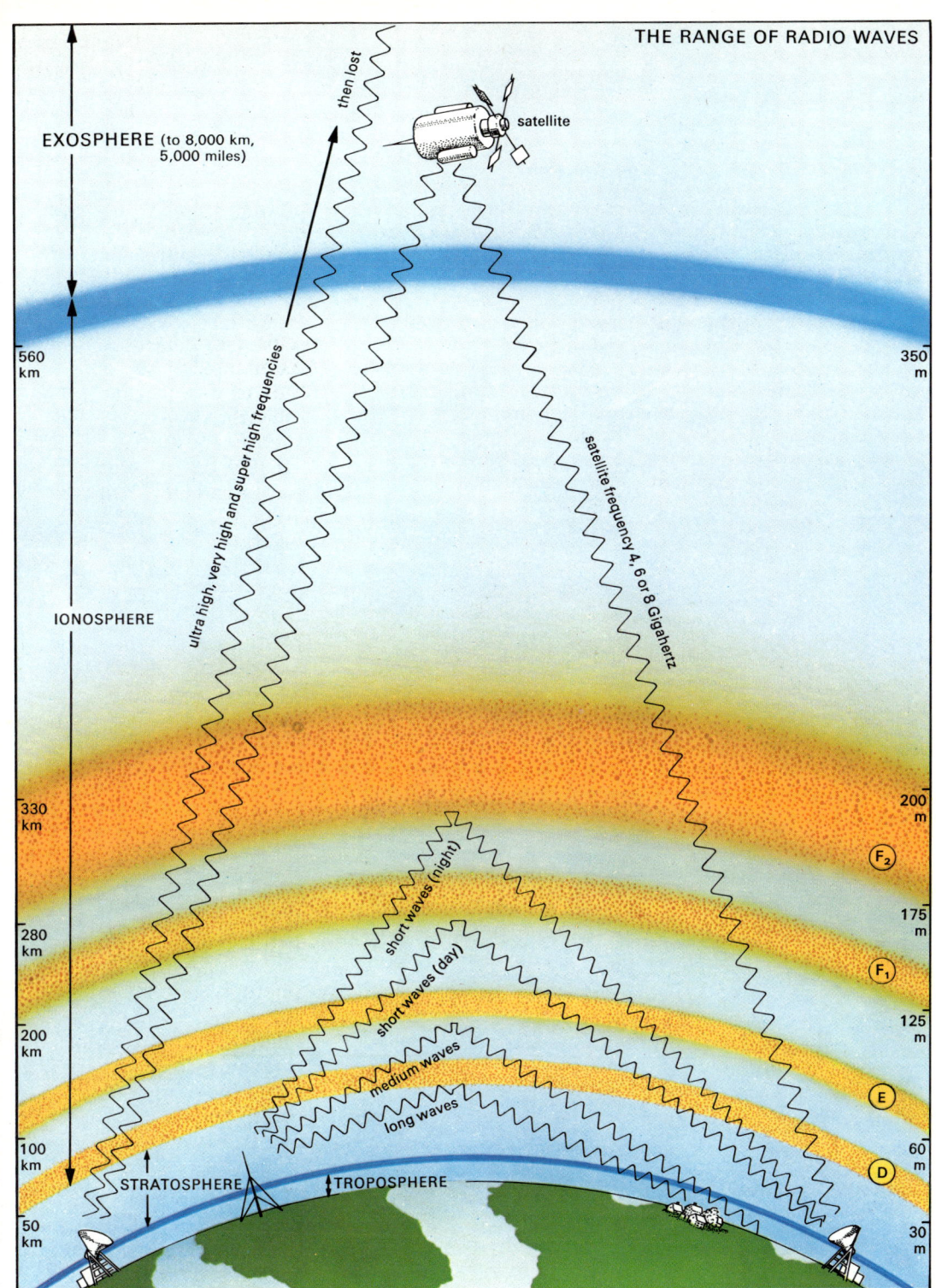

THE RANGE OF RADIO WAVES

EXOSPHERE (to 8,000 km, 5,000 miles)

then lost

satellite

560 km

350 m

IONOSPHERE

ultra high, very high and super high frequencies

satellite frequency 4, 6 or 8 Gigahertz

330 km

200 m

F₂

short waves (night)

280 km

175 m

F₁

short waves (day)

200 km

125 m

medium waves

E

long waves

100 km

60 m

D

STRATOSPHERE   TROPOSPHERE

50 km

30 m

Left: Radio waves can be transmitted considerable distances around the earth because the electrically-charged layers in the upper atmosphere, known collectively as the ionosphere, reflect them back down to distant receivers. The ionosphere is a series of layers, known as D, E, F₁ and F₂, consisting of ionized gas molecules with free electrons which were liberated when the molecules were ionized by the action of solar radiation. The height at which radio waves are reflected depends on their frequency, and the highest frequencies are not reflected at all. At night, the F₁ layer merges with F₂.

Spark transmitters

All the early wireless installations used spark transmitters. The signals were generated by starting and stopping spark discharges with a Morse key and messages were universally sent in the dots and dashes of the Morse Code. At the receiving end the detection device was the coherer, a glass tube containing fine particles of metal which had the property of varying in electrical resistance as the spark signals were received and made it possible for them to be heard on headphones quite clearly.

Ambrose Fleming, a British professor of electrical engineering had invented the diode valves which were patented in 1904. Fleming was a consultant to Marconi and it was Marconi who held the patents. Another young engineer, Lee de Forest, was also busy experimenting in America and it was he who invented the triode valve. Both valves worked better as detection devices than the coherer. But whereas Fleming's valve was a better solution than the coherer, Lee de Forest's triode valve was superior to both in that it not only detected the weak wireless signals but also amplified them. Modern broadcasting uses the thermionic valve, a much improved version of the triode, which makes possible the transmission of speech and music on a continuous modulated wave.

Guglielmo Marconi

Guglielmo Marconi was an Italian, born in Bologna, but much of his pioneering work on wireless telegraphy, which led to his later development of radio communication and broadcasting, was done outside his home country, mainly in Britain, because the Italian government declined to give him financial support when he badly needed it.

Marconi was always more of a practical person than an academic and from an early age, to the displeasure of his father, he preferred tinkering with objects to studying. It was natural therefore that he should seize on the discovery by Heinrich Hertz, a German physicist, that energy could be transmitted from place to place in the form of electromagnetic radiation, just as James Clerk Maxwell had earlier predicted, for Marconi immediately saw the practical potential of 'Hertzian waves' as a means of communication.

Marconi was 20 when he first learnt of Hertz's work and he immediately embarked on a period of intense experimentation in two attic rooms of his family's country mansion outside Bologna. He filled these with equipment, including a coil and spark gap—for creating the electromagnetic waves—and a receiver for detecting them. Soon Marconi was able to show his mother (she was a source of constant encouragement, unlike his father) how a key which was pressed at one end of a room could

cause a buzzer to sound 30 feet away.

Using his capacity for improving and inventing, Marconi gradually developed his apparatus so that he could transmit over greater and greater distances. And he soon discovered that a hill between a transmitter and receiver was no obstacle. At that stage he emigrated to England in search of support, which he got, from both the Post Office and the War Office. By 1879, when he was 23, Marconi was sending wireless signals over a distance of nine miles.

The setting up of a company by Marconi and some British relatives, and the first transmission across the English Channel, followed in quick succession. In 1899 he visited the United States to demonstrate his techniques which by that time had to compete with those developed by other people and other companies—but the mission was not a great success because Marconi was reluctant to show off his then unpatented improvements to possible rival businesses. His aim by then, however, was to transmit across the Atlantic and this he accomplished in 1901; when he was still only twenty-seven.

Marconi was closely involved in the commercial development of wireless and saw it installed in countless places including ships such as the Titanic, and the Montrose which carried the murderer Crippen to his arrest as the result of a ship-to-shore message in 1910. Marconi weathered a financial scandal surrounding his company (but not himself) in 1912 and after World War I devoted more of his time to his home country, both in a political and a technical sense. When he died in 1937 at the age of 63 the world paid the simplest and most impressive tribute it could make—two minutes of radio silence.

Far left: Marconi demonstrates his radio apparatus to the Italian government. By the mid 1850s his work was well advanced, but his financial backing eventually came mainly from Britain. Left: in 1901 Marconi (centre) and his assistants received the first signals to be broadcast across the Atlantic. They were transmitted from Cornwall and received at Signal Hill, St. John's, Newfoundland.

THE STORY OF BROADCASTING

The first American radio programme was broadcast from the experimental station at Brant Rock in Massachusetts on Christmas Eve 1906. Many experimental stations started operating when restrictions necessary for wartime purposes on the use of wavelengths were lifted at the end of World War 1. Some consider that the birth of modern broadcasting was on the evening of 2 November 1920, when station KDKA went on the air reporting returns of the Presidential election won by Harding who was opposed by Cox. Eight stations were operating by the end of 1921, and one year later, there were 564 already crowding the wavelengths.

In 1921 Marconi himself started transmissions from Marconi House in London, using the callsign 2LO which soon became famous. Within a few months the British Post Office called a meeting of manufacturers in the developing industry and an agreement was reached to start a system of broadcasting in Britain involving only one company, the British Broadcasting Company, which started transmissions with three stations in the major cities of London, Brimingham and Manchester in 1922, and soon opened other regional stations.

The number of broadcasting stations throughout the world increased from about 600 at the end of 1925 to 1300 in 1935, and there were at least 10,000 by the early 1960s. As had been predicted, overcrowding and overlapping of wavelengths in use soon became a problem.

The first international agreements involving large numbers of countries were reached in 1932 by the International Telecommunications Union, set up for that purpose. In spite of failures to agree on the allocation of wavelengths between communist and non-communist areas, further agreements in the 1940s and 1950s broadly assigned domestic broadcasting to two sets of wavelengths, 150 to 550 kilohertz on the long wave and 550 to 1660 kHz on the medium wave. External broadcasting on short wave was assigned the region between 2200 and 30,000 kHz. As wavelengths became more overcrowded, European countries and American stations particularly turned more and more to the use of very high frequencies (VHF), allocated for domestic broadcasting in the range between 87.5 and 100 MHz.

The development of the cheap portable transistor radio set brought listening—to broadcasts from all over the world—within the reach of poorer pockets. At the end of the last World War in 1945, there were about 150 million radio sets in the world; by 1972 there were at least 820 million, the vast majority of which were cheap portable transistor radios. But whereas there were around 85 or 90 radio receiving sets for every 100 people in North America, the ratio in Africa was between two and three per hundred. The problem of local languages and dialects remains very substantial; for example All-India Radio broadcasts in about 51 different languages and 82 tribal dialects.

Above: Heinrich Hertz, the German physicist, was the first to transmit and receive radio waves, 10 years after James Maxwell's predictions that light was a form of electromagnetic radiation. Although Marconi is generally accepted as the pioneer of broadcasting, radio frequencies are measured in hertz (Hz), kilohertz (kHz) and megahertz (mHz).

Modern broadcasting

Broadcasting studios are usually arranged as part of a suite which is acoustically separate from the control room. In the control room, the studio manager has direct control over the recording levels. When a whole programme is to be recorded before broadcasting, great skill is required to introduce prerecorded material at the correct time. Also, with the final editing of the recorded session, there must be no loss of sense or essential content where a reduction in programme time is required to fit the predetermined programme schedule. Next, the programmes are coordinated in the continuity suite, which, as its name implies, provides a continuous stream of broadcasting. The continuity announcer works from a preplanned schedule and ensures that, as far as it is possible, all programmes run on time. He is provided with plenty of written material advertising future programmes plus extra material which can fill in any spare time.

From the continuity suite the sound and vision signals pass through at least one switching centre, then via cable or short wave radio link to the regional transmitter stations. The signals are transmitted from here at the standard radio frequencies to the home receiver.

RADIO TRANSMISSION AND RECEPTION

Radio is the name given to the system of transmission and reception of information by the propagation of electromagnetic radiation as radio waves through space. The pioneers could scarcely have envisaged the complex array of wavelengths and frequencies that are used in broadcasting today, and the terminology can be confusing. But the basic principle of radio transmission is a simple one: a single signal source, after amplification, is used to modulate a carrier wave and after further amplification is fed to an aerial for transmission. At the receiver, the radio wave is selected (to the exclusion of all other radio waves), demodulated, amplified and fed to the speaker which reproduces the original sound.

Modulation

With radio reception, if some means were not available for distinguishing between the desired programme and all other programmes, the result would be very poor reception. Furthermore, the situation would deteriorate with the number of transmitters in a given area, especially if the desired signal was from a less powerful or more distant transmitter.

To overcome this problem, modulation is used. This effectively provides each transmission with a 'signature tone'—this is called the *carrier frequency*. Each transmitter has its own signature tone so that any transmission can be selected. The signal is in some way superimposed on this carrier wave before transmission—this is *modulation*. The receiver is 'tuned into' this carrier frequency and, with suitable electronic circuitry, segregates the carrier wave from the signal (demodulation), amplifies the latter and feeds it to the speaker.

In transmission, as with reception, numerous different techniques are possible. With one particular type of transmitter or receiver the circuit design can have even greater variety and so the descriptions below will refer only to the basic types, the major classifications being on the type of modulation employed.

Amplitude modulation

The first requirement of an amplitude modulated (AM) transmitter is a stable carrier frequency. If it is not stable, the reception at the receiver will not be consistent in quality and likely to fade and distort. Stability is provided by a crystal oscillator. Piezoelectric crystals are used, of which the quartz crsytal has by far the best characteristics. The design of quartz oscillators for these applications is similar to those used in quartz

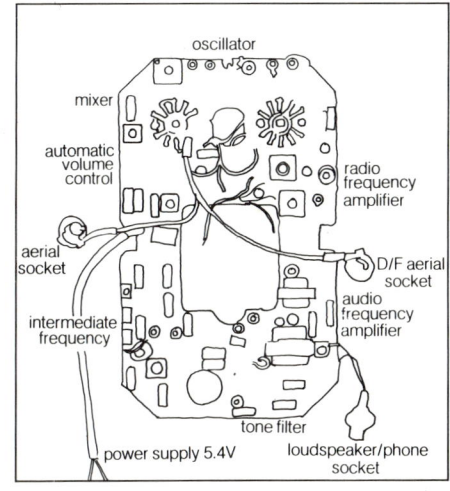

Left (and key above): a compact, highly selective and sensitive receiver for use on small marine craft. This is a superheterodyne receiver operating between 160 and 4150 kHz. It can be adapted for reception of worldwide standard time signals and for radio compass.

clocks where stability is of the utmost importance.

The voltage output from the crystal oscillator is a sine wave and this is amplified to a high power level by several amplifiers in series. Such amplifiers require special design because of the high frequencies involved (from 30 kHz in the low frequency, LF, band to upwards of 30 MHz in the very high frequency, VHF, band). They are known as radio frequency, RF, amplifiers. The greatly amplified sine wave then passes to a *modulated amplifier*.

The signal to be transmitted is first amplified using a low frequency, LF, amplifier and then passes to the *modulating amplifier*. The output from this alters the amplitude of the high power carrier sine wave, in the modulated amplifier according to the instantaneous magnitude of the signal—this is amplitude modulation. The AM signal then passes through a *matching network* and on to the aerial for transmission (see page 42).

The type of circuit described above produces what is called a double-sideband, DSB, AM transmission. This follows from the way in which the signal and carrier wave are combined essentially by *multiplication*. In general, the multiplication of one sine wave (frequency f_1) by another (frequency f_2) produces a waveform containing two frequencies (f_1+f_2) and f_1-f_2). Where the signal contains a range of frequencies (as in speech) the resulting AM signal contains the original carrier frequency, f_c, with two *sidebands* about this frequency. If, for example, the signal has frequencies up to 4 kHz (typical speech) and the carrier frequency is 100 kHz then the total frequency bandwidth of the AM signal is

8 kHz about the 100 kHz mark, that is, from 96 kHz to 104 kHz. The portions on either side of the 100 kHz mark are known as *sidebands*.

There is a certain *redundancy* in this situation because the information about the original signal is contained separately in both sidebands. Also, the transmission bandwidth is twice that which is really necessary. Where the radio spectrum is crowded (as it generally is between LF and VHF) this presents an unnecessary and extravagant waste of frequency 'space'.

Single-sideband, SSB, transmission is therefore used in some situations by filtering out one of the sidebands. Furthermore, using two such circuits with one common carrier frequency, two independent sidebands (representing two independent signals) can be superimposed about the carrier frequency for transmission. Such systems are used, for example, in remote control models—providing two separate control signals in one transmission—and for stereo transmission.

AM receivers

The receiver must be able to receive any programme from the broadcasting spectrum—this means able to select a particular carrier frequency and its sidebands but excluding everything else.

Before 'disentangling' signal from carrier it is usually necessary to amplify the aerial signals. This requires an RF amplifier. Next, the signal is demodulated by the *detector circuit* and the resulting audio signal amplified, using an LF amplifier. Frequency selection is carried out in the preamplification stage before demodulation. This is achieved with a *resonant circuit* whose resonant

Table 1: General classifications of frequencies in radio wave transmissions

band number	frequency range	general classification
4	3-30 KHz	very low frequencies (VLF)
5	30-300 KHz	low frequencies (LF)
6	300-3000 KHz	medium frequencies (MF)
7	3-30 MHz	high frequencies (HF)
8	30-300 MHz	very high frequencies (VHF)
9	300-3000 MHz	ultra high frequencies (UHF)
10	3-30 GHz	super high frequencies (SHF)
11	30-300 GHz	extra high frequencies (EHF)

Hz = hertz (cycles per second)   K = kilo (1000)
G = giga (1,000,000,000)   M = mega (1,000,000)

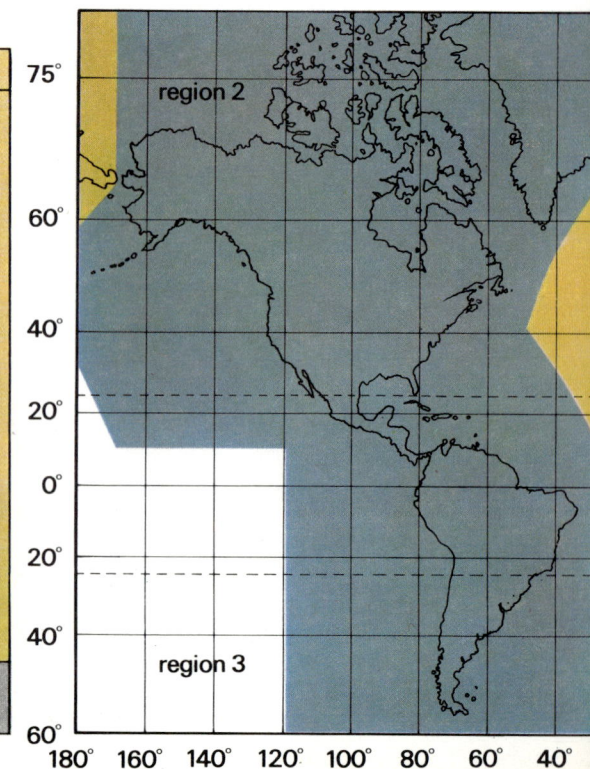

frequency is adjustable by means of a variable capacitor.

Because of the density of broadcasting, especially in the lower frequency part of the spectrum, the selectivity of the tuning circuit is important when considering high fidelity reproduction. In some systems based on the above scheme, two or more resonant circuits are coupled together through amplifier stages. They are individually tuned with variable capacitors, but these are 'ganged' together with a common control knob for ease of tuning.

Another method, used extensively, is to take the frequencies in the region required (a rough selection) and transfer them to another part of the frequency spectrum—called the *intermediate frequency* (IF). This is achieved using the heterodyne principle—where two sine waves are mixed to produce beats—and this type of receiver is known as a *supersonic heterodyne* or 'superhet' for short. The superhet principle is simply that rather than tune the circuit to the carrier frequency it is better to change the carrier frequency to suit a fixed tuned circuit. This way the tuned circuit

Below: the world is split up into three regions for the purposes of radio broadcasting. Strict monitoring of broadcasting frequencies is vital to avoid interference. Right: this chart shows the major frequency allocations of primary services in these three regions. Apart from the frequencies allocated to broadcasting (shown in red) the most important primary services include maritime (green) and aeronautical (blue) services for communications and navigation, and land communications (yellow).

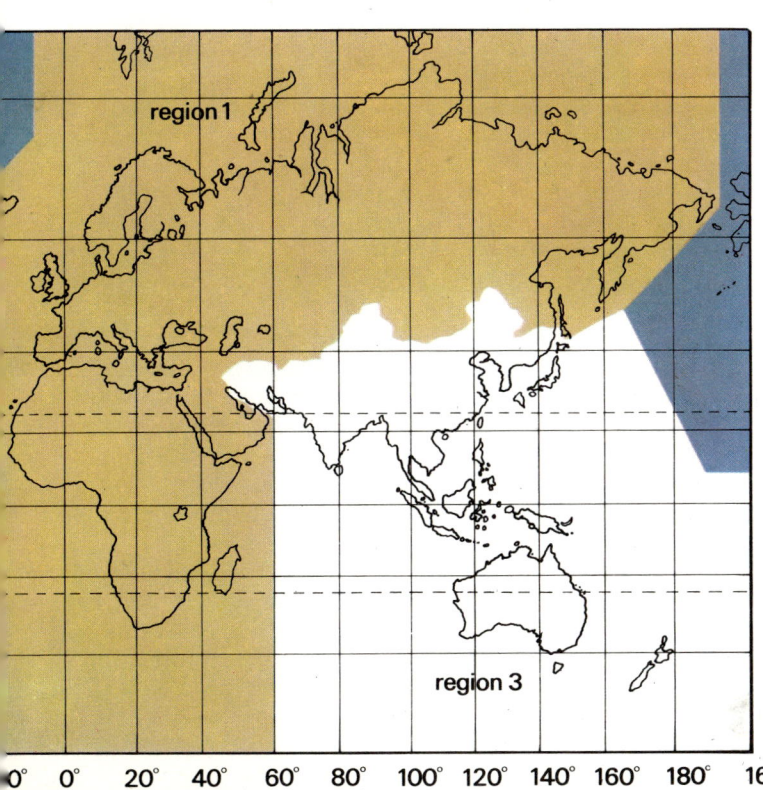

	REGION		
	ONE	TWO	THREE

UHF:BAND 9
VHF:BAND 8
HF:BAND 7
MF:BAND 6
LF:BAND 5
VLF:BAND 4

NOT ALLOCATED

region 1
region 3

0° 0° 20° 40° 60° 80° 100° 120° 140° 160° 180° 160°

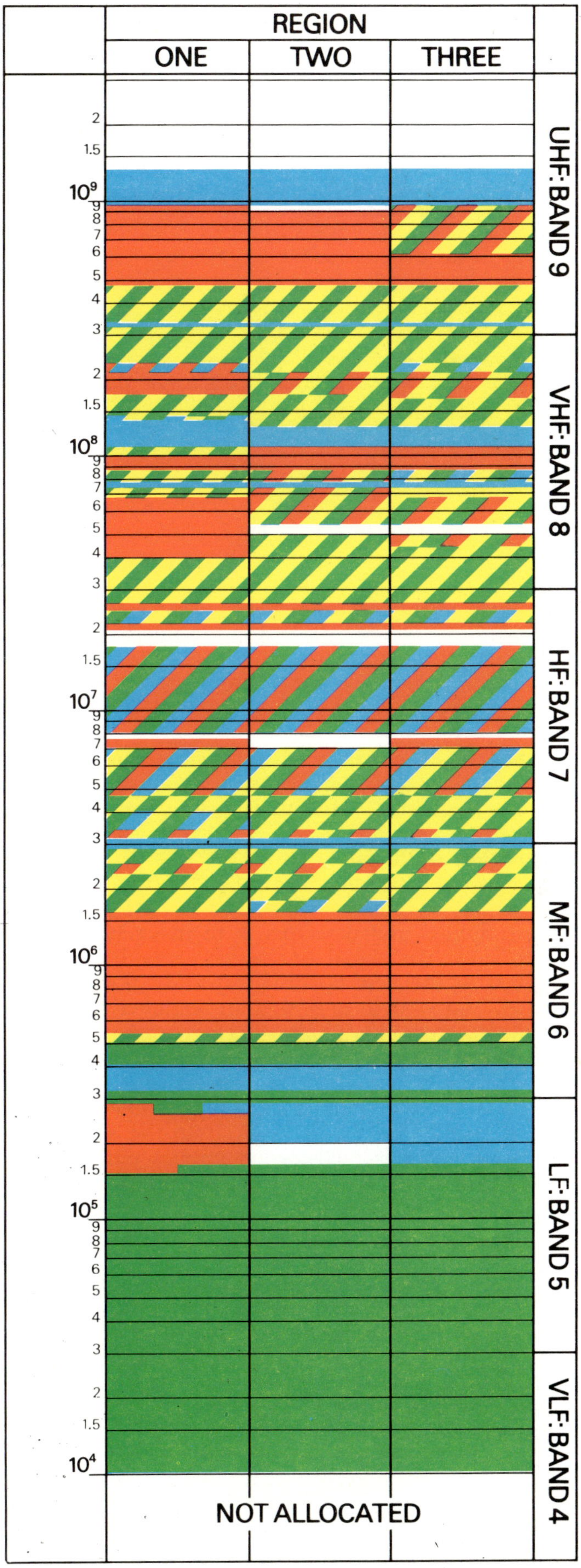

39

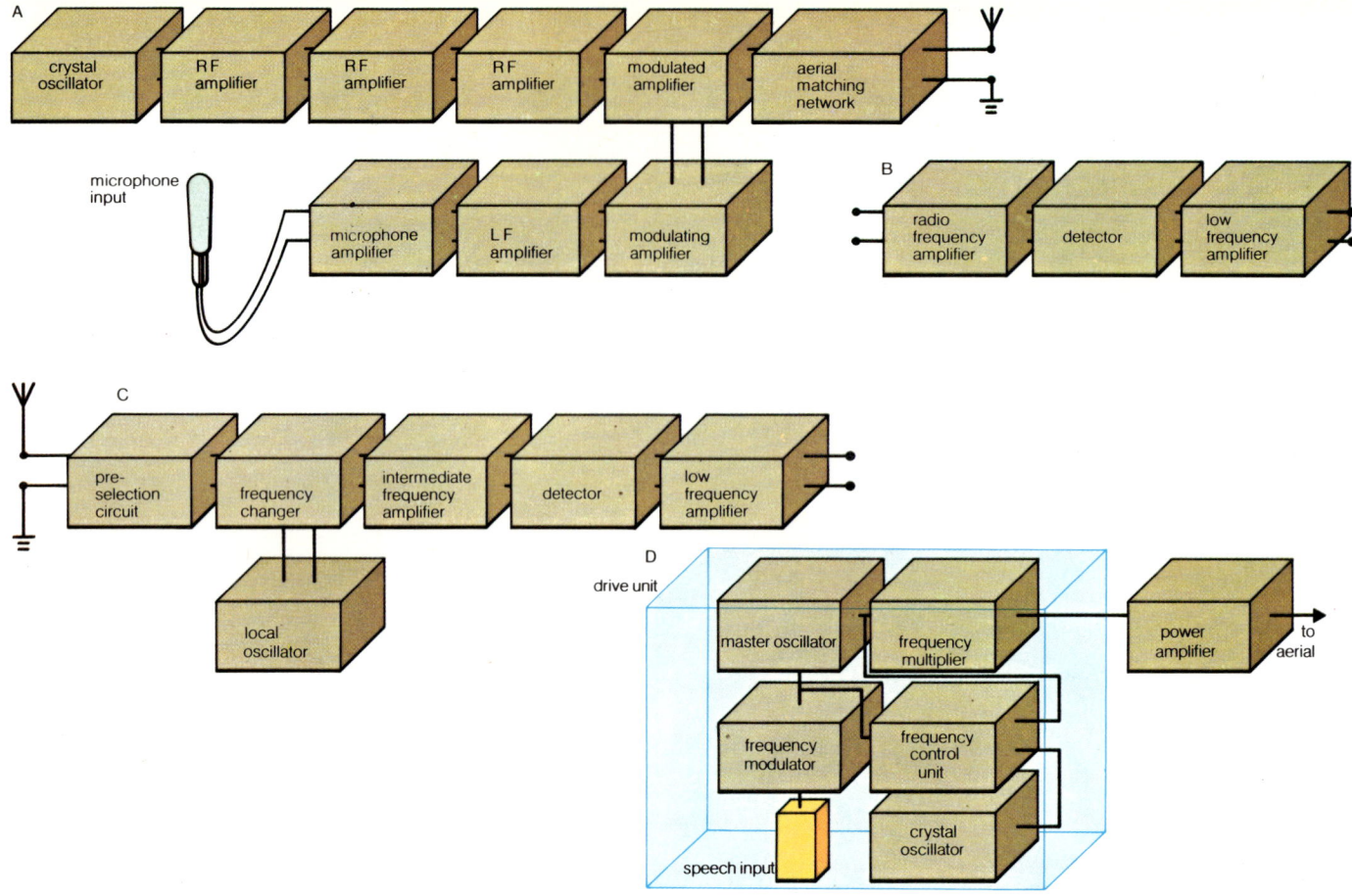

can be designed to have the best possible characteristics. The filtered signal from this stage passes to an intermediate frequency, IF, amplifier and from here on to the detector as before.

Distortion and noise

The reason for turning a simple radio principle into a complex arrangement of LF, IF, and RF amplifiers, tuned circuits and detectors is to make sure that at every stage the signal or carrier or both are being handled in the best possible way. For example, it is virtually impossible to design an amplifier which will handle low frequency (audio) and high (radio) frequency signals equally well. It must be designed to do one or the other.

The factors that an engineer looks for in an electrical circuit and in the final sounds from the speaker are *distortion* and noise. Distortion implies unfaithful reproduction and is mainly caused by non-linearities in the amplifier. For example, if a 10 volt signal is amplified to 20 volts, but a 20 volt signal is amplified to 35 volts, then the gain is not the same for all input signals (see page 45) and distortion results.

Noise is all unwanted signals. This could be interference from an electrical machine or closely packed broadcasting stations straying into the fields of reception. AM systems do not cope with noise as well as frequency modulated (FM) systems.

Frequency modulation

Both AM and FM are used extensively in radio broadcasting, but in television FM is used exclusively.

In AM, the signal modifies the amplitude of a constant frequency carrier wave (in a sound wave, amplitude is loudness and frequency is pitch). The signal is

Above: block diagrams of basic units in radio transmitters and receivers. A and B show simple AM transmitter and receiver. A more sophisticated AM receiver, the supersonic heterodyne or superhet, is shown in C. An FM transmitter is shown in D—here the carrier frequency is altered according to the amplitude of (speech) signal. Right: circuit diagram of a simple AM receiver showing the functions of the various components. The input from the aerial is transformer coupled to the first of two tuning stages which reject neighbouring broadcasts. The 'accepted' signal goes to an RF amplifier and then on to a second tuning circuit. The signal now has sufficient amplitude to be demodulated by detector circuit using a diode detector (R2, C2 and grid circuit of second valve). This valve also acts as AF amplifier and after more amplification (third valve), the audio signal goes to the speaker.

transmitted in this modulated form and to recover the original signal at the receiver it must be amplitude *demodulated* (demodulation is the reverse operation to modulation). In FM, the carrier wave is of constant amplitude and the signal is coded in the frequency fluctuations about a central (carrier) frequency. Again, to recover the original signal it must be demodulated—this time by frequency demodulation.

The complete radio frequency spectrum from low frequencies, LF, to ultra high frequencies, UHF (that is, from 10,000 Hz to 1,000,000,000 Hz) can accommodate over 50,000 AM channels even without duplication. Because the broadcasts can be limited to a specific region or country, those same channels can be used elsewhere without too much interference (depending

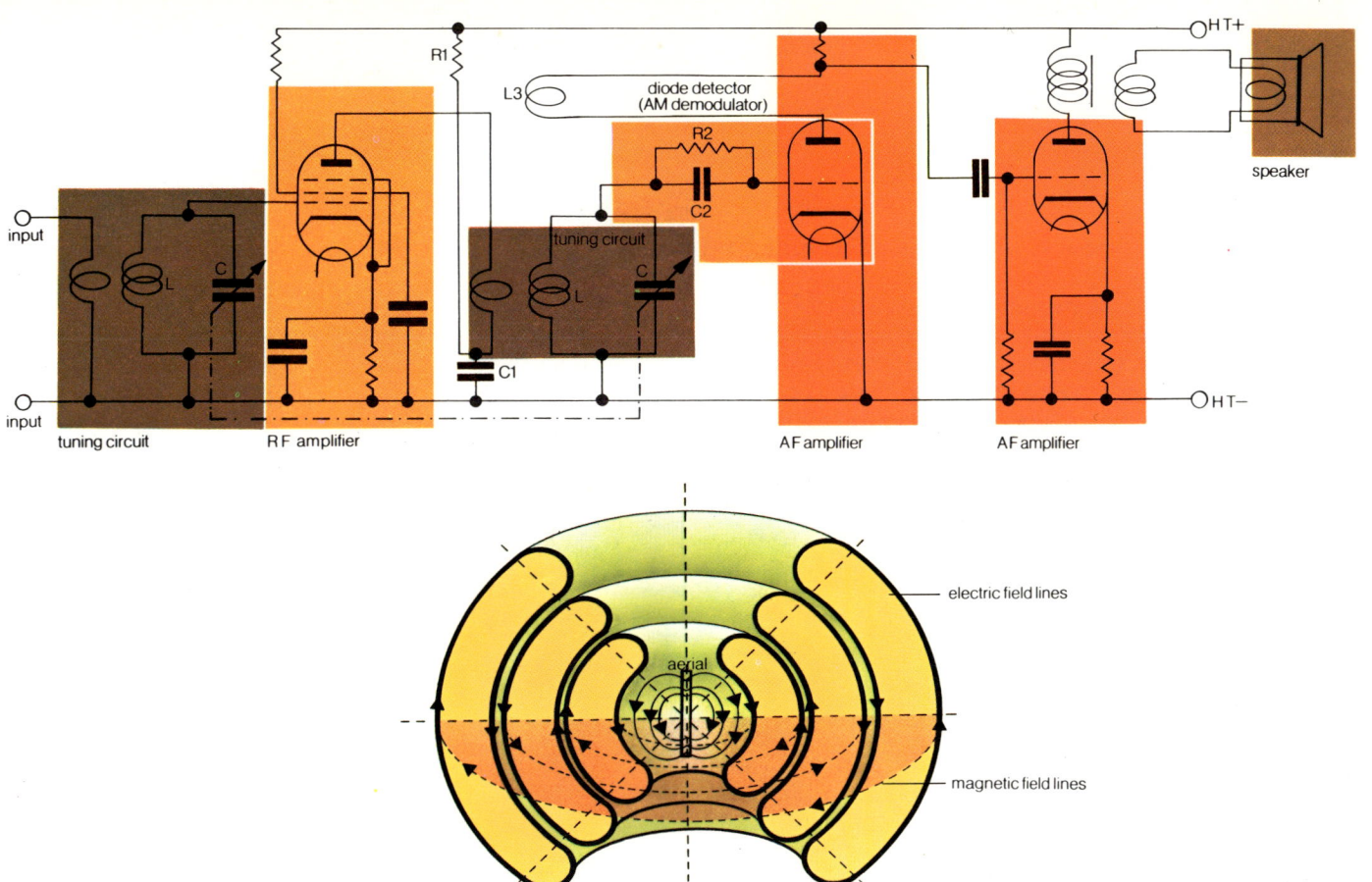

input

tuning circuit

R1

L3

diode detector
(AM demodulator)

R2

C2

tuning circuit

L

C

C1

R F amplifier

HT+

speaker

AF amplifier

AF amplifier

HT−

electric field lines

aerial

magnetic field lines

on the power of the transmitter). Tight control is, however, exercised in the allocation of radio frequencies throughout the world.

In FM, the carrier wave is made to change in frequency around a central frequency. The change in frequency is made proportional to the amplitude of the signal to be encoded. For example, if the frequency changes by 1 kHz for every one volt of input signal amplitude, then an amplitude of five volts produces a change in frequency of 5 kHz. If the input signal to be encoded is a 2 kHz sinusoidal wave-form with a peak amplitude of ± 10 volts, then the frequency fluctuations are ± 10 kHz about the carrier frequency. With a carrier frequency of 1 MHz (1 MHz = 1000 kHz) this would mean fluctuations from 1.01 MHz to 0.99 MHz and back again 2000 times a second.

To achieve this in practice some means is required to change the frequency of an oscillator according to the amplitude of the signal. In high fidelity (hi-fi) FM broadcasting, the circuit can be extremely complicated to provide the required quality of reproduction. But there are several ways of achieving an approximate and cheap equivalent. A simple oscillator, for example, can be constructed using a tuned inductor-capacitor (LC) circuit in the feedback path of an amplifier with positive feedback. The oscillator frequency is determined by the values of inductance and capacitance. By varying either the inductance or the capacitance the oscillator frequency can be changed. One way to achieve this is to use a valve [vacuum tube] where the effective capacitance between anode and cathode is dependent on grid voltage. This uses the characteristics of a valve but similar arrangements are possible using transistors.

Demodulation

Demodulation and the recovery of the original signal, are achieved by the reverse operations to modulation. Here, a change in the FM signal frequency is made to produce a change in output voltage. One technique is to use a tuned LC circuit which is tuned to the central carrier frequency. When this circuit is fed with an un-modulated FM signal (that is, constant carrier frequency), the circuit oscillates 'in harmony' with the signal—the oscillations are of maximum amplitude. A modulated FM signal will, however, have a frequency slightly different from the tuned circuit and the circuit will oscillate with a smaller amplitude. By detecting these variations in amplitude using a rectifier and low pass filter (low frequency with respect to the carrier frequency) the original sound can be recovered.

FM versus AM

FM systems offer a far greater immunity to noise and general interference from other broadcasting channels than AM. This is, however, only gained at the expense of a larger channel 'bandwidth', which is required if the signal is to be reconstructed faithfully at the receiver. Typically, an FM channel for sound reproduction has a bandwidth of 200 kHz, compared with 20 kHz for AM. For television the bandwidth is much higher.

FM was first applied by E. H. Armstrong during the 1930s. Its development was delayed by the necessary high frequency carrier wave required (as FM requires a channel bandwidth of 200 kHz it can only be used extensively with carrier frequencies above 1 MHz). FM is mainly used in the VHF and UHF frequency bands, that is, above 10 MHz. By the 1930s AM had become so well entrenched in Britain that it took another 20 years before FM gained commercial acceptance.

Aerials [antenna] and matching networks

When a stone is thrown into a pond the wave ripples spread out in concentric rings. A similar process occurs when an alternating current travels along a conductor except that the ripples are now electromagnetic in nature. The aerial [antenna] is the 'conductor' in this case and the alternating current is the AM or FM signal from the last amplifier stage in the transmitter.

Basically, a transmitting aerial converts the electrical signals from a transmitter into an electromagnetic wave, which spreads out from it. A receiving aerial intercepts this wave and converts it back into electrical signals that can be amplified and decoded by a receiver.

A radio transmitter produces its signal in the form of an alternating electric current, that is, one which oscillates rapidly back and forth along its wire. The rate of this oscillation can be anything from tens of thousands of times a second to thousands of millions of times a second. The rate is known as the frequency and is measured in *kilohertz* or *kilocycles* (thousands of times a second) or, for higher frequencies, in *megahertz* or *megacycles* (millions of times a second).

The oscillating current in the transmitting aerial produces an electromagnetic wave around it, which spreads out from it like the ripples in a pond This wave, which is shown in the diagram, sets up electric and magnetic fields. The lines of the electric field run along the aerial and those of the magnetic field around it. Both the electric and magnetic fields oscillate in time with the electric current.

Wherever this wave comes into contact with a receiving aerial, it induces a small electric current in it, which alternates back and forth along the aerial in time with the oscillations of the wave. Although this current is much weaker than the one in the transmitting aerial, it can be picked up by the amplifier of the radio tuned to receive it.

The air is full of radio waves at all frequencies, which the aerial picks up indiscriminately. Each radio or television set has a means of selecting a narrow band of frequencies at any one time—this is what happens when a particular signal is tuned in. Each set can be tuned within a certain frequency range, and will only respond to signals in that range.

Each frequency is associated with a wavelength. This is because the waves, as they radiate out from the aerial at a certain frequency travelling at the speed of light,

Right: the principles of FM radio. The modulator produces a carrier wave, and alters its frequency in proportion to the changes in amplitude of the signal waveform, to produce the modulated wave. The demodulator reverses the process, producing an output signal whose amplitude changes in proportion to the frequency variations of the FM wave. In this way the original signal is reproduced faithfully.

42

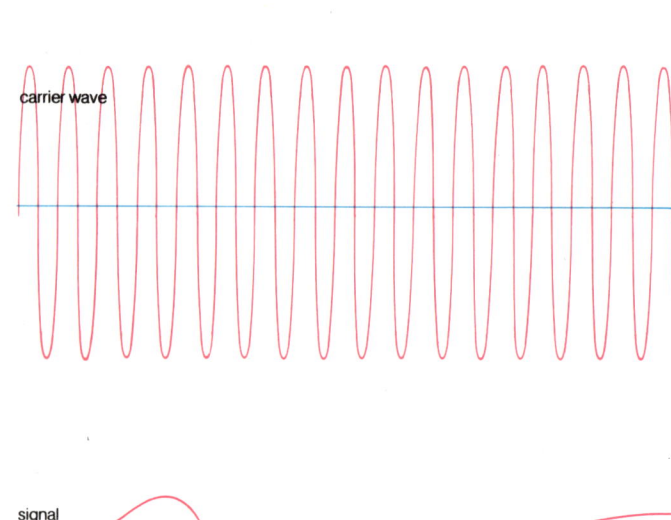

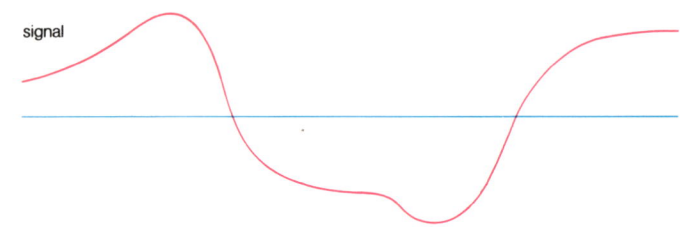

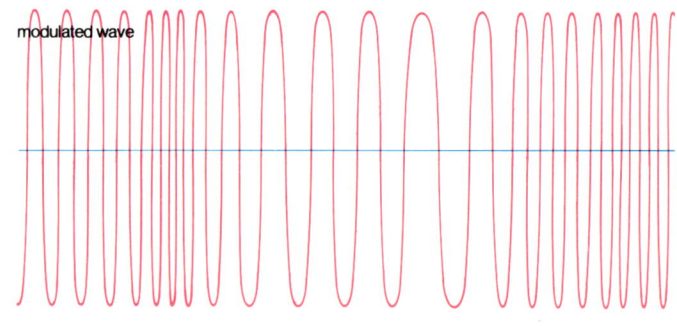

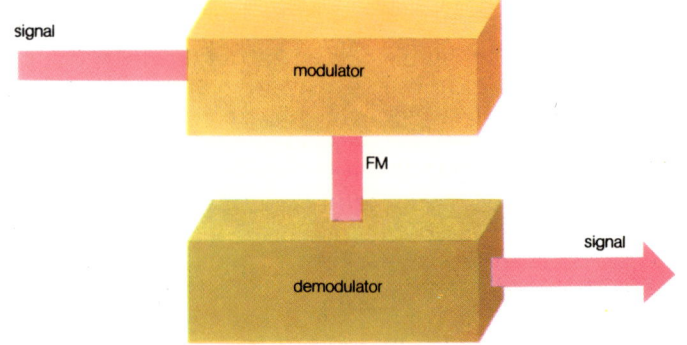

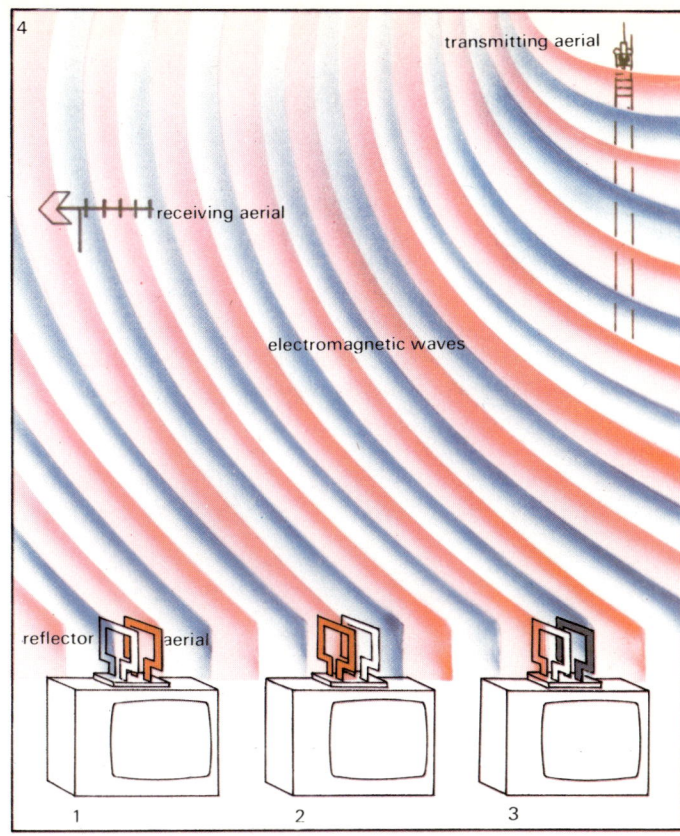

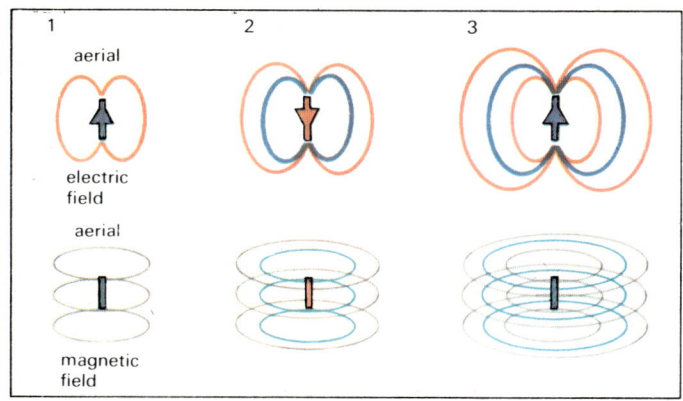

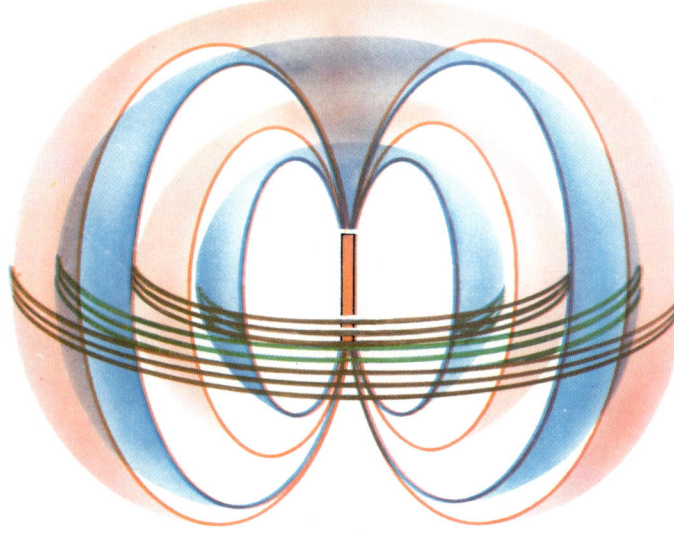

Top right: an aerial radiates both an electric field (shown in red and blue) and a magnetic field (shown in green and brown). The polarity of these fields changes with the direction of the electric current in the aerial. This results in waves spreading out in all directions (1,2,3). The wavelength is the distance from 'crest' to 'crest' of the waves (from one red line to the next). Above: this diagram shows the shape that the two fields take together. Top: the waves spread out from the transmitting aerial and can be picked up by any properly aligned receiving aerial within range. In this diagram, a simple set-top TV aerial with one reflector shows how the 'crest' of a wave strikes the aerial (1) and the reflector a moment later (2), and is then reflected back with opposite polarity to reach the main aerial at the same time as the 'trough' (3).

space themselves a certain constant distance apart. The higher the frequency, the shorter the wavelength (the product of the two being always equal to the speed of light). A transmission with a frequency of 1000 kHz has a wavelength of 984 ft (300 m).

Electricity travels along a wire at a similar speed. It will therefore greatly increase the efficiency of an aerial if its length is correctly related to the wavelength of the signal it receives or transmits. Ideally, aerials are exactly one half or one quarter of the wavelength they receive or transmit.

Receiving aerials inside domestic radios cannot be even one quarter as long as the wavelengths, and in any case have to work over a wide range of wavelengths. But fortunately, the signal from the transmitter is so powerful that it can be received on a comparatively inefficient aerial.

Types of aerial

The same principles apply to transmitting and receiving aerials. The simplest form of aerial is a single elevated wire. This type of aerial was introduced in the early days of radio by Marconi, who found that by using a wire instead of a small metal cylinder as he had done previously, he increased the range of his transmitter from one hundred yards to one mile.

This type of single element aerial is called a *monopole*. It is connected to only one terminal of the transmitter; the other terminal is connected to earth. This arrangement does not stop current flowing in the aerial; it streams between the aerial and the ground as if across a capacitor, and sets up an electromagnetic field between the two. The ground here is said to be used as a *counterpoise*. Car radio aerials use the car body.

Two-element aerials called *dipoles* are also used. These consist of two rods of equal length (again half-, quarter-, or eighth-wave) set end to end a few inches apart. One rod is connected to each terminal of the transmitter, but they are not connected to each other. The field forms about both rods, linking them. No earthing is needed, since the rods counterpoise each other; they are said to be *balanced-fed*.

A transmitting aerial may be set either vertically or horizontally, provided the receiving aerial is set the same way. Vertically set aerials transmit *vertically polarized* waves, which have little effect on a horizontal receiving aerial (and vice versa). For the best results, the receiving aerial should be set at exactly the same angle as the transmitting aerial.

This *directivity* (sensitivity to angle) of an aerial is very clearly shown in the comparatively inefficient aerials of portable radios. These may be of two types: the *loop aerial*, a long loop of wire wound many times around the interior of the cabinet, and the *ferrite rod* aerial, where the wire is wound around a magnetic material which increases its efficiency. For the best reception, the plane of the loop, or a plane at right angles to the ferrite rod, should pass through the transmitter. The performance of a portable radio depends very much on the way it is pointing.

Television detector vans use the directivity of swivelling loop aerials connected to powerful receivers to locate the faint radio signals broadcast by the magnetic coils of a television set. The operator rotates the loop until the strongest signal is received. He can then tell in which direction the set lies by the way the loop is pointing.

Directivity has other uses, too. Reception of a broadcast is often impaired by interference from another transmitter with nearly the same frequency. Medium and long wave radio signals follow the curve of the earth and can travel hundreds, or even thousands of miles with comparatively little loss of strength, which can cause serious 'overcrowding' problems.

The shorter wavelengths or very high and ultra-high frequency transmissions (vhf and uhf), which are used for hi-fi radio and television broadcasts, will only travel in straight lines, and stop at the horizon. This means that there have to be large numbers of vhf and uhf transmitters to cover a country, which can cause reception problems to someone half way between two transmitters sending different programmes. Both problems can be solved by using a strongly directional receiving aerial lined up with the desired transmitter.

Top: TV (405 lines) and VHF radio relay station aerial at Kinlochleven in Scotland. This is a low power transmitter (2 to 5w) situated for local reception (1 to 2 miles) in mountainous areas. Right: A Marconi high frequency (HF: 3 to 30 MHz) curtain array.

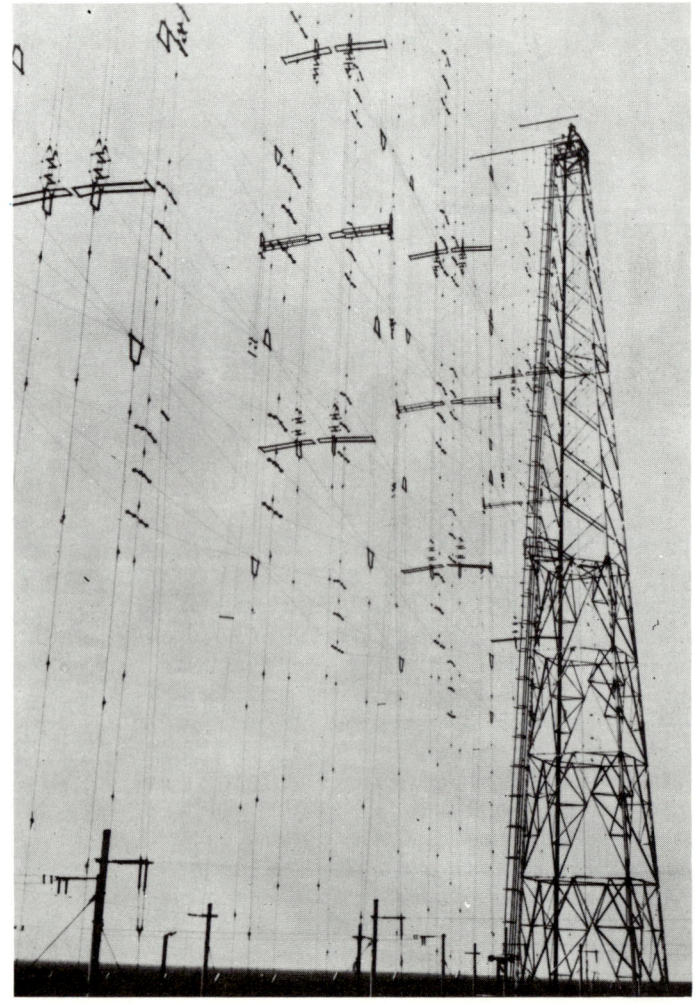

AMPLIFIERS

An amplifier is a device for increasing the strength of a weak signal fed into it. Electronic amplifiers are used in radio and television receivers, record players, tape recorders, radar, analogue computers and electronic equipment generally. All electronic amplifiers work in much the same way, though they differ widely in design. Gain (degree of amplification) can be measured as a proportional increase in voltage (the usual method for amplifiers), in current or in wattage—total electrical power.

The heart of an amplifier, and the device that actually does the amplifying, is either a thermionic valve [vacuum tube] or a transistor. Nearly all electronic amplifiers have several of these plus a set of resistors, capacitors, potentiometers and related devices to control the flow of electricity through the basic amplifying components.

Valves [tubes] and transistors use different principles to perform the same function. Basically, they act as variable switches where the flow of a small current through one part of the device controls the flow of a larger current through another part. When the small current flows, the large current, which is drawn from a separate power source, flows too. When the small current stops flowing, the large one is shut off, and when the small current flows at, say, half power, so does the large one.

The proportion of the smaller current to the larger one is constant in a linear amplifier, the most usual type. So if the small current is modulated by adding a signal from a record, tape or other source, the signal will be reproduced more or less faithfully at a much higher power in the form of a modulation of the large current. This large current can then be fed to a loudspeaker to convert it into sound.

Valves [tubes]

The term *thermionic valve* (vacuum tube) is used to describe a variety of electronic devices, but they all have two distinct characteristics: they are all enclosed in a sealed glass container which has been pumped free of air (electrical connections to the internal parts being through the base of the container), and they contain a *thermionic electron emitter*. This is usually a specially treated metal which emits electrons when it is heated with an electric heater, an effect which had been demonstrated by J J Thomson in 1877.

The first practical valve is generally attributed to J. A. Fleming, who produced a diode in 1904. In this device the thermionic emitter was a carbon or tungsten filament which was heated to about 2500°C by passing an electric current through it. Also within the valve was a metal plate called the *plate electrode*. This was placed about one inch away from the filament and the whole construction was mounted in an evacuated glass bulb. If the plate was then made positive with respect to the filament by means of an external battery, the negatively charged electrons from the filament would be attracted to the plate and an electric current would flow. If the

plate was made negative, then the electrons would be repelled and no current would flow. The diode thus behaved as a valve, that is, permitting current to flow in one direction only. The Fleming diode was used a great deal in the early days of radio communication as a detector in amplitude modulated (AM) receivers, but it was not capable of amplifying the small signals it detected.

In 1907, the American Lee de Forest introduced a third electrode called the control electrode or *grid*. This was a perforated plate or wire grid placed between the *anode* (positive electrode) and the *cathode* (negative electrode) of a diode, thus forming a *triode*. This control grid was held at a small negative voltage with respect to the cathode, the anode being made positive with respect to the cathode. Electrons emitted by the cathode would be attracted by the positive anode, but they would first have to overcome the repulsion effect of the negative grid. As a result, the number of electrons reaching the anode could be increased or decreased by varying the voltage on the grid.

The grid was placed nearer to the cathode than the anode so that a small variation in grid voltage caused a much larger variation in anode to cathode current. The triode could therefore be used as an amplifier. This in turn made practical the broadcasting of sound. When it was announced that music could now be broadcast on the wireless, musicians promptly dubbed the device 'de Forest's prime evil'.

Better evacuation of the glass tube was achieved, making possible cooler operation and the use of more efficient materials in the emitters. Despite these improvements, the triodes could not be used at frequencies greater than about 1 megahertz (1 MHz—1 million cycles per second). In 1927, A W Hull introduced the four electrode valve or *tetrode*. He placed an additional *screen* electrode between the anode and grid of a triode where it provided an electrostatic shield between the grid and anode and greatly improved the frequency range of the valve.

Finally, in 1928, a fifth electrode or *suppressor* was introduced, forming a *pentode* valve. The extra electrode was placed between the screen and anode and improved the performance of the valve at low anode voltages. This form of the valve has proved to have very good characteristics over a wide frequency range and is the most common form of valve in general use today.

As an electronic device the valve has many uses—as an amplifying device in radio, television, telecommunications, radar, oscillators, computing, and many other applications. It suffers, however, from a number of physical drawbacks. It is rather fragile and therefore easily damaged by shock and vibration, and is generally large in size, requiring a great deal of power for its heaters. Both these characteristics make it unsuitable for portable battery operation. In addition, the valve heater has a definite life and when it fails the valve has to be replaced. The transistor, however, has none of

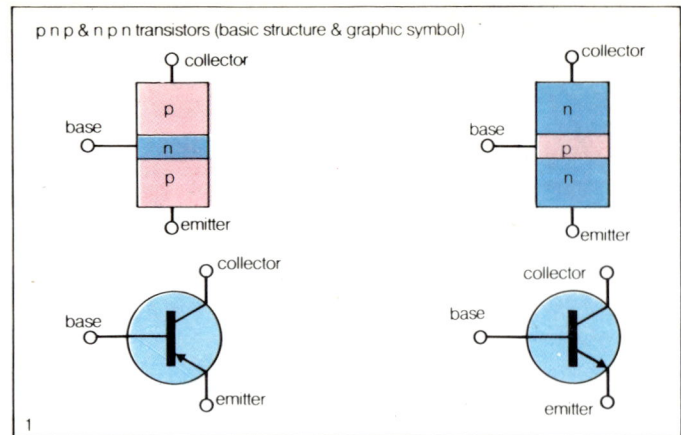

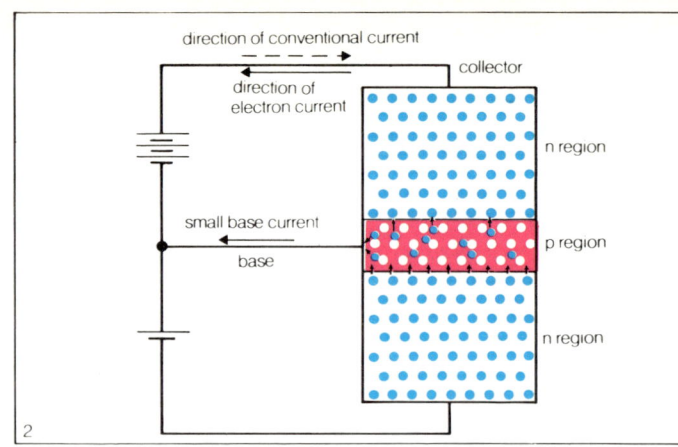

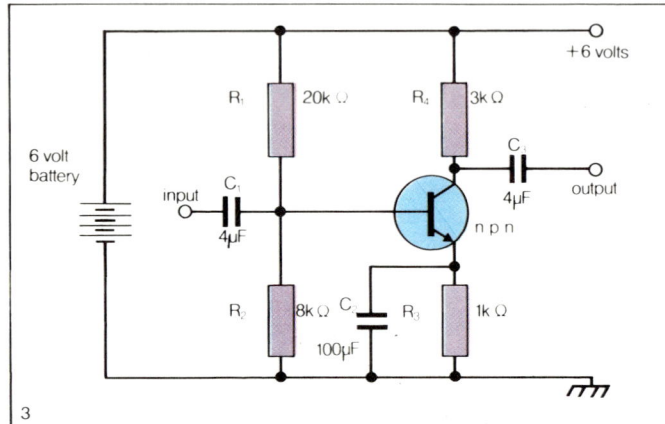

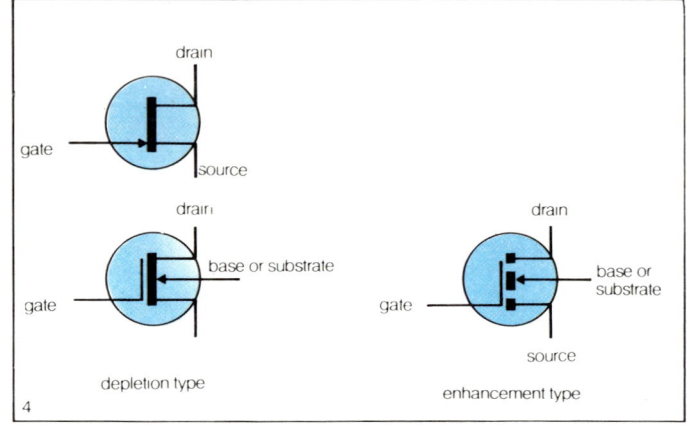

these disadvantages and since about 1960, when it became available in commercial quantities, has superseded the valve in very many fields.

The valve is still used in high voltage applications such as television and in high power applications such as radio and radar transmission. It still has various special uses, for example in atomic particle detectors such as the geiger counter and photo-multiplier tube.

Transistors

Almost as a by-product of research into solid-state physics, the transistor was developed as a substitute for the valve at the US Bell Telephone laboratories in 1948. Transistors are made of semiconductors.

The term semiconductors is applied to a variety of chemical elements and compounds, of which the most important are silicon, germanium and gallium arsenide. Their common property is an electrical conductivity, determined by the number of elementary positive charges ('holes' or 'vacancies'), or negative charges (electrons) which are 'free' to move. The density of these 'free carriers' is dependent upon the structure of the material, its impurity content and its temperature. A semiconductor with a predominance of free electrons is called 'n-type'; those containing mostly holes are called 'p-type'. If a defect-free crystal of a perfectly pure semiconductor is heated, free carriers are generated as electron-hole pairs, and the material is said to be *intrinsic*. A suitable chemical impurity will cause an imbalance, and the material becomes p or n type.

It was the development of the pn junction which sparked the progress in solid-state electronics which is still going on today. This consists of an interface of ultra-pure semiconductor between n and p type material. When an operating voltage is applied across

it, electrons and holes in great numbers, equivalent to a large current, can cross the junction. The p and n regions are then called *majority carriers* and the condition is called *forward bias*. When the voltage is applied in the opposite direction, the junction is a *depletion area* and this is a *reverse bias*. The three regions of the transistor are called the *emitter, base* and *collector*.

Semiconductor materials also contain *minority carriers*, that is, holes in n-type material and electrons in p-type. A reverse bias enhances the flow of minority carriers, giving rise to a *leakage current*. Another important process in all semiconductors is *recombination*, in which holes and electrons cancel each other out. This is increased at crystal defects, surfaces and sites of certain impurity atoms. For reasons such as these, the design and manufacture of transistors is a highly precise business, and the finished product must be carefully controlled or even graded, like eggs. This is why the number of transistors in a radio is not by itself a guarantee of quality.

Transistors have largely superseded valves in most applications since they became widely available around 1960, because they run cooler, use less current, take up less space and last indefinitely. Some hi-fi enthusiasts still maintain that valves ('tubes') make better-sounding amplifiers, but the 'tube-testing' machines which used to be found in large American drug stores are a thing of the past.

Resistors

Resistors are used to set the relationship between voltage and current in an electrical circuit. The value of a resistor is known as the resistance, and is measured in ohms. The majority of resistors are linear, but some designs alter their value sharply when current is passed

Left: (1) the basic structures and graphic symbols for pnp and npn transistors. (2) action of a bipolar npn transistor biased for normal operation as in an amplifier (3). R_1, R_2, R_3 and R_4 are resistors. (4) graphic symbols for various types of n-channel field effect transistors.

and are therefore used to protect electrical equipment from sudden surges of power. Transistors, for example, could easily be damaged by accidentally short-circuiting the terminals on a hi-fi amplifier, so resistance protection is designed into such units.

When current is passed through a resistor, power is dissipated and appears as heat. Resistors are manufactured in a wide variety of sizes and colour-coded according to their power-handling capacity. They are made of a variety of materials and fillers from powdered carbon black to metal alloys on a ceramic base, according to the fixed precision required.

Variable resistors are called potentiometers, or 'pots', and employ a sliding contact on the surface of a resistance wire wound on to a base, or in the most modern type, on a glaze printed on to a ceramic base.

Glazes are also used as the basis of the newest types of fixed resistor. A paste of resistive material is screen-printed on to a ceramic base, and then heat-treated; this forms a glaze in a pattern determined by the screen. The process is cheap and capable of mass-production, both for individual resistors and for networks of more than one component.

Capacitors

Electrical capacitance is an electrostatic phenomenon, and is concerned with the storage of electrical charge and the behaviour of electrons at rest. Capacitors (formerly called condensers) consist essentially of two parallel plates which possess a certain 'capacity' to store an electric charge. They are used as control devices in amplifiers and other electronic equipment. For example, the frequency dependent properties of a capacitor in an AC circuit has led to its use in the suppression of radio interference. It allows high frequency currents to be filtered through it but at the same time blocks the low frequency and DC currents.

Amplifiers in practice

A simple amplifier would not normally produce enough gain for practical purposes. It might reach a 30 times increase in voltage. But an ordinary hi-fi amplifier operating in normal conditions would probably give a 100,000 times voltage increase. Some special-purpose amplifiers have much higher gains than this. Large gains are produced by using an amplifier consisting of several stages. The output of the first stage is passed to the second stage and amplified further, and so on through as many stages as are needed to yield the necessary gain.

A hi-fi amplifier usually consists of two stages, the first a pre-amplifier with a fixed gain setting which boosts the incoming signal from the record, tape or radio to a level at which it can be handled by the second stage, or basic amplifier, which provides sufficient power to drive the speakers. This stage includes a volume control to adjust the final gain.

Amplifiers are normally designed with an inbuilt gain much higher than is actually needed or used. This is then moderated by the use of negative feedback, where a portion of the output signal is fed back to the input with a reversed polarity (current direction) to reduce the gain. In this way, the volume can be controlled by varying the amount of negative feedback. More importantly, distortion will be reduced and any changes in the supply voltage or the electronic components will have less effect on the gain. In addition, if more gain is available than normally needed, the peak power (for when loud sounds are reproduced) will be of higher quality.

If positive feedback were used, part of the output signal being fed back to the input with the *same* polarity to *boost* the gain, the result would probably be to produce unwanted oscillations, which are sometimes heard in public address systems as a loud howling noise. This is caused by the output boosting the input, the input increasing the output accordingly and so on up to uncontrollable levels, causing the amplifier to stop working. In public address systems this is caused by sound from the loudspeakers (the output end) reaching the microphone (the input end).

The quality of a linear amplifier is assessed by its ability to magnify the input signal 'faithfully', that is, without altering its essential shape. To give faithful reproduction, an amplifier must respond to all the frequencies provided by the signal, giving an equal response to all of them. In the case of a musical instrument, this means reproducing a complicated set of overtones. In practice, it means that a hi-fi amplifier must respond equally to the whole range of audible frequencies, from about 30 Hz to 18 kHz (30–18,000 cycles per second). This range of frequency response is known as the bandwidth. No actual amplifier can live up to this ideal, but high quality hi-fi amplifiers come close. The frequency response can be partially altered by adjusting the treble and bass controls.

The video amplifiers used to form the pictures of TV and radar receivers have an enormous frequency bandwidth from 0 Hz (that is, direct current) to 6 MHz (6,000,000 cycles per second).

Amplifiers also suffer from harmonic distortion— output at frequencies twice, three or more times that of the signal—and from amplifier noise, a random jumble of different frequencies independent of the input signal. This is called 'white noise' because it includes all frequencies, just as white light includes light waves of all frequencies between red and violet. Amplifier noise can never be totally eliminated. It can always be heard in a sound amplifier as a slight hiss. But a good hi-fi amplifier can have a signal-to-noise ratio better than 3,000,000 to 1. For a 10 watt amplifier this would mean a noise power of less than 3 microwatts.

THE AGE OF TELEVISION

TELEVISION BROADCASTING

Although J. L. Baird was the first man to transmit a television picture in 1926 he was actually using a patent taken out as long ago as 1884. The British Broadcasting Corporation was not slow to take up the challenge of the new technology.

In 1929 the BBC began its first experimental television transmissions and in 1936 the world's first regular public high definition television service, using at first 240 lines and later 405 lines was introduced. Transmissions were broadcast from Alexandra Palace in north London.

During the 1930s about twelve experimental television stations began transmissions in the United States, broadcasting drama, sporting events, and even politics, though no commercial receivers were yet available. Then at the end of World War 2 in 1945, twelve VHF channels were allocated to TV in the United States (from 50 to 216 MHz). By 1948 twenty TV stations were on the air, 80 more were partially completed and soon due to start broadcasting and 300 were applying for licences. Eventually 70 more channels were allocated for TV, the number of channels allocated to cities varying in proportion with the population.

In Britain, although there are only three main programme channels, there are 15 independent regional stations relaying and originating programmes. In a typical television studio today the visual sources come from four to six studio cameras, with maybe more outside broadcast units contributing to the programme. Videotape recordings, made earlier from TV cameras or ordinary film (with or without soundtrack), can be prepared on special machines called telecine machines, and may replace live TV camera pictures several times in a single programme.

A major advance in broadcasting technology came in 1962 when the second communications satellite to be launched, Telstar 2, first enabled television pictures to be transmitted between Europe and America. Satellites are now in regular use for international communications and broadcasting (see page 105).

The third world

Each nation has its own separate and highly individual story to tell when it comes to the development of broadcasting. But to give an idea of the disparity between the richer and poorer parts of the world, in 1969 there were 112 regular television transmitters working in Africa,

Below: the mechanical scanning section of Baird's first television apparatus of 1925. Below right: a television camera fitted with an iconoscope tube, now replaced by the image orthicon tube. The camera lens focuses the image on a signal plate which is scanned by an electron beam.

BLACK AND WHITE TELEVISION

340 in Latin America, 3050 in North America and 6515 in Europe. The advent of village sets is beginning to make television a powerful educational medium in some areas, but it will be a long time before it begins to approach the power of radio.

The significance of modern broadcasting techniques in such areas is potentially enormous. United States calculations have shown that schools or further education colleges in remote areas could be provided with all the equipment required for full scale educational television by satellite at a cost of £1 ($1.70) per person in the area per year. The United Nations has a centre for research and training in satellite communications in northern India set up for the same purpose.

Modern broadcasting

The first successful television transmissions, carried out by John Logie Baird between 1928 and 1935, were composed of only 30 lines and small details could not be reproduced: this was known as a *low-definition* system. Several hundred lines are needed to give definition comparable with that of 16mm or 35mm film.

The world's first *high-definition* service (using 405 lines) was launched by the BBC in the autumn of 1936 from Alexandra Palace in North London. This service has remained in operation since then, except for an interruption between 1939 and 1946 caused by World War 2. In 1964 the BBC introduced its second television programme using the 625 line system: this gave better definition than the 405 line system and the new line standards agreed with those used by many other broadcasting authorities, so facilitating the international exchange of television programmes.

The first regular colour television service began in the USA in January 1954, in Japan in 1960 and in Great Britain and a number of European countries in 1967. Thus it is nearly half a century since Bairds' original black and white transmissions, and during this time development has been such that in Great Britain in early 1975 there were nearly 17.5 million television receivers (7 million were colour) and colour transmissions were available to 95% of the population.

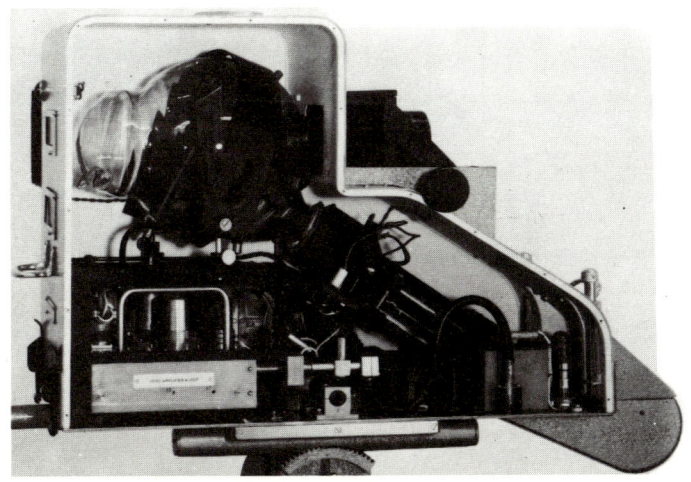

Television is a highly complex subject, and in this description of the fundamental principles a number of simplifications have been made in the interests of clarity.

Close examination of a newspaper pictures shows it to be composed of a large number of dots arranged in a regular geometric pattern. The dots are very small in almost-white areas of the picture but are large and almost touching in very dark areas, intermediate sizes of dot giving the various shades of grey between black and white. At normal viewing distances individual dots are too small to be seen and the picture appears continuous. An alternative way of reproducing a photograph would be to have dots of constant size but of various degrees of grey between black and white.

This technique of dividing the picture into very small *elements* is used in television. Information about the degree of grey (or alternatively of the degree of brightness) of each element is sent to the receiving end where it is used to build up a reproduction of the original scene.

Television camera

The first process is the creation of an optical image of the scene to be televised. This is normally formed by the zoom lens of a television camera and the image is focused on the *target* of the *camera tube*. The target is of *photo-emissive* or *photo-conductive* material and generates a pattern of electrical voltages on the rear surface, the voltage of any point being proportional to the brightness of the corresponding point in the optical image on the front surface of the target.

The target is *scanned* by an *electron beam* generated in the camera tube, the beam moving over the rear surface of the target in precisely the same way that the eye moves over a printed page in reading. Thus the beam moves from left to right across the image, returns rapidly to the left again and scans a second line immediately under the previous line and continues in this manner until the bottom of the image is reached. The beam now returns to the top of the image and begins the process again.

The greater the number of lines used in one complete scan of the target, the higher is the definition of the television system. In most European countries 625 lines are used and the definition is very good. Each complete scan of the target is accomplished (in Europe) in 1/25th second so that 25 complete pictures are transmitted every second (compared with 24 in movie film). In the USA the picture is composed of 525 lines and 30 pictures are transmitted per second. (In practice, each picture is scanned twice, in alternate stripes like the red and white parts of the American flag, so that a rate of 25 pictures a second involves 50 scans a second, but this is purely a device to reduce flicker.)

As the target is scanned the voltages representing the detail in the optical image are neutralized by the scanning beam and are, in effect, transferred to the output terminal of the camera tube. Thus the tube output

51

arrangement of zoom lens and camera tube in a black-and-white television camera

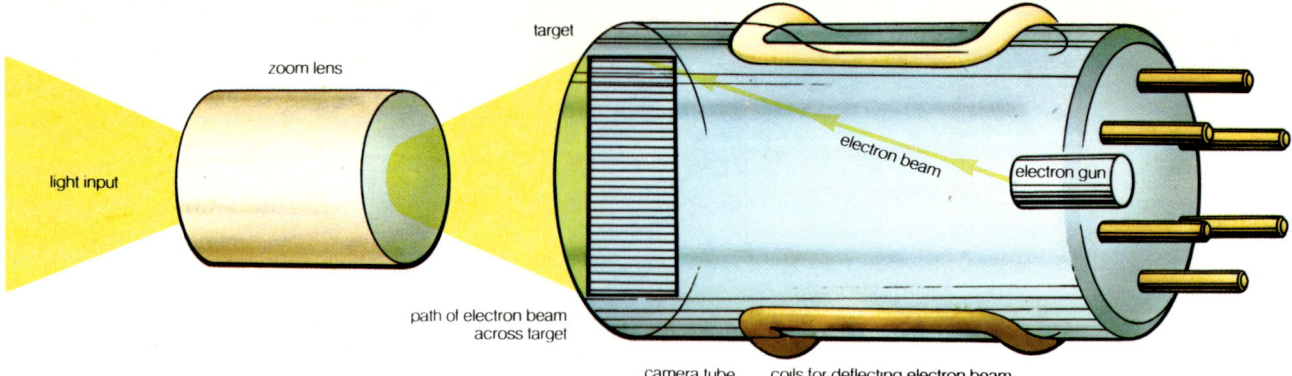

zoom lens

target

light input

electron beam

electron gun

path of electron beam across target

camera tube

coils for deflecting electron beam

waveform of camera tube output. i.e. a picture signal

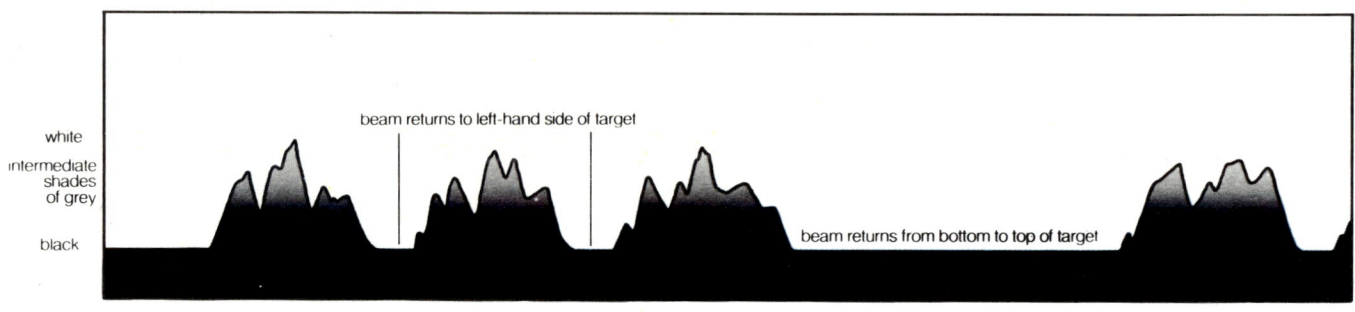

white

intermediate shades of grey

black

beam returns to left-hand side of target

beam returns from bottom to top of target

waveform of video signal i.e. a picture signal and sync signal

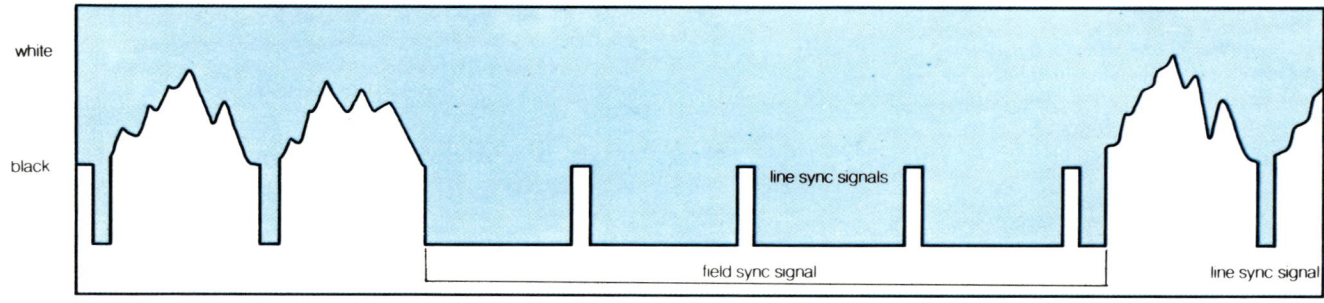

white

black

line sync signals

field sync signal

line sync signal

simplified block diagram for a black-and-white television receiver

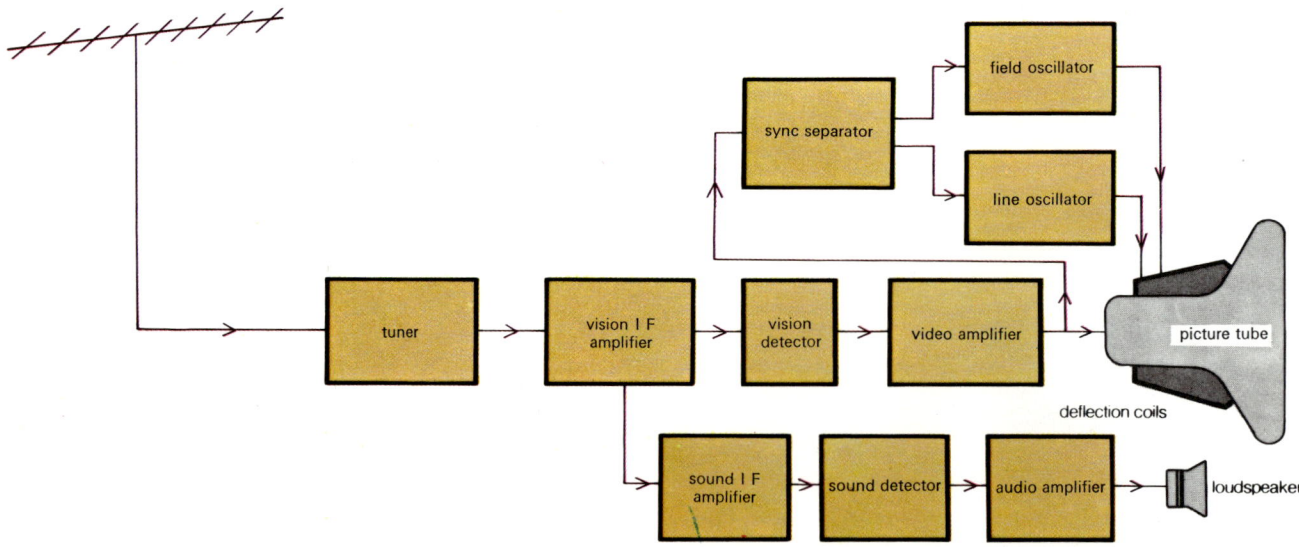

sync separator

field oscillator

line oscillator

tuner

vision I F amplifier

vision detector

video amplifier

picture tube

deflection coils

sound I F amplifier

sound detector

audio amplifier

loudspeaker

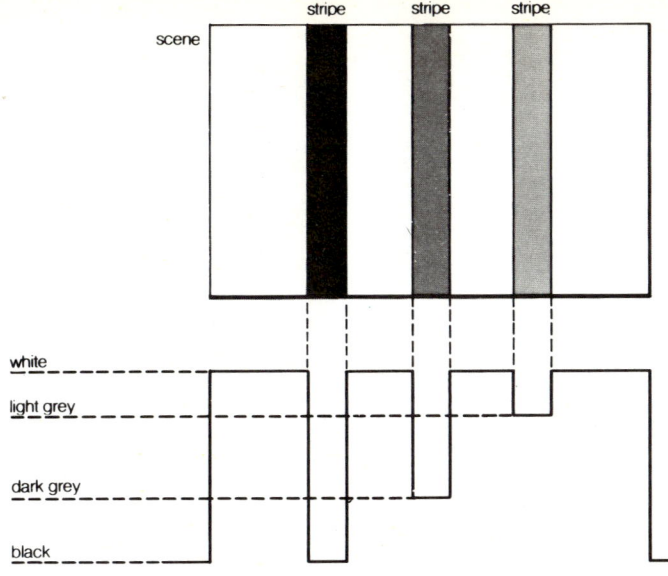

picture signal for a scene containing a black, dark grey and light grey stripe

scene — stripe stripe stripe

white
light grey
dark grey
black

picture signal representing scene

two types of amplitude modulation used for video signals

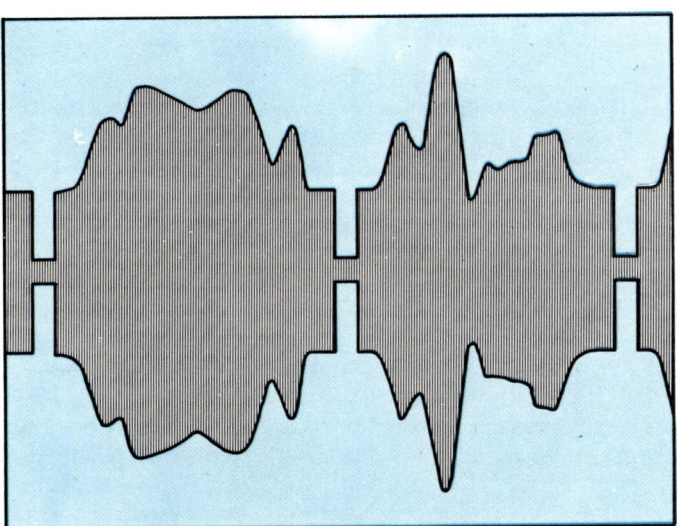

positive modulation

negative modulation

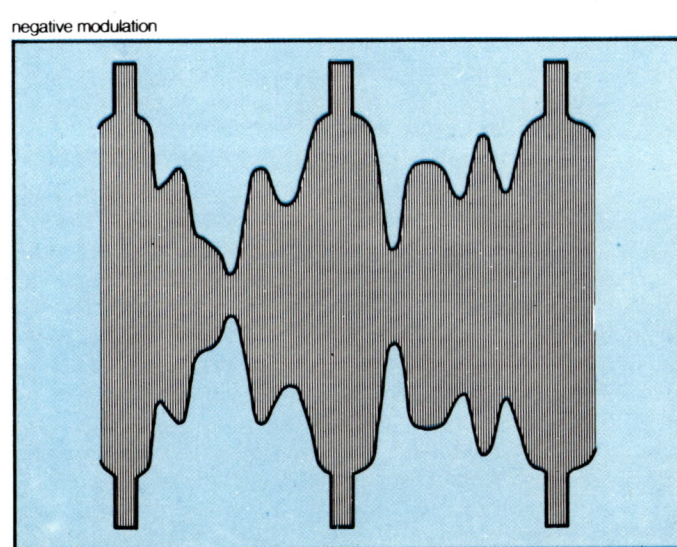

consists of a varying voltage which represents the way in which the brightness varies along the scanning lines of the optical image: this varying voltage is known as a *picture signal*. It is interrupted for a brief interval every time the beam returns to the left hand side of the image and, for a longer interval, every time it returns to the top of the image.

To show how the detail in a picture can be represented by such a signal consider a very simple picture consisting of a uniform white background with three separate vertical stripes, one black, the second dark grey, and the third light grey. Such a picture has no detail in the vertical direction and the detail along all the scanning (horizontal) lines is the same. Each line begins with a period of white level, then black level when the first stripe is encountered, white level again, then dark grey level at the second stripe, white level again, light grey level at the third stripe and finally white level. Thus the picture signal for this simple scene has a waveform consisting of a series of pulses. The signal is a maximum during white areas, a minimum during black areas, with two levels in between for light and dark grey.

In a normal detail television picture the picture signal is different for each scanning line. Moreover if there is movement in the picture the waveform for any line varies with time. To reproduce the picture at the receiver (the television set) a *picture tube* (or cathode ray tube—CRT) is employed which also contains an electron beam focused on a screen, which scans it in exactly the same pattern as the camera tube beam.

Cathode ray tube

Cathode ray tubes are used not only in television sets but also for radar displays and scientific instruments such as oscilloscopes.

A CRT consists of an evacuated (emptied of air) glass tube with a flat screen at one end coated on its inside with a fluorescent material. At the other end of the tube is an electron gun (see diagram) which projects a beam of electrons down the tube towards the

Left: when light from a scene hits the camera target, the target becomes positively charged. An electron beam scans the target in a regular manner and converts this charged pattern into an electrical signal—this is the picture signal. The picture signal varies from its maximum value (white) to its minimum value (black). With line sync and field sync signals added this becomes the video signal containing all the information to control a picture tube (CRT) and reproduce the original scene. For broadcasting, however, the video signal must first be amplitude modulated. Two types of modulation—known as positive and negative—are possible. The choice of modulation is important when considering colour transmissions. At the receiver, line sync and field sync signals are separated from the picture signal and control the scanning pattern in the picture tube.

screen. The electrons, striking the fluorescent screen excite the atoms of the screen's material and cause it to glow—thus producing the visual display. The intensity of the glow is proportional to the intensity of the electron beam which is controlled by an element within the electron gun.

The components so far mentioned would be unable to make a useful display. The electron beam on leaving the gun is divergent, that is it spreads out, producing a large dim spot on the screen. It must therefore be focused by a *focusing system* which makes the electron beam converge to a fine point at the surface of the screen. Also a *deflection system* is required so that the electron beam (and therefore the spot on the screen) can be moved around.

Electron gun
An electron gun works on the same principle as the electronic valve [vacuum tube]. It has basically three components: a cathode, grid and anode. The anode is maintained at a high positive voltage with respect to the cathode, which is made of the reactive alkali metal caesium. When the cathode is heated by a small heating element, the caesium gives off electrons. The electrons, which are negatively charged particles, move towards the anode. In the centre of this anode is a small hole through which some of the electrons pass, forming a diverging beam in the direction of the screen. The intensity of the beam is controlled by the grid placed between the cathode and the anode. By varying the voltage on the grid the flow of electrons to the anode can be controlled.

Focusing system
The diverging electron beam can be focused using either an electrostatic or a magnetic field 'lens' in the same way that a glass lens is used for focusing light. In both cases a carefully shaped field pattern is established which bends the electrons moving through the field into a converging beam.

Deflection systems
Deflection is also achieved using either an electrostatic or magnetic field. Two such systems are required: one

to deflect the electron beam horizontally (left or right) and the other to deflect the beam vertically (up or down). In this way, all points on the screen can be covered by the electron beam.

With electrostatic focusing and deflection the required elements must be positioned within the evacuated tube. With magnetic systems, however, it is possible to position them externally, thus making construction simpler and cheaper.

Fluorescent materials
CRTs producing black and white displays commonly use silver activated zinc sulphide and silver activated zinc-cadmium sulphide as fluorescent materials. When mixed in the correct proportions, these produce a bluish white glow under excitation.

In a television receiver the appearance of a continuous picture is created by scanning the screen with the electron beam in a series of horizontal lines—varying the intensity of the beam while scanning. Because of the speed with which this is done, the eye perceives a complete picture with various shades of brightness—the individual lines being too fine and close to distinguish easily.

With TV CRTs the choice of materials is important because of a phenomenon called afterglow or *persistence*, where the material continues to glow for a while after the electron beam has been removed. The persistence of the screen material helps to maintain the picture continuity between scans. Television screens are scanned at a repetitive rate of about 25 times a second. If the persistence or glow time is much greater than 1/25 second, blurring will occur when fast actions are being displayed. On the other hand, a persistence much less than 1/25 second will lead to 'flickering' as the picture fades away before being rescanned.

Sound accompaniment
In many closed-circuit applications of television, the picture provides all the information that is required and there is no need for any sound accompaniment. In television broadcasting, however, sound is essential and is radiated from a separate transmitter, which commonly

Far left: the control room of a television station at Pago Pago in American Samoa. Centre: television transmitting equipment. The klystrons (red) are used to generate an ultra high frequency (UHF) carrier wave which is then modulated with the audio and video signals. This is fed to powerful transmission aerials which transmit the signal to receiving aerials. The receiver separates out the video and sound signals as described right, and demodulates the signals to reproduce the original scene and sound track. Frequency modulation and the general principles of aerials and matching networks are described on pages 40–44. Right: monitor screens display the outputs from cameras and telecine machines so that these can be selected and integrated as necessary.

uses the same transmitting aerial as the vision transmitter. Sometimes, as in the British 405 line system, the sound is radiated by amplitude modulation but for the 625 line system, frequency modulation (see page 40), is used for the sound accompaniment. One advantage of using FM is that the *inter-carrier method* of sound reception (described later) can be used in the receiver.

Television channels

The sound carrier frequency is placed near that of the vision so that both signals can be amplified simultaneously in the early stages of receivers and the two signals are together regarded as constituting a *television channel*. The *frequency band* occupied by a channel depends on the spacing of the sound and vision carriers and on the frequency band of the vision signal. For the 405 line system channels are spaced at 5 MHz intervals and for the 625 line system at 8 MHz intervals. Sound radio transmissions are usually identified by their *wavelength* (in the medium wave band) or *carrier frequency* (in the very high frequency, VHF, band) but television transmissions are known by their channel numbers. It is, however, unnecessary to know the numbers because channel selection on most receivers is by push buttons labelled by the programme: for example BBC1, IBA, and so on.

Black and white receiver

Various operations must be carried out on the video signal and in practice may be achieved by one or more valves [vacuum tubes], one or more transistors or by integrated circuits. Early receivers used valves only and later receivers employed a mixture of valves and transistors. Most modern receivers use transistors only or a mixture of transistors and integrated circuits.

Television receivers operate on the *superheterodyne principle*, that is, most of the amplification and *selectivity* of the receiver is provided by an amplifier known as the *intermediate frequency* (IF) amplifier (see page 45). The carrier frequency of every signal selected by the tuner is changed to the IF value applied to the IF amplifier. The tuner contains a *frequency changer* stage and a preceding carrier frequency amplifier known as a *radio frequency* (RF) amplifier.

Channel selection in the tuner is commonly controlled by push buttons or multi-position rotary selectors, but continuous tuning is sometimes provided, particularly in portable receivers. The video and sound signals for the selected channel are amplified together in the early stages of the receiver but are divorced later and handled by separate circuits. The video signal is abstracted from the modulated carrier by the *vision detector*, and after further amplification, is applied to the picture tube. The sync signals are removed from the video signal in the *sync-separator* stage and the line sync signals are applied to the line *oscillator* to lock it at the correct frequency. The output of the line oscillator is fed to deflection coils clamped around the neck of the picture tube and these are responsible for horizontal scanning. The frequency of the line oscillator can be adjusted by a control (called line hold or horizontal hold) to bring it into the range in which locking occurs. The field oscillator (responsible for vertical deflection) is similarly locked, the frequency control being labelled field (or frame) hold, or vertical hold. The sound signal (assumed amplitude modulated) is abstracted from the modulated carrier by the sound detector and, after amplification, is applied to the loudspeaker.

John Logie Baird

John Logie Baird was the first man to demonstrate that television was a practical possibility. The son of a minister, he was born at Helensburgh, near Glasgow on 13 August 1888. He served as an apprentice engineer in a Glasgow factory, and studied at Glasgow University and the Royal Technical College (now the University of Strathclyde).

Dogged by ill-health, Baird was declared unfit for military service in 1914, and soon decided to leave his work as an electrical engineer and set himself up as an inventor. In 1923, exhausted by his various enterprises and ordered to recuperate after a complete breakdown, he concentrated on the idea of sending pictures by radio waves.

In that year he produced his first crude apparatus, using a scanning disc pierced with holes, in which the shadow of a cross was recorded and transferred to a screen. The following year, in a small workshop in Hastings, he gave the first demonstration of television, and in 1925, with a capital of £500 he formed a company called Television Limited. He approached the Marconi organization with his ideas, but was told that they were not interested in developing television.

Baird achieved a breakthrough in 1926, when the BBC (British Broadcasting Corporation) agreed to broadcast a picture from his transmitter to a receiver, the first wireless transmission of television. In 1927 the Baird Television Development Company was formed, and in 1928 a short wave television transmission was sent from London to New York. A year earlier, in Glasgow, Baird had demonstrated his first colour television set.

It was clear to all concerned that television, to be a success, needed the co-

operation of the BBC, and several experiments were arranged. The first public transmission was made on 30 September, 1929, with a speech by Sir Ambrose Fleming, the inventor of the radio valve [vacuum tube]. At this time there were fewer than 30 television sets in the country capable of receiving it, but as news of the invention spread, and test transmissions continued, the Baird Company received orders for thousands of receivers. On 14 July, 1930, the first television play was transmitted.

By this time the Marconi-EMI company, in association with the Radio Corporation of America, had produced cathode ray receivers along the lines of modern sets and were posing a serious challenge to Baird's mechanical scanning method. For his part, Baird saw no future in the cathode ray tube system. Anxious to score some more 'firsts', Baird televised the Derby horserace in 1931 and 1932. The second transmission was seen by 5000 people in the Metropole Theatre, London on an improved large screen, and was reported as 'the most thrilling demonstration of the possibilities of television yet witnessed'. In 1934, however, the BBC decided to adopt the Marconi-EMI system, and Baird never forgave them for this decision.

Baird died at Bexhill on 14 June 1946, while working on colour and stereoscopic (three dimensional) television systems. Although his mechanical scanning method was abandoned commercially in his own lifetime, he is rightly known as the 'father of television'.

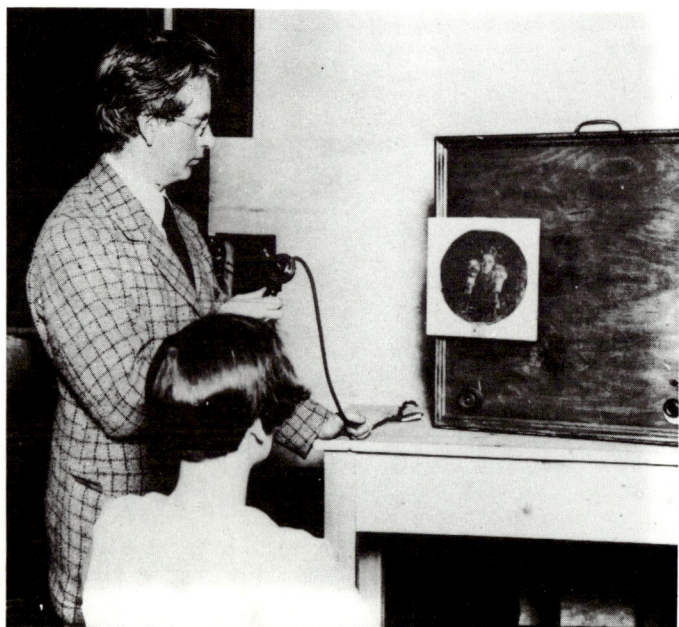

Top: John Logie Baird, 1888-1946. Left: Baird demonstrates his television apparatus in 1926. The image of his assistant can be seen between the two dolls.

COLOUR TELEVISION

Below: a modern, portable colour television camera. This camera automatically aligns the images from the picture tubes and balances the colour.

Countries which have only recently started their television service can profit from recent advances and can begin with colour: South Africa is an example of such a country. It is more usual, however, for colour television to be introduced into a country which has already had a black and white service for many years. To enable a colour service to co-exist with black and white television, a number of technical requirements must be met: first, the colour transmissions must fit into the frequency band of existing black and white channels; second, black and white receivers must give a satisfactory black and white picture when tuned to colour transmissions (known as *compatibility*); and third, colour receivers must give good black and white pictures when tuned to black and white transmissions (known as *reverse compatibility*).

Colour information

To satisfy these requirements the colour television system is basically the black and white one already described, to which additional signals have been added to provide information on colour. Indeed, the picture given by a colour television receiver is fundamentally black and white with areas filled in by colour.

To enable a receiver to reproduce the correct colour for each coloured area of the image it must be given two items of information: the basic colour (or *hue*) and its strength (or *saturation*). The hue (whether it is red, yellow, green or whatever) is determined by the position of the colour in the spectrum. Saturation is a measure of the strength or weakness of the colour. If the hue is red, the colour may be crimson, pink or some intermediate shade. In other words it is the extent to which the colour is diluted by white. Crimson is a saturated colour and pink unsaturated.

Information about the hue and saturation of every coloured area of the picture must therefore be sent to the receiving end. This information is not sent directly in the form of measurements of hue and saturation but as follows.

R, G and B signals

Green paint can be made by mixing blue and yellow paint, and purple by mixing blue and red. In fact by using only three primary colours it is possible, by varying the proportions of each, to produce practically all known colours. This principle is used in colour printing: it is also used in colour television and the colours chosen for television are red, green and blue (generally abbreviated to R, G and B). It is necessary, therefore, to analyse the image of the original coloured scene and for each coloured area to measure what fraction of its colour is contributed by red, green and blue.

This analysis is carried out in the colour television camera. The image is split into its red, green and blue components with *dichronic mirrors*. These are mirrors of special construction which can reflect light belonging to particular regions of the spectrum but permit the remainder to pass through unhindered. The red, green

and blue images so obtained are focused on the targets of three identical camera tubes, each containing an electron beam as in the black and white system. The three beams are focused on their respective targets and scan them in exact synchronism. From the tubes three picture signals are obtained, one representing the red content of the picture, another the green content and the third the blue content. By combining these outputs, we get a signal representing the black and white content

57

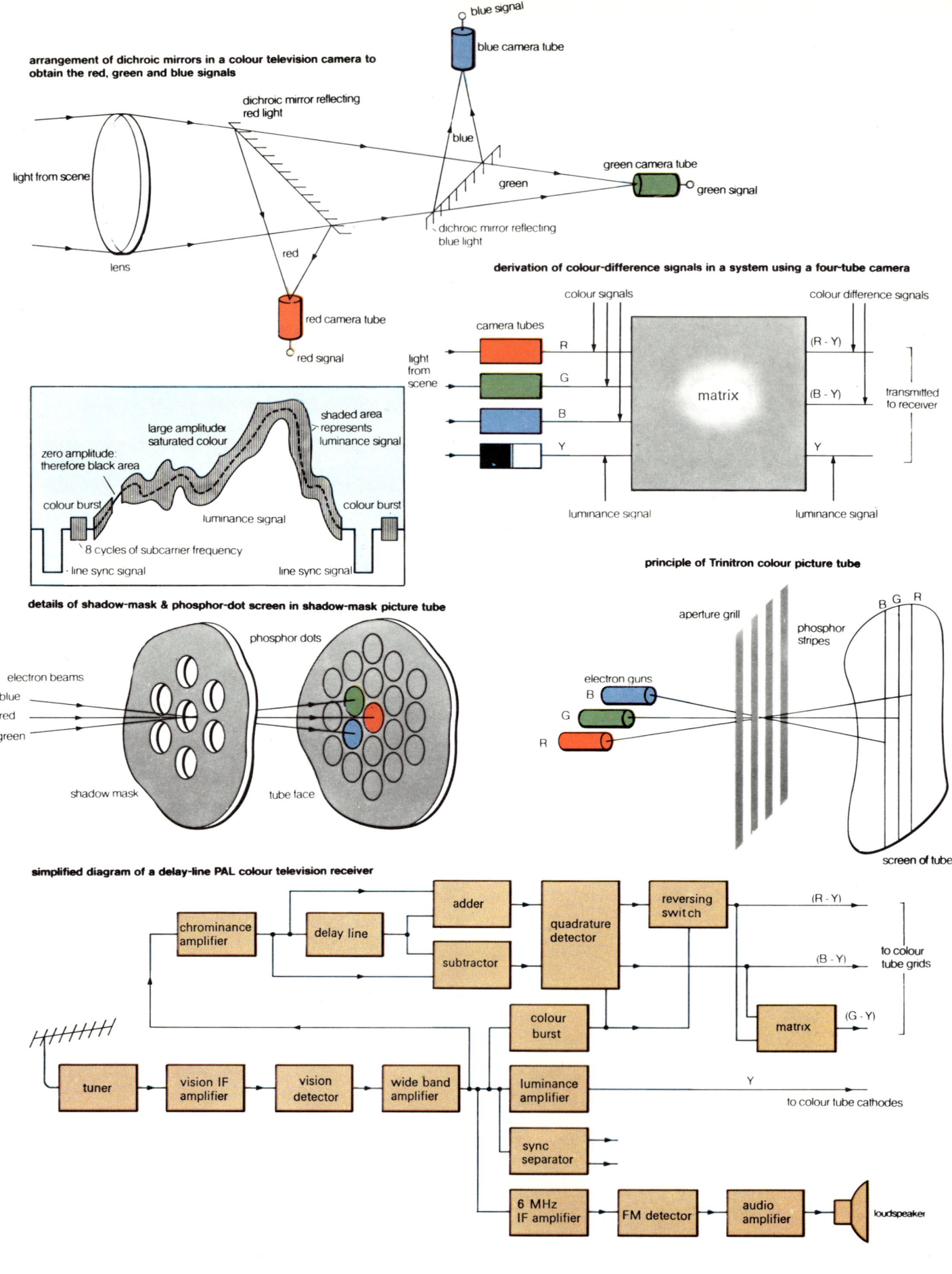

arrangement of dichroic mirrors in a colour television camera to obtain the red, green and blue signals

blue signal

blue camera tube

dichroic mirror reflecting red light

light from scene

blue

green camera tube

green signal

green

dichroic mirror reflecting blue light

lens

red

red camera tube

red signal

derivation of colour-difference signals in a system using a four-tube camera

colour signals

colour difference signals

camera tubes

light from scene

R

G

B

Y

matrix

(R - Y)

(B - Y)

Y

transmitted to receiver

luminance signal

luminance signal

large amplitude: saturated colour

shaded area represents luminance signal

zero amplitude: therefore black area

colour burst

8 cycles of subcarrier frequency

line sync signal

luminance signal

colour burst

line sync signal

details of shadow-mask & phosphor-dot screen in shadow-mask picture tube

phosphor dots

electron beams

blue

red

green

shadow mask

tube face

principle of Trinitron colour picture tube

aperture grill

phosphor stripes

electron guns

B

G

R

B G R

screen of tube

simplified diagram of a delay-line PAL colour television receiver

chrominance amplifier

delay line

adder

subtractor

quadrature detector

reversing switch

(R - Y)

(B - Y)

to colour tube grids

colour burst

matrix

(G - Y)

tuner

vision IF amplifier

vision detector

wide band amplifier

luminance amplifier

Y

to colour tube cathodes

sync separator

6 MHz IF amplifier

FM detector

audio amplifier

loudspeaker

of the picture, as from a single tube black and white television camera, and this combined signal, known as the *luminance* signal, is the basic signal transmitted in a colour television system: it is the luminance signal which is accepted and displayed by a black and white receiver tuned to a colour transmission.

Four tube camera

To obtain a good luminance signal from a three tube camera, all three scanning beams, must, at every instant, be scanning the same element of the same line of the optical image. This is difficult to ensure but the difficulty can be avoided by using a four tube camera.

In this the red, green and blue tubes are used only to give colour information. The fourth tube is fed with the original coloured image and produces a picture signal output as in black and white television: this output is used as the luminance signal. It is, of course, essential for all four beams to be synchronized and for all four optical images to be carefully aligned, but lack of alignment between the luminance and colour tubes does not degrade the quality of the luminance signal.

Transmission of colour information

The three outputs of the colour camera tubes must be transmitted to the receiving end because a colour picture tube requires red, green and blue inputs. To transmit information about three varying quantities such as the red, green and blue content of the picture requires three separate signals. These signals need not, however, be the R, G and B picture signals themselves. Any three signals which contain R, G and B will do because from these the R, G and B signals can be obtained by algebraic operations in a circuit known as a *matrix*.

The operation of the matrix is similar to that of the algebra used in solving simultaneous equations. One signal involving R, G and B already exists as the luminance signal, usually represented by Y. Two other signals are therefore required, and the two selected are the (R–Y) and (B–Y) signals, known as *colour-difference signals*. A subcarrier is used to transmit the two colour difference signals and a number of methods have been devised for modulating the subcarrier by two independent signals and for recovering them at the

Left: the colour content of a scene can be recorded and reproduced if information about the red (R), green (G) and blue (B) primary colours is known. In a colour camera this information is obtained from dichroic mirrors (optical filters). A luminance signal (Y) is also required. This is obtained from a black and white camera tube. As Y is the sum of R, G and B, only two other independent signals need to be transmitted. For convenience, these are the colour difference signals (R–Y) and (B–Y). For transmission, the Y signal forms the basic signal for compatibility with black and white transmissions, and the colour difference signals are combined on to a subcarrier frequency. At the receiver (R–Y), (B–Y) and Y are separated and (G–Y) is generated from these.

receiver. To keep the colour transmission within the channel, the colour subcarrier is located within the frequency band of the video signal and its frequency is carefully chosen and maintained to prevent it and the modulating signals from causing interference with the luminance signal.

NTSC system

The first colour television system was the NTSC (National Television System Committee) introduced into the USA in 1954 and still used there and in Japan, Canada and Mexico. In this system the colour subcarrier is amplitude-modulated by the two colour difference signals by a method known as *quadrature modulation*.

The method involves resolving the carrier wave into two components with a 90° phase difference between them. Each component is then separately amplitude modulated by a colour difference signal. One of the features of the system is that during modulation the subcarrier itself is suppressed. This is permissible because the colour information is obtained in the *sidebands*. The suppression of the subcarrier improves the quality of the compatible black and white picture by removing the fine pattern which it would otherwise produce on the receiver screen.

After modulation the two colour difference signals are combined to form the *chrominance signal*. The colour difference signals can be recovered at the receiver in a circuit known as a *quadrature detector*. This requires for its operation a reference signal very accurately locked to the subcarrier frequency. A few cycles of the subcarrier are therefore transmitted immediately after each line sync signal: this is known as the *colour burst*.

During transmission the chrominance signal is superimposed on the luminance signal. The effect of quadrature modulation and the subsequent combination of the two colour difference signals is to produce a new signal at the subcarrier frequency, the amplitude and phase of which convey the colour information. The hue is represented by the phase of the chrominance signal relative to that of the colour burst, and the saturation is represented by the amplitude of the chrominance signal.

The system works well but has one disadvantage—any variations in the phase of the chrominance signal are interpreted by the receiver as changes in hue. Unwanted phase changes do occur in transmitting equipment (particularly videotape machines) and in the receiver itself. It is therefore essential in an NTSC receiver to have an over-riding phase control which can be manually adjusted to give correct hues. This control is normally set to give good rendering of flesh colour (according to the viewer's preference) and all other colours are then automatically correct.

PAL (phase alternating line) system

To overcome the effects on reproduced hue of unwanted phase changes in the chrominance signal, the

Telefunken Laboratories in Hanover developed a system of automatic compensation which is so effective that PAL receivers do not have and do not need a hue control. This is the colour system used in the United Kingdom, Australia and most of the European countries (except those using the SECAM system).

The method used is to reverse the polarity of the (R–Y) signal on alternate lines at the transmitting end. The reversal is achieved by an electronic switch and a similar switch (operated at the same instants) is required at the receiver to restore the original polarity.

Suppose there is an unwanted phase change which would cause the hues along a particular line of the displayed picture to be too red. Then, as a result of the polarity reversal, on the next line the reproduced hues would not be red enough. If the picture signals for these two lines are averaged, the resulting picture signal is free of phase error and if the averaged picture signal is displayed the picture so obtained is free of errors in hue, This is the technique used in PAL.

To enable a comparison to be made between the picture signals for successive lines, the receiver incorporates a delay device which introduces a time lag equal to the duration of one line (64 microseconds in the 625 line system). Thus, while the picture signal for a particular line is being transmitted, that for the previous line is being delivered from the delay device. The picture signals for both lines are thus available at the same time and the receiver is able not only to produce the average of the two but to separate the (R–Y) and (B–Y) signals in a most ingenious manner described later. The delay device is usually a glass block and the delay is achieved by propagating ultrasonic waves through it. The chrominance signal (frequency 4.43 MHz) is injected into one end of the block by a piezo-electric transducer. The need to introduce a delay device makes a PAL colour receiver more complex and more expensive than an NTSC receiver.

SECAM system

The third system of chrominance modulation is that developed in France and used in that country, in the German Democratic Republic, in Hungary, Algeria and the USSR. This is known as SECAM (système en couleurs à mémoire). The (R–Y) and (B–Y) colour difference signals are sent during alternate lines and by *frequency modulation* (FM) of the chrominance subcarrier. The SECAM receiver is simpler than a PAL receiver in that FM detectors are used to recover the colour information, but an electronic switch and a line-time delay device are necessary to ensure that (R–Y) and (B–Y) signals are present simultaneously.

The system is immune from the effects of phase distortion but there is a slight loss of definition because half the colour information is not used. Moreover a SECAM picture when reproduced on a black and white receiver is not so satisfactory as from the other two systems: it is not possible with SECAM to suppress the colour subcarrier as in NTSC and PAL.

Shadow-mask picture tube

There are several different types of colour picture but the most popular is the *shadow-mask* type. This has three electron guns, one for each of the primary colours, arranged in delta formation, that is, at the corners of an equilateral triangle. The three electron beams are focused on the screen and scan it as in a black and white tube. Very near the screen there is a shadow mask: this is a metal plate containing about half a million small holes arranged in a regular pattern.

Associated with each hole is a group of three *phosphor* dots, known as a *trida*, on the inside of the tube face. One of these dots glows red when struck by the electron beam, another glows green and the third blue. The arrangement is such that the beam from the red gun can strike only the red dots, that from the green gun on the green dots and so on. The intensity of the three beams is controlled by the R, G and B signals generated in the receiver decoder. If there is a saturated blue area in the scene, then the red and green signals go to zero when the corresponding area of the tube face is scanned, and only the blue gun operates in this area. If the area is an un-saturated blue then the red and green signals are present also as the area is scanned so as to provide the white light which desaturates the blue: the red and green colours combine with part of the blue colour to produce white which combines with the remainder of the (saturated) blue to produce light (unsaturated) blue.

The dot structure of the tube face coating is too small to be seen at normal viewing distances and the effect is that the tube face is fully filled with picture. If, however, the tube face is examined through a magnifying glass the dot structure can easily be seen.

The shadow-mask tube has three electron beams and can thus produce three images; one red, one green and one blue. Ideally these images should be perfectly superimposed so as to reproduce the colours of the original scene. A very large number of adjustments, known as *convergence* adjustments, are necessary to secure perfect registration of the three *primary* images and special *pattern generators* are used to facilitate these adjustments.

Trinitron picture tube

In the Sony Trinitron tube the red, green and blue phosphors are deposited on the inner face of the tube in the form of vertical stripes, several hundred in number. In place of the shadow-mask there is a metal grill with vertical slots, one for each group of three phosphor stripes. The electron gun is required to produce three beams in a horizontal line; this greatly simplifies the design which consists of a single gun (compared with three in the shadow-mask tube) with three cathodes arranged in line. This tube can be made very compact and is thus suitable for use in portable colour television receivers. Convergence adjustments are simpler than on a shadow-mask tube. The system is, however, more suitable for small screens than large ones because

above a certain size the vertical phosphor stripes become obtrusively visible.

Colour television receivers

The PAL colour television receiver (incorporating a delay line) has a tuner, vision intermediate frequency (IF) amplifier, vision detector, sync separator, line and field deflection circuits as in a black and white receiver. Sound is, however, transmitted by frequency modulation of a carrier displaced by 6 MHz from the vision carrier: this makes possible the *inter-carrier* method of sound reception. All the circuits before the vision detector and the amplifier following it have a frequency band wide enough to accept the vision and sound signals. As a result of the detection process the sound signal emerges from the detector as a frequency-modulated carrier of 6 MHz. A sound IF amplifier, tuned to 6 MHz, can thus be used after the wideband amplifier to select the sound signal. An FM detector followed by an audio amplifier are then necessary, to provide a signal for the loudspeaker.

From the wideband amplifier the chrominance signal is selected by a filter and is applied to the delay line. The circuit surrounding the delay line is interesting because it provides a most effective method of separating the two colour difference signals while they are still in the form of modulated carriers. The (R–Y) signal is reversed in polarity on alternate lines and so if the direct signal is added to that which has passed through the delay line, the two signals cancel, leaving only the (B–Y) signal. The (B–Y) signal is not subjected to polarity reversal and thus the direct (B–Y) signal is in phase with that which has traversed the delay device. Cancellation of the (B–Y) signals can thus be achieved

by subtracting the direct and delayed signals, leaving only the (R–Y) signal.

Associated with the quadrature detector is the (R–Y) polarity-reversing switch which eliminates any phase errors. The switch is operated from the colour burst as indicated. The only effect of this phase-error cancelling circuit is a small, usually imperceptible, reduction in colour saturation in reproduced pictures.

It is possible to use a matrix which accepts the (R–Y), (B–Y) and Y signals and derives from them the corresponding R, G and B signals which can be applied directly to the input of the colour picture tube. It is more usual, however, to design the matrix to produce the third colour difference signal (G–Y). The picture tube *grids* are now fed with the (R–Y), (G–Y) and (B–Y) signals and the *cathodes* are fed with the Y signal. The Y signal is thus common to each grid and cathode and so cancels: in effect, therefore the grids are fed with the R, G and B signals as required. This elaborate method of driving the tube is adopted in the interests of reverse compatibility. If the colour receiver is tuned to a black and white transmission, a circuit detects the absence of the subcarrier and 'kills' the colour difference circuits so that no signals are fed to the picture tube grids. The Y (luminance) signal is still applied to the tube cathodes as in a black and white receiver: thus the colour receiver reproduces a black and white signal in black and white.

TELEVISION TECHNIQUES

The preceding chapters have explained how a television image is built up of lines. This technique of picture presentation makes possible a number of special effects which are exploited in television programme production.

A number of these effects are means of replacing one image by another. This can be done instantaneously (a technique known as a 'cut') or the first image can gradually disappear at the same time as the second appears: this is known as a 'cross fade'. Two images can be superimposed or the left hand half of one image can share the screen with the right hand half of another image. This 'split screen' technique is commonly used in television plays to show the players at two ends of a telephone conversation. A vertical line separates the two half images in this example but it could be a horizontal or diagonal line. It is possible to make the image separating line move across the screen, eliminating one image and apparently, 'uncovering' the other: this is known as a 'wipe'. All the facilities so far mentioned are available on *vision mixing desks* using techniques such as *inlay* and *colour separation overlay*.

Inlay

It is possible in television to eliminate any area of one image and to replace it by the corresponding area of another and there are two techniques which can be used to achieve this. One method, employed in black and white television, uses a cathode ray tube, the screen of which is scanned by an electron beam synchronized with the beams in each of the camera tubes producing the images to be 'married'. The electron beam in the cathode ray tube is not modulated and the

Above: flight arrival and departure times are displayed on colour television screens at an airport terminal. This kind of display is invaluable wherever data has to be constantly changed and updated. Similar information screens are widely used to give stock market prices, train times, and for various monitoring functions in industry.

screen is therefore uniformly illuminated by the 405 or 625 scanning lines. A photoelectric cell near the centre of the screen responds to the light from the screen, and the electrical output of the cell operates (after amplification) a changeover switch which substitutes one camera output for the other.

If half the cathode ray tube screen is covered by an opaque card with a straight vertical edge, the photocell will be illuminated while half of each line is scanned and in darkness while the other half is scanned. The switchover from one camera output to the other therefore occurs at the middle of each line and the composite image obtained from this system consists of the left hand half of one camera output and the right hand half of the other. By moving the card, a wipe effect can be obtained and by using various shapes of mask on the cathode ray tube screen a number of interesting effects can be produced. For example, suppose that one camera is focused on an indoor scene such as a room with a window and that the mask is made to fit precisely the window area. In the final picture the window area is in fact the corresponding area from the second camera and this could be a country scene (from a still photograph or transparency) or even a street scene containing moving traffic from a *telecine* or video-

Left: Closed circuit television is widely used for educational purposes. The camera (top) enables students to see what the teacher is writing even if they are in another room. This picture shows a language centre. Below left: principle of inlay equipment. For simplicity, the changeover switch is shown as a mechanical type. In colour separation overlay equipment (bottom) the blue area of the scene of camera 1 is replaced by the scene of camera 2. As with inlay equipment, switchover is achieved electronically and not mechanically as this would not be fast enough.

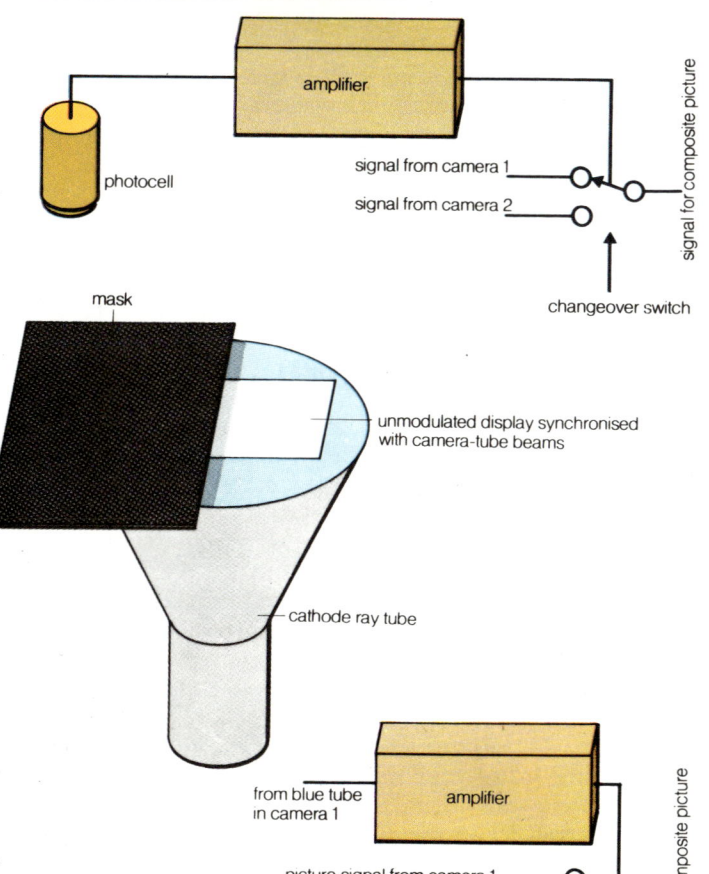

tape machine. This system of marrying parts of two images is known as *inlay*.

Colour separation overlay

The second method of marrying parts of two images is used in colour television and does not require a cathode ray tube and mask. The parts of scene 1 which are not required in the final picture are coloured a particular shade of blue and the output of the blue tube in the colour television camera is used to control the changeover switch. For example, it could be arranged that every time a blue area of scene 1 is scanned the switch selects the output of camera 2. This system, known as *colour separation overlay*, is particularly useful in news programmes where it is required to show, for example, the newsreader apparently sitting in front of the Houses of Parliament. The newsreader is, in fact, seated in front of a plain blue background and camera 2 is focused on a photograph or transparency of the Houses of Parliament. The system works well but care must be taken to see that none of the newsreader's clothing contains any area of blue. In place of a blue tie, for example, viewers would see the corresponding area of the Houses of Parliament apparently through a hole in the newsreader.

Caption machines

The obvious way of producing *captions* for displaying on a television screen is to have them drawn by caption artists. The resulting lettering can be displayed to a television camera or can be photographed and made into a transparency which can then be viewed by a camera or can be put into a *slide scanner*. Both processes turn the lettering into a video signal which can then be

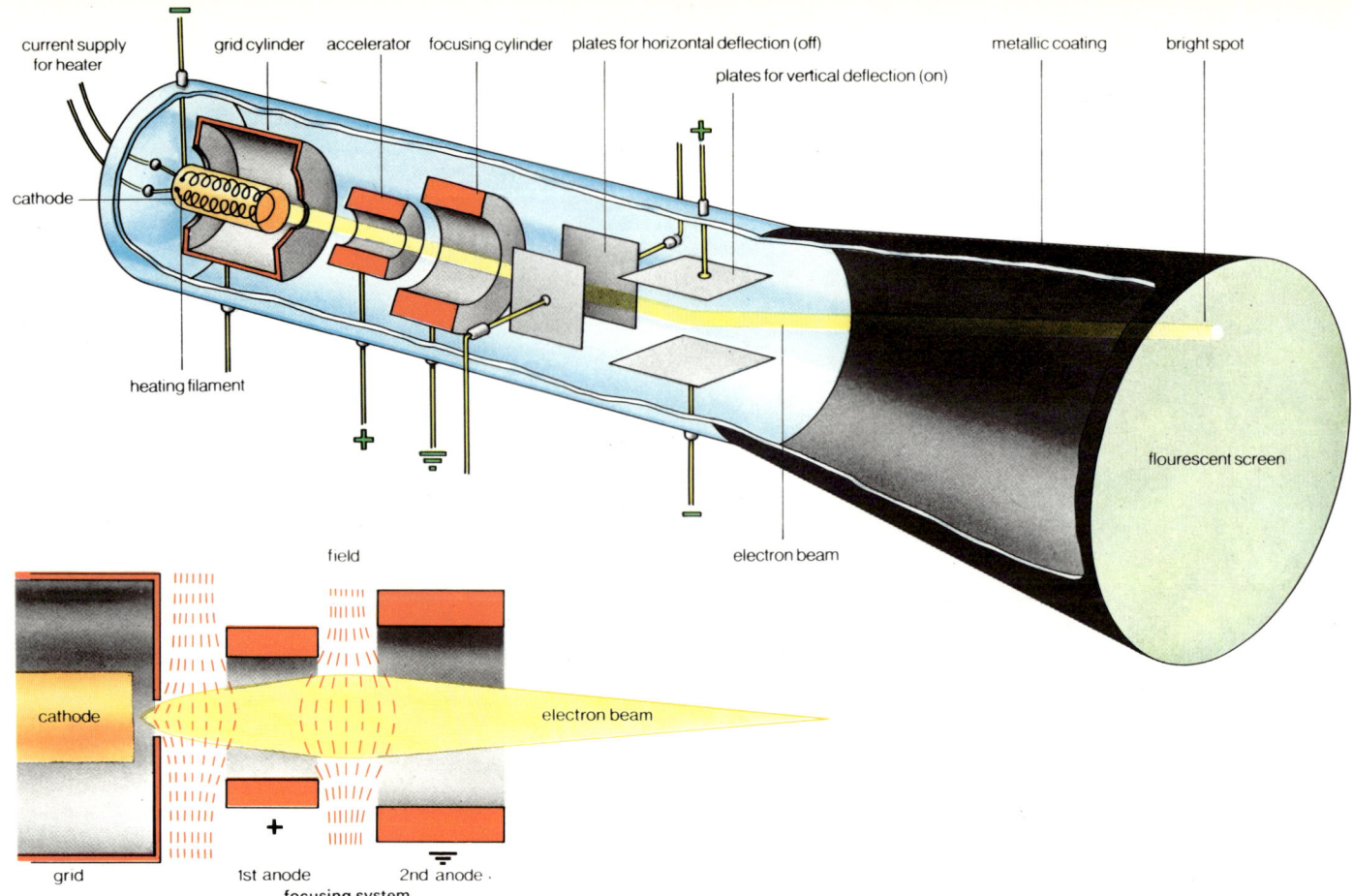

current supply for heater · grid cylinder · accelerator · focusing cylinder · plates for horizontal deflection (off) · metallic coating · bright spot

plates for vertical deflection (on)

cathode

heating filament

flourescent screen

electron beam

field

cathode

electron beam

grid · 1st anode · 2nd anode

focusing system

mixed with the video signal for a scene if the caption is required to be superimposed on the scene. Both processes, however, take time, and have now been eliminated by a technique in which captions are generated electronically.

The new machine has keys similar to those of a typewriter but when the key for a particular letter is struck the machine generates the video signal for that letter. If the video signal is fed to a television receiver the letter is displayed on the screen. Once a key is struck the machine continues to generate the relevant video waveforms so that the letter persists on the screen. By striking a succession of keys up to 25 letters can be produced in a row across the screen. This is often all that is required in a caption at the bottom of a picture but if necessary the machine can fill the screen with 14 rows of lettering. A useful feature of the machine is that captions can be prepared in advance in the form of magnetic tape or a perforated tape which can be fed into a tape reader to generate the video signals when required.

Test signals

It has already been mentioned that not all the 625 lines are seen on a receiver screen. A number are lost because the picture tube beam is cut off during the field sync signal. These unused lines can be used for transmitting information which is ignored by the television receiver.

One type of information which is transmitted in this way is a series of engineering test signals. When the television signal is received at a transmitter, the test signals give information about the performance of the various circuits and equipment throughout which the

Above: the electrostatic focusing system of a cathode ray tube creates a curved electric field which bends the divergent beam of electrons, emitted from the electron gun, into a convergent beam which comes to a point at the surface of the screen. Deflection is achieved by the vertical and horizontal deflection plates. Cathode ray tubes are used not only in domestic television sets but also in various monitoring systems, closed circuit television and radar displays. Above, right: a closed circuit televion system is used to train operating staff at Hillingdon Hospital, Uxbridge, in Great Britain. A large number of students can watch the progress of an operation without having to be present in the operating theatre.

signal has passed since its origination at a television studio centre. This signal gives engineers at the transmitter useful information about any shortcomings so that they can take remedial action.

A more recent development is the installation of computerized equipment at the transmitter which can simply assess the performance of the chain of equipment through which the signal has passed and can itself take executive action such as switching the signal to an alternative route.

Ceefax and Oracle

These are the names given to an information service which is already available on a trial basis in Britain. The service goes under the general name of 'Teletext'. It makes use of signals which are transmitted during the field sync signal and are thus ignored by conventional television receivers. The signals can, however, be selected by suitable equipment attached to or built into a television receiver and can then be displayed on the

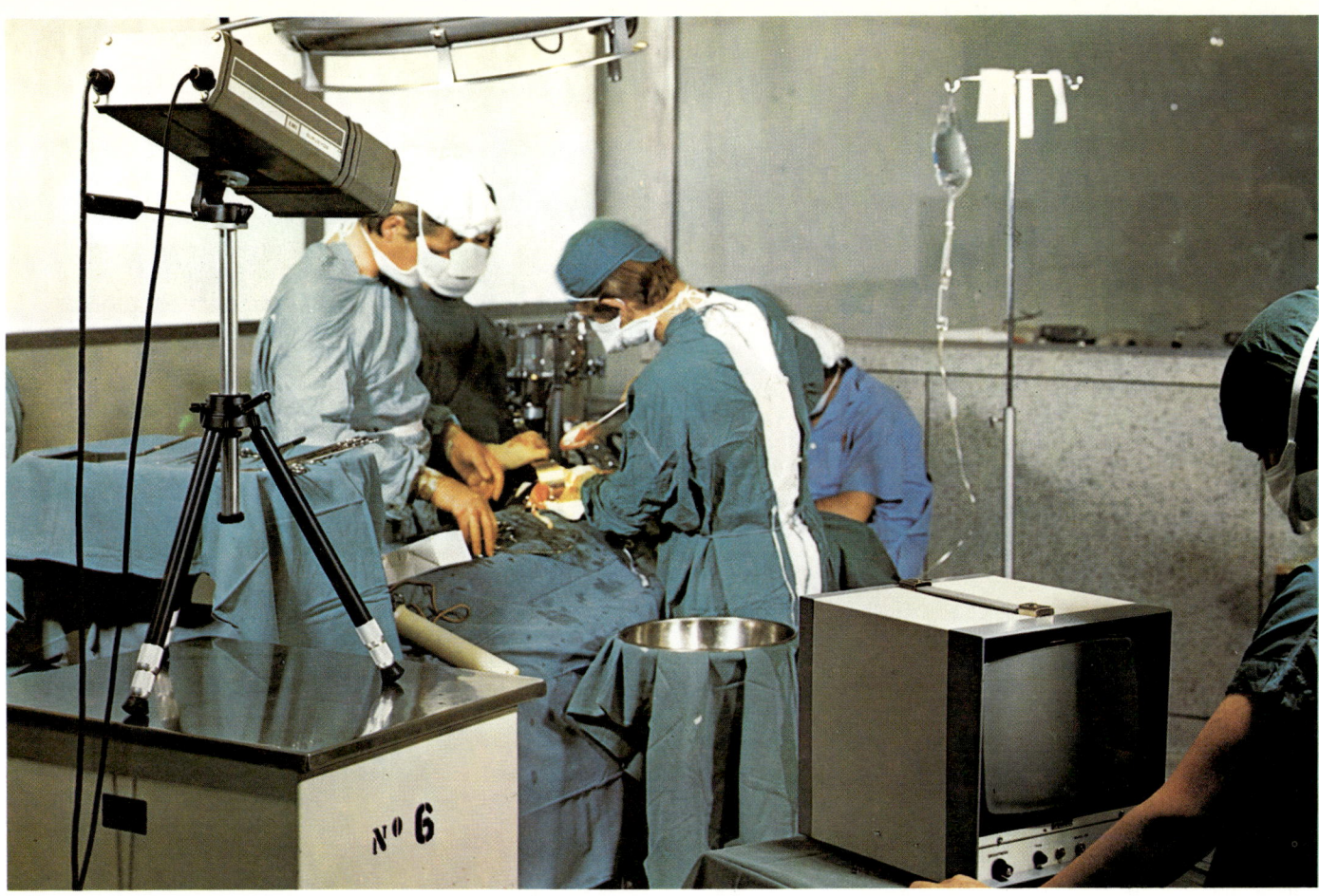

screen in place of the normal picture or superimposed on it.

When displayed the signals take the form of a series of pages of information, from one to 100, and the desired page can be selected by push buttons. Each page can have up to 24 lines of information with up to 40 characters in each. Pages can be devoted to news items, weather forecasts, sports results, stock exchange and so on. An advantage of this system is that the information can be continuously updated and can change while it is being displayed.

Viewdata

A third system is now being developed by the British Post Office. The subscriber to this system will be able to call up information on the telephone and receive a printed display on a domestic television set wired to his telephone. Viewdata will not suffer from the restriction of the television companies' systems, which can only display a limited amount of information because only two of the 625 lines are at present available for this use. Viewdata has the additional advantage of being two-way: only the material specifically requested by the individual subscriber is sent down the line. This enables the Post Office to offer currently at least 75,000 pages of data, a service which holds tremendous potential not only for the general public but for businesses which require databanks of technical information and would be willing to pay for the facility.

It remains to be seen whether these services will turn out to be in direct competition with each other, how much advertising will be required to finance them, and whether indeed they could pose a threat to the whole newspaper industry. The final judge will be the public,

who may decide that they don't wish to pay for the new service. But access to information is what the 'wired city' of the future is all about, and it seems likely that such systems could revolutionize the way we receive news bulletins and the whole business of information storage and retrieval.

Closed-circuit television

Television techniques have extensive use other than in broadcasting. There are many occasions when it is useful to be able to see what is happening at a distant point. This can be achieved readily by use of a television camera connected to one or more receivers. Normally it is not necessary to have a radio link between camera and receiver as in television broadcasting. A direct connection is all that is necessary and this gives what is known as *closed-circuit television*.

In industry, for example, television enables processes to be watched at points where it would be inconvenient or dangerous to put a human observer. Traffic control can be simplified by mounting television cameras at strategic points and observing the traffic flow at a central control room. Television can aid security, too: systems of closed-circuit televisions are used in shops and enable one operator to watch the whole floor area of large premises. Television is used in prisons to enable guards to survey the perimeter fence. It is extensively used for displaying information, particularly where there is frequent need to update the information, for example, in airports and railway stations for showing timetables. Television is used in hospitals for teaching purposes: a camera can be mounted above an operating table to enable students to watch the progress of an operation on receivers. In the UK, the Open University makes extensive use of television but, because the students are scattered over the entire country, the normal television broadcasting network is used to distribute the programmes. Various monitoring systems are discussed under Telemetry, page 90.

Television projection

An eidophor is an extremely thin film of oil acted upon by an electric field to give its surface a controlled irregularity on a microscopic scale. This oil film is the basis of a complicated but ingenious system which can convert a TV signal into a display on a cinema screen—

the word *eidophor* is Greek for 'image bearer'. It is very difficult to project a TV picture, because the original picture is created on the face of the picture tube by the phosphor screen being struck by electrons. There is no beam of light involved, and the intensity of illumination is quite low.

In the eidophor projection system the incoming TV signal is amplified in the usual way and supplied to an electron gun, but instead of directing this at a phosphor-coated screen it is aimed at the eidophor oil film. The electron bombardment creates local electrostatic charges on the oil film, and these mutually repel each other to curve the film surface in a way that, in effect, converts the oil film into an extremely fine-grain lens or mirror (depending on whether the film is on a transparent glass plate or a reflecting surface) producing a duplicate of the TV picture. The film slowly rotates, so that the incident beam of electrons is always able to act on a fresh surface. Unlike a conventional TV system, the electron beam is not modified in intensity. Instead, it is focused or defocused by the signal strength: a bright spot on the image is represented by a sharply focused beam, giving maximum deflection of the surface. The film emerging from the electron beam gradually loses its charge and 'picture', but it is swept absolutely flat by a knife blade before it re-enters the beam. This flat surface gives no picture at all.

This unique fine-grain variable lens or mirror is thus able to serve as the controller for an extremely powerful beam of light which can be projected on the screen. There are different ways of doing this, but all involve a slatted screen or mirror which as far as possible, arrests all light except that 'structured' by passing through, or being reflected, by the eidophor film.

A typical mirror has six slats, each about $\frac{1}{2}$-inch (13mm) wide, arranged at $45°$ like the slats of a half-open venetian blind. The light source, invariably an arc lamp such as a xenon arc, is reflected off the angled slats on to the eidophor surface. It reflects back towards the slats in such a way that if there is no deflection of the beam by the eidophor, the light will be stopped by the slats. If, however, there is a slight deflection caused by the electron beam, the light will not be interrupted by the slats and will pass through a projection lens on to the screen. This screen may be as large as 30 × 40 ft (9 × 12m)—as in a cinema.

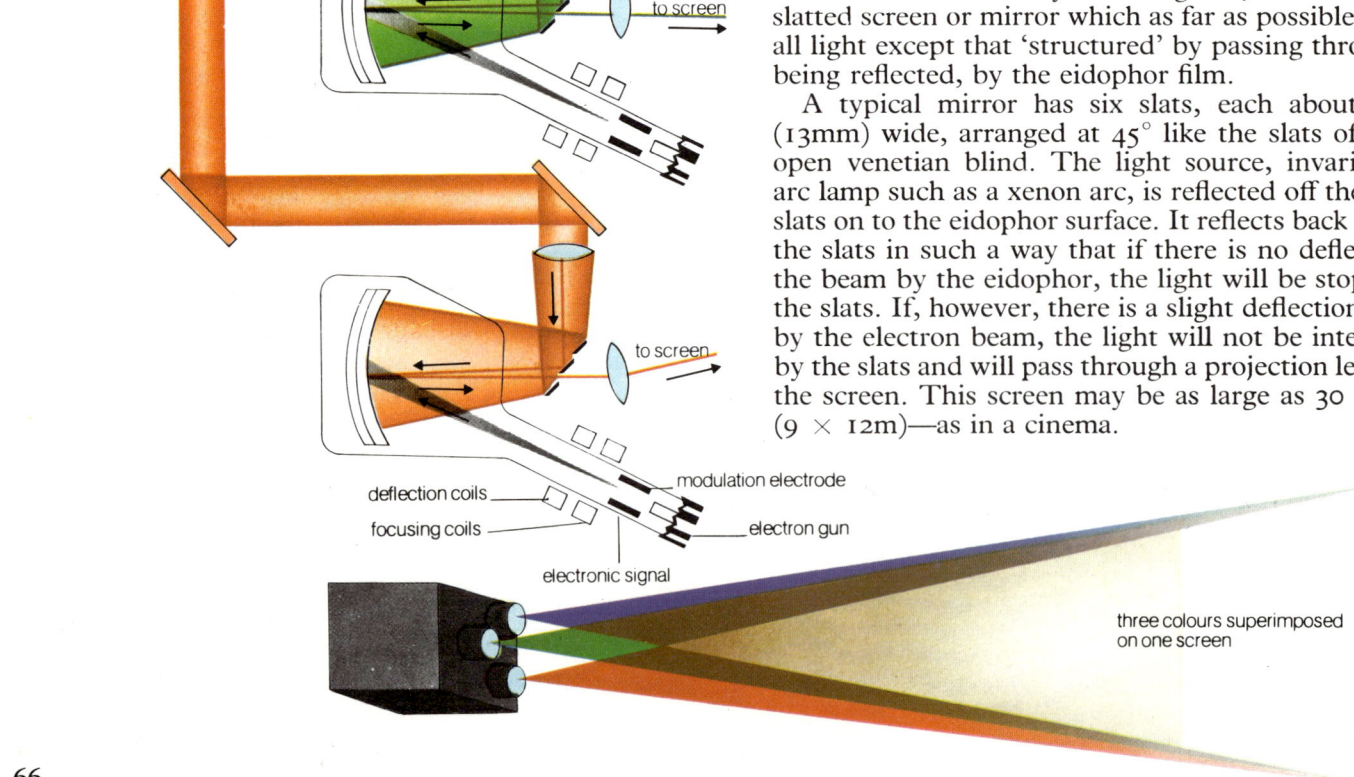

xenon lamp (light source)

dichroic mirrors

projection lens

to screen

mirror strips

to screen

to screen

deflection coils

focusing coils

modulation electrode

electron gun

electronic signal

three colours superimposed on one screen

Projecting colour

A normal colour TV set, as we have seen, uses three electron guns, aimed at red, green and blue phosphors on the TV screen. Three separate electron guns and eidophors are used in the large-screen system, again each dealing with an image which is to be projected in one colour only. To avoid problems of matching up three light sources, only one arc lamp is used, but its light is split into the three colours by a system of dichroic optical filters. These beams are then reflected on to their respective eidophors and recombine on the screen to give a full colour picture.

The eidophor is just one of several ways of producing a large picture display controlled by a TV signal, the output of a computer or some other dynamic source. Such a picture, to be useful, must change in 'real time'; that is it must faithfully reproduce the incoming signal and must not lag behind. The eidophor has the great advantage of being capable of electronic control in the purest sense, in that the controlling medium is a beam of free electrons. On the other hand, this means that the central portion of the equipment must be sealed and operated under a high vacuum. Developments of the eidophor are aimed at greater simplicity and the ability to operate at ordinary atmospheric pressure. Broad research programmes are trying to perfect rival schemes such as electroluminescent displays, displays using liquid crystals, solid state light systems (mostly based upon various kinds of LED, light emitting diode) and displays generated by fibre optics.

Far left: schematic diagram of a colour eidophor projector. The light from the lamp is split into three colours by a filter system similar to those in a colour TV camera, and each beam is then reflected on to the eidophor mirror. It may either be reflected straight back the way it came, or, if the electron beam is distorting the oil film, it will be focused by the projector lens on to the main screen. A single beam is shown for each colour in this simplified diagram.

Above left: a colour eidophor projector. The three plated casings contain the electron gun assemblies, one for each colour. Each assembly has three units, so that if the gun in use fails another can be rotated into place within seconds. Above each gun is the projector lens for that colour; the same 2.5kW lamp is used for all three systems. Above: the big screen TV system in operation. It has many uses, from the televising of sporting events to operations and conferences.

VIDEO RECORDING

The earliest video recording appeared in 1928 when John Logie Baird developed the Phonodisc. This was a 10 inch (25 cm), 78 rpm record, in every way similar to the acoustic discs already being produced for conventional sound recording at that time. The difference was that the low definition, 30-line television signal was recorded as a hill-and-dale audio modulation on the bottom of the groove which, if replayed through a loudspeaker would have produced a warbling musical note. Despite its novelty, the Phonodisc failed to be a commercial success for the same reasons that the 30-line system was abandoned in 1936 in favour of the high definition, 405-line system.

Modern video recording appeared during the 1950s with the development of magnetic tape machines 'stretched' beyond their normal audio recording capabilities, to record the very high frequency video signals which carry the information for black and white colour television pictures.

The main difficulty associated with recording a high definition video signal is not only the upper limit of the frequencies involved, which extends to 6MHz (6 million cycles a second) but also the range of frequencies, which cover about 20 octaves. The first magnetic video machine recorded its signals longitudinally on the tape and since, up to that time, the design of these machines had been based on audio recording principles, where the range of signals is only ten octaves, some method had to be devised to divide the wide bandwidth of the video signal up so that it could be recorded on a number of parallel 'tracks' on the tape.

Nevertheless, even after this division of information had been achieved, the machine still had to be capable of recording frequencies in excess of 1.5 MHz. This necessitated extremely high tape speeds, at times up to 240 inches per second (240 ips – 6.1 m/sec). A number of these longitudinal-recording machines were made in the early 1950s and successfully recorded and replayed colour television signals.

However in 1956, Ginsberg and Dolby of Ampex developed a new machine that was to revolutionize the world of professional video recording. The Ampex VTR (Video Tape Recorder) had a relatively low tape speed of 15 ips (38cm/sec). The width of the tape was 2 inches (5cm) and it was guided across the front of the head assembly and drawn into a semi-circular shape by a vacuum guide.

The head assembly consists of a small electric motor rotating a drum which carries four record-replay heads arranged at 90° intervals. These heads scan in turn, across the width of the tape as it passes through the guide assembly. As one head leaves the top edge of the tape, the next head on the drum crosses the bottom edge. By carefully synchronizing the speed of the head and that of the tape, the changeover is made to occur during a line blanking period, thus avoiding interference to the picture.

On early machines, the signals to the head were fed

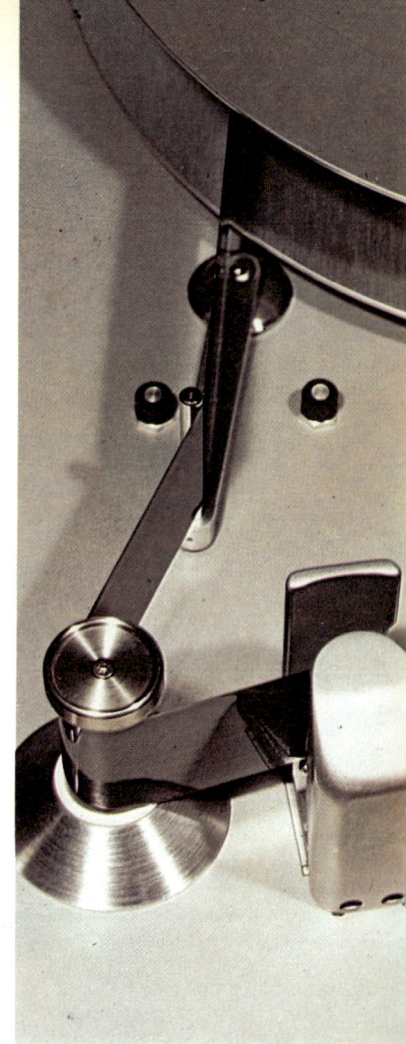

Right: the helical recording system, an alternative technique for achieving high head to tape speeds. The tape is wound on a spiral and a drum. The head or heads are situated in a slot in this drum and, as they rotate, they sweep across the tape at an angle of about 3° to the length of the tape. Below, right: closed circuit television systems with video recording facilities are becoming very popular in educational institutions and local community groups. With microelectronics all items to be found in professional studios can be made portable: monitors, mixing consoles, special effects machines and VTRs.

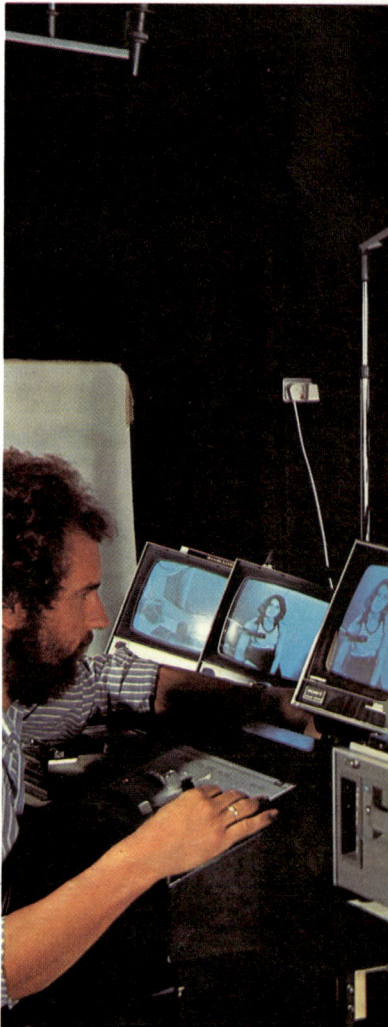

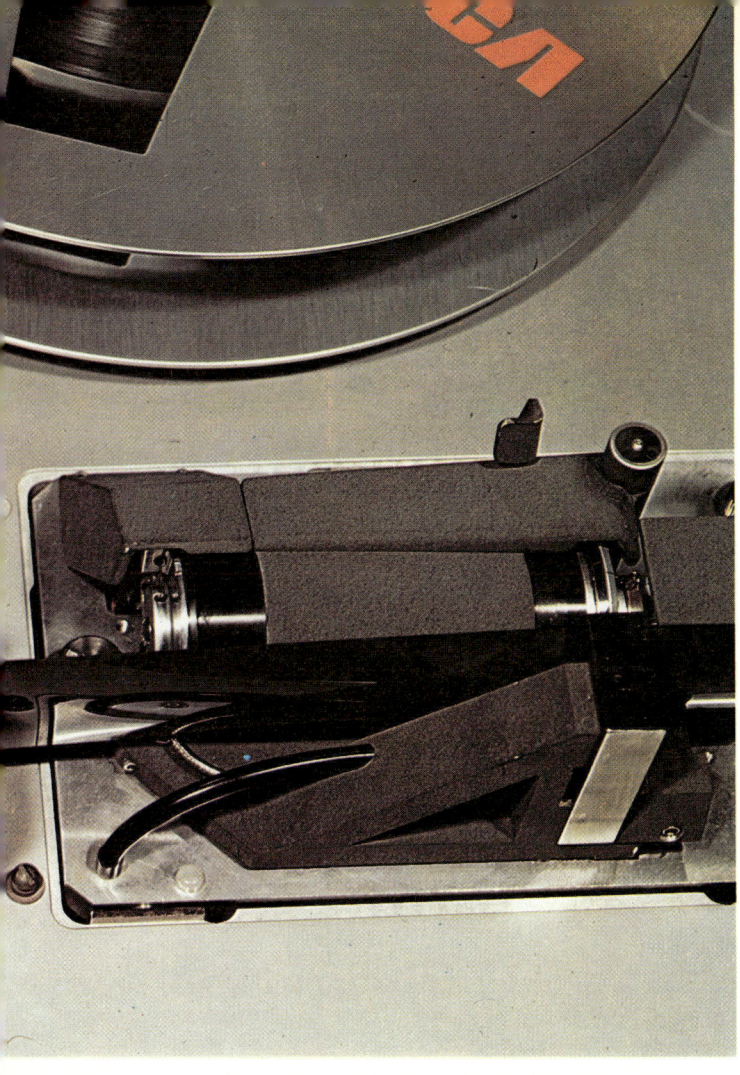

through slip rings on an extension to the motor shaft. In more modern machines, this is achieved through special transformers. This transverse recording machine is economical on tape and, from the arrangement of heads on the drum, is termed a quadruplex VTR.

The quadruplex VTR achieves a tape to head speed of approximately 1550 ips (39.4 m/sec), and is thus capable of recording much higher frequencies than achieved in the original longitudinal recording machines. But the video signals require a certain amount of pre-processing before they are fed to the recording heads.

The input video signal from the camera is first used to frequency-modulate a carrier frequency of about 50 MHz. The resulting band of frequencies extends from 49.1 to 52.1 MHz, and since this range of frequencies is rather high for even the high tape to head speed achieved by the Ampex recorder, it is converted down to the range 6.3 to 9.3 MHz. The prime purpose of first modulating the signal in this fashion is to avoid some of the potential signal error problems caused by variations in head to tape speed.

The processed band of frequencies is fed simultaneously to all the recording heads, which then convert the original electrical signal into a magnetic recording on the tape. During the recording process it is not necessary to provide an exact relationship between tape speed and the speed at which the heads rotate. This means that on replay, some method needs to be arranged to permit accurate synchronism of the rotating replay heads to locate them directly over the right portion of the recorded tracks.

This is achieved by longitudinally recording a control track along one edge of the tape, using a head placed a short distance away from the rotating video head. This recording consists of an audio signal, whose frequency is proportional to the actual rotational speed of the recording heads. On replay, the signal obtained from this control track is compared with a signal derived from a photoelectric sensor on the drive motor shaft of the video head assembly. Deviations between the two create error signals in the comparator which will alter the speed of the head drive motor to reduce and eliminate the locational error.

Similarly, audio signals carrying the sound information are recorded longitudinally on the other edge of the tape, using a conventional audio head. This type of recording machine is now manufactured under licence by several other companies, and is in regular use in all television broadcast organizations. Further developments of this system have occurred, including modifications to the head assembly, which have improved the overall performance. In addition, experimental work is under way investigating the possibilities of recording colour television signals in the form of digital pulses, in a similar fashion to data storage computers. This is a field in which new techniques are superseding the old very rapidly.

Helical recording system

Unfortunately, the type of magnetic tape video recorder just described is too complex and consumes too much tape to make it a suitable machine for use in anything other than broadcast situations. An alternative form of recording video signals was therefore developed around 1959, this being called the helical recording system.

Helical scanning is achieved by wrapping the tape around a drum in a spiral fashion. The drum is split into two by a slot which passes round its circumference and in which the recording head, or heads, rotates. Thus, if the 'wrap' angle is chosen with the correct degree of rise from one side of the drum to the other, the combination of the forward movement of the tape and the rotation of the head across the tape produces a track which is aligned to the horizontal by about 3°.

One of the major difficulties with the helical recording system is the variety of standards available in the different machines on the market. The wrap angle can vary from between 90° to 360° and the head assembly can have from one to four heads, and each track on the tape can have one or several television fields contained along its length. Because the head-to-tape speed is much slower in the helical scan system than in the quadruplex recording system, the resolution of the picture is markedly inferior.

This is because the maximum bandwidth of the domestic variety of machine is about 3 MHz, half of that attained in the broadcast machines. As a result, a variety of complex methods of signal processing is required to rearrange the content of the original 6 MHz bandwidth to something more suited to the bandwidth of the domestic machine. At the moment, the situation is very confused as far as standards are concerned for helical-scan recording systems.

There are three major systems at the moment: the Philips, EIAJ and the Sony U-Matic. The Philips system is suitable for 625-line PAL and 525-line NTSC system and the Sony U-Matic is suitable for 525-line NTSC and 625-line PAL television systems. In the case of the Philips system, a cassette is used containing two reels, one above the other. The half-inch (1.25 cm) wide tape is drawn out of the cassette in a loop and located in the operating position around the drum, by loading pins.

The EIAJ standard mainly refers to a half-inch, open-reel tape machine. Although it uses the same helical scanning principles as the Philips VCR, the tape is loaded on reels in much the same way as a conventional audio tape recorder. A few cassette machines have been produced using this particular standard, but have not proved popular. The third system originates from Sony and is called the U-Matic. The $\frac{3}{4}$ inch (1.9 cm) tape is contained within a cassette with the spools side by side, and a loop is drawn out and round the drum forming the shape of the letter U.

Both the Philips and the Sory systems are capable of recording colour video signals. Since they are pri-

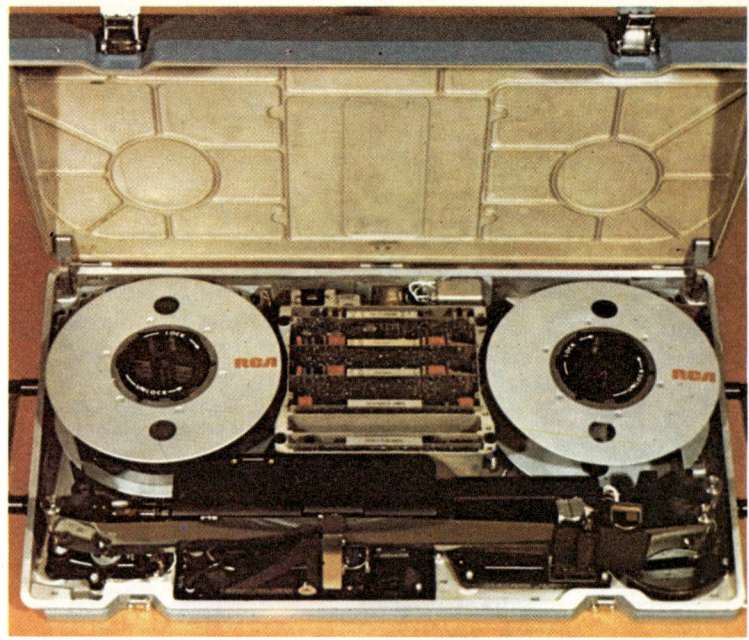

marily designed for recording television broadcasts in a private home, most of the models incorporate a small television tuner. The incoming signals from the aerial can be fed to the input of the video recorder, where they are demodulated and the video signal extracted. The video signal is then processed for recording on to the tape at frequencies ranging from 3-4.7 MHz, depending on th type of recorder. In the two systems capable of recording colour, the colour information is recorded as an amplitude modulation of 650 kHz bandwidth for the Philips system, or 500 kHz for the Sony system.

Video discs

Since the development of the helical scan recorder, other experimental video recording or playback only systems have appeared in prototype form. One is the joint venture disc system developed by Decca and AEG Telefunken, and called Teldec. Essentially it is a return to the Phonodisc version of video recording, with a number of important refinements enabling the high signal frequencies, up to 3 MHz, to be recorded and played back.

The disc is made from thin plastic of a diameter of either 8 or 12 inches (20 or 30 cm). It is rotated at a speed of 1500 rpm for a 50 Hz mains supply and 1800 rpm for a 60 Hz supply. The pickup arm and stylus is fixed in its vertical position and so the disc is raised against the stylus by a cushion of air. Since the disc is flexible, the stylus deforms the disc whilst detecting the hill and dale modulation in the groove. As these pass, they produce variations in pressure against the transducer, which is mounted on the pickup arm. These variations in pressure are converted into an electrical form suitable for processing in the video amplifiers. Both colour and black and white 625 line pictures may be recorded, although it is probable that initially, only black and white programmes will be produced. Like the conventional audio disc, home recording is not practical. The recording and duplication of the Teldec discs is almost identical to that used in the audio record industry.

Other forms of disc playback system are also being developed, a notable example being the Philips video-

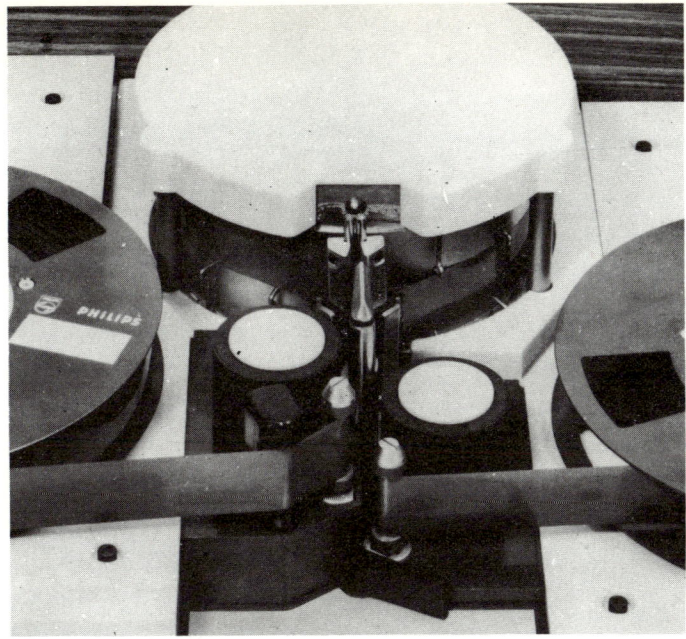

CABLE TELEVISION

Television as most homes receive it is 'broadcast' using VHF or UHF radio waves for both sound and picture. These waves are picked up by the aerial (antenna), usually mounted directionally on the roof, which relays the signal to the TV set. But where reception is poor or community TV programmes are desired another system has been developed—cable television. Programmes are relayed by a wired system which is similar in principle (but may be more complex in operation) to the electricity supply or the telephone. The system is used most extensively in the United States.

Development

Wired radio started as a supplementary means of distributing radio to listeners in the larger European towns in the early 1930s; by 1950 there were about a million subscribers in Britain alone. In the case of sound programmes, signals at high power can be distributed on groups of several pairs of cables (multipair cables), each pair going to one receiver, which consists of little more than a selector switch and a loudspeaker. This could thus, before the days of the transistor, be competitive

disc. This differs from the Teldec system, in that no direct contact is made with the disc when reading the information. The video signal is recorded in the form of a spiral track of depressions, the spacing of these representing the black and white information in the picture, and the length of which represents the colour information in the picture. The disc itself is made from plastic plated with a highly reflective metal surface.

The playback machine contains a helium-neon laser which provides an extremely small and powerful spot of light to shine on the disc. The laser beam is centred on the spiral track by an electronic servomechanism, and the reflection, which varies in intensity as the disc rotates and the depressions pass under the laser beam, is picked up by a photo-electric diode which converts the varying intensity of the reflection into an electrical signal. Again, this is a playback only system and since the 'reading' of the disc is achieved without mechanical contact, there is no wear and the disc should theoretically last indefinitely.

The rotational speed of the Philips video disc is about 25 rps and each revolution of the disc provides sufficient information to reproduce one complete picture frame consisting of two interlaced fields (or partial frames).

Other optical disc systems, said to be compatible, are also being developed in conjunction with Philips. The main difference is in the disc itself; in one system, the variation in light intensity picked up by the photo-electric diode is achieved by variable opacity in an essentially plastic disc material.

Other systems

The above represents a description of some of the methods of recording video signals. For special purposes, such as slow-motion, for stop-frame pictures as used in television broadcasts of football matches, magnetic disc recorders have been created which carry recordings of short length, but which can be 'accessed' extremely quickly. Optical film methods of recording video, such as holography, are also being experimented with, whilst the proponents of the magnetic recording systems are exploring the possibilities of recording television pictures in a digital form.

Above left: this video recording system has a rotating drum with 4 heads around it. The heads scan across the tape which is curved around the drum by a vacuum guide. Below: in some countries, notably America and Canada, CATV cables are strung on existing telephone poles with other services.

in total cost to the use of ordinary tunable radio sets. The natural development was to adapt the systems for television, particularly in the USA, where populated areas are further apart than in Europe and thus less easy to cover with broadcast TV. For this purpose multipair cables were again installed which could carry television picture signals on a high frequency (HF) carrier wave with a frequency near 5 MHz as well as the sound signals at audio frequency. The receivers (usually rented) can again be simpler than conventional ones, and some 2000 or more subscribers may be fed from the same distribution amplifier unit.

Besides the high frequency (HF) multipair system described above, there is the method of direct distribution of programmes modulated (as in broadcast transmissions) on carriers at very high frequency (VHF), that is, within the 30 to 300 MHz range of frequencies or, in some cases, at ultra high frequencies (UHF) up to about 850 MHz. These signals can all be carried on a single coaxial cable just as they are in the lead from an individual domestic antenna, and conventional television receivers, with tuners, are used to select the desired channel. Each amplifier unit in the system, however, cannot supply more than 100 to 150 subscribers. A large system needs many amplifiers in series, with automatic gain control to preserve the level of each programme signal at around one or two millivolts at each subscriber's outlet. This system has been developed in the USA and also in Europe mainly for areas with problems in broadcast transmissions, and is termed CATV—originally called community antenna system but now most often used to describe cable television.

In the USA and Britain more than 10% of households receive television programmes by cable; the larger proportion (60%) of subscribers in Britain are supplied by HF systems. Cable television is also used and being further developed in other European countries, notably Belgium, Denmark, Switzerland and Ireland, as well as the USSR which has for many years employed cable extensively for sound programmes.

Economic and technical aspects

In cable systems as in conventional broadcasting many homes can be served cheaply in large towns, but the investment per household rises appreciably in remoter and less densely populated areas, which may require long runs of cable or broadcast stations serving relatively few people. The VHF system may be a little cheaper to install, but does not have the benefit of simplified receivers; the total rented cost of feed plus receiver is thus comparable in the two systems.

A problem in VHF systems is the selection of frequency channels for distribution. Using the same channels as for broadcasting in the area would require careful screening of the cables and receiver to prevent broadcast signals being picked up as interference. These might cause 'ghost' images, rather like the reflections in air transmission which cause secondary images on a

TV screen. Therefore different frequency channels are generally used and (with the need to avoid channels causing mutual interference) a well known problem with receivers—it may be necessary to use non-standard or UHF channels.

In the HF system a different problem arises. An economic design of distribution cable has a capacity for only six television programmes. Where more are required, more than one cable is needed. If, as in the USA, more than twelve channels are required, it is better to use a single coaxial cable to carry the television signal plus a pair of telephone type wires to each subscriber, who is provided with a selector, operating like a telephone dial, to ensure that the programme he desires is switched to his feed line. The distribution of all programmes need only go as far as a number of junction boxes containing the dial-operated switches.

Future developments

Cable television has tended to be attractive in difficult broadcasting reception areas—even in towns where there are many high buildings—but it has not yet been able to offer the majority of viewers marked saving in cost over good broadcast transmissions. One future development is direct broadcasting from communications satellites; for this, cable television could offer greater savings over individual reception. In the 1960s, the growth of cable television was seen as one of the

most exciting developments in the field of communications. Since wiring to houses is expensive, it is natural to consider exploiting its use also for facilities not available from normal broadcasting. Apart from additional original programmes (which are expensive to provide if they are to compete with broadcast programmes) further signals or data may be provided to the subscriber. If signals can be sent back from the subscriber (*bi-directional systems*), then these data facilities could be more detailed and given on demand through code signals dialled by the user (see also the various 'Teletext' systems now being developed such as Ceefax, Oracle and Viewdata, page 64). Viewer reaction to programmes can be obtained quickly, and the system might be extended to obtain electricity and gas meter readings, or provide two-way educational programmes.

There are other less welcome implications: for example, advertisers could indulge in a new form of inertia selling, whereby the viewer need only press a button or flick a switch to order advertising material or even buy an item featured on his television set. Advertising revenue would in any case be vital to exploit the full potential of cable television in this way, unless massive government aid were forthcoming. Preliminary estimates suggest that the equipment investment cost per subscriber would be at least twice as much for bi-directional as for simple distribution systems.

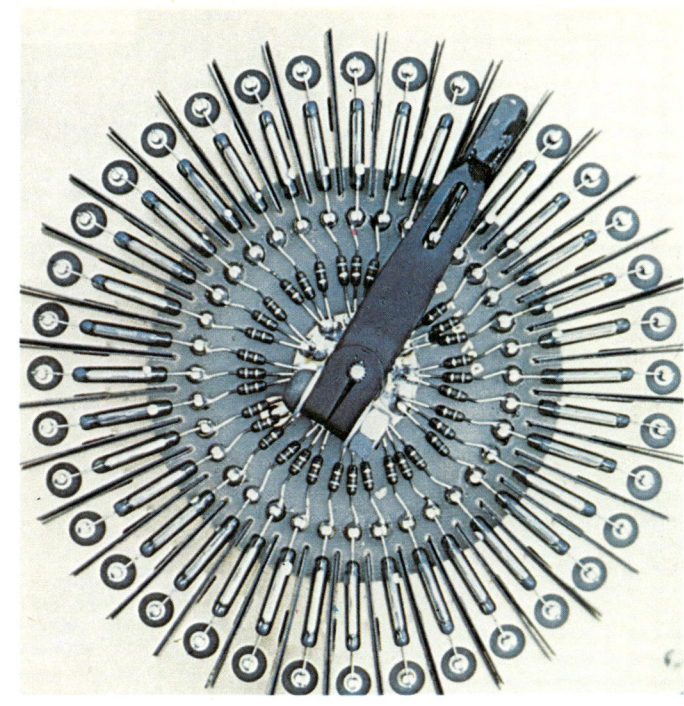

Above: this selector switch enables up to 36 different programmes to be selected in a cable TV system. The switch has 36 reed relays mounted radially with a rotating selector arm containing a small magnet which operates the contacts to connect up each channel. The switch can be situated in the home or operated remotely. Below, left: these aerials at Brussels, Belgium, receive broadcasts from Germany and Luxembourg for distribution to the home via cables. Below, right: an alpha-numeric Ceefax display on a Sony Trinitron tube.

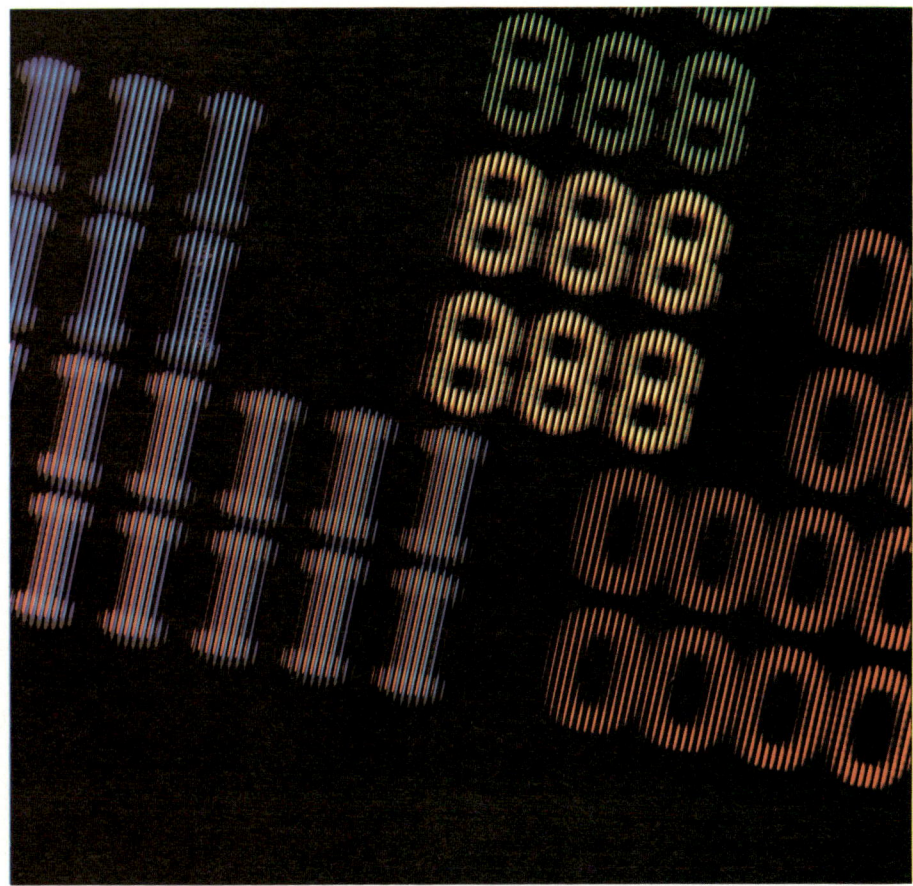

COMMUNICATIONS IN WAR,

COMMERCE & EDUCATION

RADIO TELEPHONE

Communications are not of course limited to the media. Many technological advances, notably radar, have been developed as a result of wartime research and have since found other peacetime applications. Radar in wartime gave an early warning of the approach of enemy aircraft: today it is also used for air traffic control, by shipping and in meteorology. Similarly, we are reminded that radio has many uses in business and public service when occasionally we pick up local police or taxi service messages on our domestic TV or radio sets.

The early pioneers could never have envisaged the ways in which their technology would expand and diversify to cover just about every field of human interest and human endeavour. We have already seen how the Cooke and Wheatstone telegraph systems were the forerunners of telex, and how closed-circuit television has become a valuable security aid in department stores and prisons. Closed-circuit television also has important uses in education—educational aids based on CCTV, film, tapes and radio are now big business. Educational broadcasts on the normal broadcasting network including radio programmes for the blind, and sub-titled television programmes for the deaf, have proved extremely valuable. Perhaps the greatest triumph in this field has been Britain's Open University, which has enabled thousands of people to study for a university degree in their own homes.

Undoubtedly communications will continue to expand, affecting more and more areas of our lives. This section examines some of those applications today in business, in defence and in education.

As the name implies, a radio telephone is a device used for telephoning, but without any connecting telephone wires as it operates on radio transmission and reception. Radio techniques are used today in many different fields, from the simple 'two-way' unit installed, for example, in a taxi cab to the highly developed systems for communicating speech and data to and from astronauts in space.

History

While there is some evidence of earlier use, it is true that, like many other technological developments, radio telephones were developed seriously during wartime for military applications. During World War 2, the ability to communicate with aircraft, ships and vehicles was essential. Often, the distances between the radio stations were quite short and therefore did not require the high power transmitters used in broadcasting. Low powered very high frequency (VHF) radio telephone systems were therefore developed which operated over some tens of miles rather than hundreds of miles.

Immediately after World War 2, the need to improve communications in the police and fire services resulted in further applications of the wartime developments. In 1947, the British Post Office licensed the very first commercial radio telephone systems—for a fleet of tugs on the river Tyne and for a taxi company in Cambridge. It

Above: the control room of the City Police Force in Edinburgh, Scotland, showing the radio telephone control consoles and the computer data display terminals. Right: French tennis champion J René Lacoste on board the liner 'France' using the radio telephone to talk to Madame Lenglen who was on the liner 'Paris' over 200 miles (322 km) away. This photograph was taken in 1927.

was soon realized by industry and service organizations that here was a tool that could be used for commercial benefits, improving efficiency and enabling an operator to utilize his workforce and vehicles to much greater effect. Radio telephones are now used extensively by transport companies, local authorities, doctors and vets—in fact, they are used in any sphere where there is a need to communicate with people on the move.

With the development of the transistor and subsequently the transistor radio, cheap and compact radio transmitter receivers became a possibility. In the United States, a 'citizens' band was allocated—generally in the 27 to 28 MHz bands—which could be used freely by all citizens. Without control over the allocation of frequencies the result is a communications jungle. At the other extreme most countries maintain strict control over frequency allocation and have no citizens' bands.

Frequency and range

In general, radio telephony utilizes the VHF (30 MHz to 300 MHz) and the UHF (ultra high frequencies—300 MHz to 3000 MHz) bands. VHF and UHF propagation is effectively 'line of sight' and therefore limited by geographical obstructions and manmade obstructions, such as buildings.

With the increasing demand for radio telephones, the governments of each country have applied stringent controls on how and where they are used. These controls are necessary where essential services are concerned because these must not be hindered by interference. The frequency spectrum is therefore divided into bands and these are allocated to a particular category of user. The efficiency of different bands varies considerably with different applications—for example the higher the frequency, the shorter the range. This is because as the waveforms become shorter (that is, fre-

quency increases) absorption of the signal by the Earth in the form of intervening hills becomes greater.

When relatively large areas need to be covered it is advantageous to use lower frequencies. In Britain, local authorities covering rural areas tend to use frequencies in the 70 to 80 MHz band, whereas in small towns where there are concentrations of buildings and the distances involved are much shorter, frequencies in the 450 to 470 MHz are better suited.

The government licensing authority will allocate a user a very small portion of the band best suited to the type of application—this portion is called a channel. When land radio telephone systems started up, these channels were spaced every 100 kHz, but today, with improved technology and vastly increased demand, they can be spaced every 12.5 kHz. In 1947 there were 10 channels for every 1 MHz and today there are 80 channels.

The technical standard of the radio telephone must be such that it will operate only within its own channel and not drift on to an adjacent channel, causing interference to other users.

The basic radio telephone consists of a transmitter and receiver, like radio. The transmitter generates the required radio frequency, suitably modulated with speech. This is fed to the aerial where it is radiated as radio waves (electromagnetic radiation). At the receiver, the specific transmission or signal is selected while rejecting all unwanted frequencies. The signal is then demodulated and the audio signal fed to the speaker.

Radio telephone system

The system should be carefully planned and relevant factors should be taken into consideration; range required, topography of the area and so on. Probably the most important of these is the selection of the base antenna site. This is normally on high ground, a hill top or a high rise building. Often, lofty masts are erected to provide the extra height to achieve the desired range; however, the licensing authorities often restrict the range of the system to avoid interference to other users on the same frequency but who are located in a different geographical area. Typical ranges of radio telephone systems vary from one mile (1.6 km) for a police pocket set to 30 to 40 miles (between 48 and 64 km) for a transport operator.

More sophisticated systems are continually being developed, and in many parts of the world it is now possible to dial from a radio telephone (installed in a vehicle, for example) into the telephone system and speak to any telephone subscriber in the world. Ambulances are equipped with equipment enabling vital medical data such as heart condition, blood pressure, blood group and so on to be transmitted over the radio telephone. The surgeons and doctors based in the hospital can therefore assess the condition of the patient before he reaches the hospital, thus saving vital time and lives.

RADAR

Radar, an acronym derived from *Radio Detection and Ranging*, means the detection and location of remote objects by the reflection of radio waves. Radar proper came into existence in the 1930s principally as a resultof recognizing the need to have warning of air attack long before the hostile aircraft could be seen or heard, and was made possible by the existence of sufficiently advanced radio techniques. That objects were capable of reflecting radio waves had long been known, and indeed the principle of reflection was the means used for studying the ionized layers in the upper atmosphere, which are important in long distance communication.

Sir Robert Watson-Watt, the 'father' of British radar, had engaged in such research. Asked to comment on the possibility of a 'death ray' in the form of powerful radio waves as a defence against air atatck, he pointed out that while this was totally impracticable, it was quite feasible to use radio waves to detect an aircraft long before it could be seen. Out of this suggestion arose the British chain of Early Warning radar stations which were operational at the outbreak of the War in 1939 and were a vital factor in winning the Battle of Britain. While most of the major powers had discovered radar principles before the War and had made efforts to develop them for military uses, the British defence chain was probably the most advanced operationally in 1939, and must have saved countless lives.

Understanding microwaves

To understand how radar works it is important to understand the distinction between radio waves of the frequency used in broadcasting and microwaves. Microwaves are another form of electromagnetic radiation—they are part of the whole spectrum which includes light and radio waves (see diagram, page 33), but have wavelengths approximately midway between the two; longer than infra-red and shorter than the wavelength of broadcast radio. They share some of the properties of both. Like radio waves they can be used for communication, while like infra-red they can be used for cooking.

Microwaves have wavelengths between 30 cm and 1 mm, that is, frequencies between 1 GHz (1000 MHz) and 300 GHz. These divisions are rather arbitrary, and have no physical significance. Infra-red radiation, however, is normally produced by heat, while microwaves are produced electronically.

Right: A diagram showing the basic principles of radar. A stream of transmitted pulses are reflected by any object they encounter. The reflected pulses are picked up by the antenna when it is in the receive mode (controlled by the transmit/receive cell), amplified and displayed. Two displays are shown.

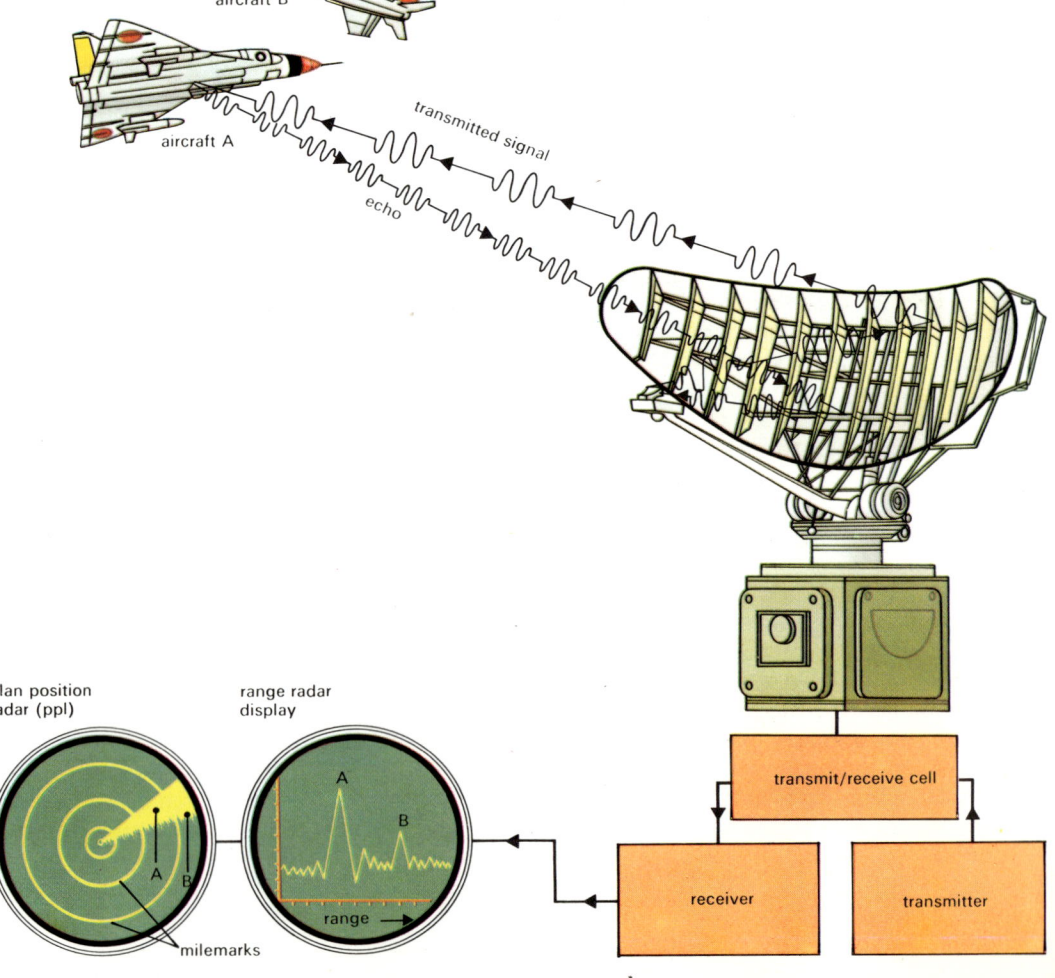

Below: a radar system which enables strike aircraft to fly safely at very low altitudes to avoid detection by enemy defence systems.

Their earliest application, and still probably the most important, was in the science of radar, but today micro-waves transmit information from space probes back to earth, and there is no doubt that their most exciting modern applications are in the expanding fields of com-munications satellites and space exploration, both of which will be described later.

Generation and amplification

The actual generation and amplification of microwaves is achieved by a variety of devices, each designed for a specific purpose. As with radio waves, the devices pro-duce rapidly oscillating electron currents, the frequency of the oscillation being the same as that of the frequency of radiation desired. The high power microwave sources have been developed from the thermionic valve [vacuum tube]. These developments took place in the early 1920s to overcome the deficiencies of the more conventional radio valve in its various forms when used to produce high powers at the higher frequencies de-manded by the rapidly expanding communications industry, and resulted in the *magnetron, klystron* and *travelling wave tube*. While the magnetron is a self sustaining oscillator tube capable of producing pulses of power well in excess of a megawatt, both the klystron and travelling wave tube are essentially amplifying devices capable of producing output powers of several kilowatts. Very low power microwave sources may be derived from either low power versions of the klystron or *reflex klystron*, or the *maser*. In addition there are many forms of solid state microwave sources, which are very compact and which exploit the *Gunn effect* for their operation.

Propagation of microwaves

Microwaves can be modulated, just like longer radio waves. Since light, radio and microwaves all obey the laws of optics, covering absorption, reflection, refraction and diffraction, many of which depend upon the wave-length being used, microwaves have characteristics which make them useful in particular situations. For example, they can be beamed rather more easily than longer wavelengths—the aerials [antennas] are of less cumbersome size—and are thus useful for setting up a communications network, rather than for general broadcasting.

The most common medium through which micro-waves are passed (the *propagation medium*) is the *troposphere*, the lowest region of the Earth's atmosphere. For most of the time this is an extremely complex and uneven region to microwaves because of the widely differing meteorological structures, such as fronts and temperature inversions, within the region. By virtue of its constituent gas and water vapour content, each part of the troposphere may have a different *radio refractive index* from its neighbour. As a result, the phenomena of reflection, refraction and so on, become extremely complex. Indeed certain microwave transmissions may be subject to various forms of 'scattering' due to either these meteorological structures or rain, snow and so on.

It is, however, the gas and water vapour components present in the region which influence the choice of suitable wavelengths to be used for transmission within this medium. At certain wavelengths the absorption of the medium is high.

While microwaves will generally pass through con-siderable distances of the troposphere, they cannot be reflected by the ionosphere, like longer radio waves. Consequently, microwave communications are restric-ted to comparatively short distances, of the order of 500 km, since they can only pass beyond the horizon by scattering and diffraction effects.

Microwave circuits

All sources of microwave energy require the use, in their design and construction, of very special electric circuit techniques which exploit both the electric and magnetic field properties of the wave. These techniques are necessary since both the physical dimensions and the electrical properties of the materials used in the construction of the more conventional electric circuit conductors (wires and cables), inductors, capacitors and resistors are such that these components do not retain their basic electrical properties when carrying alternat-ing currents at microwave frequencies.

Perhaps the most distinctive feature of any micro-wave 'circuit' is the array of 'conductors' which carry or *guide* the signal between the components. These 'conductors' take the form of waveguides, which are pipe-like structures, having either rectangular or circu-lar cross sections, usually constructed of material of high electrical conductivity and to a very high degree of precision. The effects of capacitance and inductance are introduced into waveguide 'circuits' by siting posts, 79

stubs, annuli and so on, in the waveguide. The physical dimensions of these devices and their positions in relation to the guided field structure determine the type of effect that they are to produce. Microwave aerials are usually also quite different from the more conventional types in that, although they may have many different forms, most employ parabolic reflecting surfaces which are irradiated from waveguide *feeds* at their foci to produce highly directional beams.

Microwaves in radar

It was the development of radar which initiated the application of microwaves in a variety of widely differing areas. Since World War 2, even the original simple radar principle of detecting and ranging a reflecting target has been developed to the point that the positions, speeds and courses of targets, moving at very high speeds at considerable distances from a radar installation, may now be continually recorded to accuracies of a few metres. In contrast, it is now possible to determine the position of a housefly at a range of about 2 km with microwave radar. It is therefore possible to use modern radar for all types of target observation. As a result, most major air and sea ports throughout the world are equipped to operate full traffic control, both local and distant, on all types of vehicles or vessels using the ports (see page 85). Similarly, most of the world's aircraft and ships carry microwave radar as a navigational aid and also as a bad weather or storm detector. The ability to detect the positions of intense meteorological activity in the atmosphere has also contributed in recent years to the formation of the new science of radio meteorology where microwave radar has proved to be

a valuable aid in the study of meteorology of our atmosphere.

Basic principles of radar

While it is possible to use both *continuous* waves such as are used in broadcasting and interrupted or *pulsed* signals in which the radio waves are emitted in short bursts or impulses, the way radar works is probably most easily understood in terms of pulsed radio signals. A radio transmitter connected to a directional aerial [antenna] (an aerial which concentrates its radiation in a beam along a particular direction) sends out a stream of short pulses of radio waves. Each pulse will normally be a few millionths of a second long but may be even shorter, and the pulses are separated by a time interval which is substantially longer than the time it takes for radio waves to travel to any object (or 'target') of interest and back.

Any object in the path of the transmitted beam reflects some of the energy falling on it back to a radio receiver located near the transmitter. In the receiver there is thus a stream of reflected pulses slightly displaced in time, with respect to the stream of transmitted pulses, by a short interval corresponding to the time any one pulse takes to travel from the transmitter to the target and back. This is a measure of the range of the target. If the transmitting and receiving aerials are both beamed in the same direction, only targets lying in the beam reflect any signals and so the direction in which the target lies is obtained.

In practice, a single aerial is usually used for both transmission and reception, the receiver being momentarily 'suppressed' during the brief period of the transmitted pulse but re-activated in time to receive any echo pulses. The device used for this purpose is a form of switch triggered by the transmitter pulse and called a *TR cell* (Transmit–Receive cell). The single beamed aerial will normally be rotated in *azimuth* (horizontally) at a steady rate and is then said to be scanning. This is the common arrangement for *search* or *surveillance* radars. In practice the aerial beam is one or two degrees wide in azimuth but extends in elevation from the horizon to perhaps $15°$ or $20°$ elevation. This is the so-called *fan-beam*. It produces two-dimensional information only (range and bearing).

Below: microwaves are used extensively in communications and broadcasting. This outside television unit has a parabolic microwave aerial for transmitting broadcasts to the broadcasting centre.

It is possible to devise more elaborate systems which give three-dimensional information (range, bearing and elevation). In one form the 15° wide vertical 'fan' is divided up into a number of individual narrow beams (1° to 2° wide), this 'stack' of beams being simultaneously scanned in azimuth as before. In more advanced systems the elevation information is obtained by scanning a narrow pencil beam up and down in elevation at a rapid rate while rotating it in azimuth at a much slower rate. In this way a volume of sky is scanned by the narrow cone. The azimuthal scanning is usually carried out mechanically while the elevation scanning is done by varying the radio frequency, the aerial having been designed so that the direction of its beam in elevation is controlled by the radio frequency used.

In search radars with a rotating beamed aerial, the direction of a target is obtained from the direction of maximum received signal. When greater angular precision is required other arrangements are possible. For example two directional beams can be arranged so as to partially overlap. In the overlapping area, very accurate measurement of direction is possible by taking the ratio of the signals received in the two aerials. The two partially overlapping beams may be made to rotate or 'spin' about the equi-signal line (along the centre of the overlapping area), producing what is known as a *conical scanning aerial*, commonly used in many anti-aircraft fire-control tracking radars.

Radars for fire-control purposes must follow a target continuously once it has been picked up or *acquired*. Such a radar is called a *tracking* radar and usually has an aerial beam which is a narrow cone or pencil shape.

Once the radar has found a target the beam can be made to follow it automatically; it is said to be 'locked-on' to the target.

The transmitter of a pulse radar must be capable of producing short pulses of radio energy of high intensity but at substantial intervals of time. For example, typically the pulses may each be four microseconds long spaced at intervals of four milliseconds. With these figures, the transmitter is actually operating for only 1/1000 of the total time. This is called the *duty cycle*. The 'mean' power of the transmitter will be only 1/1000 of the 'peak' power. The two most important types of transmitting tubes used in radar are the *cavity magnetron*, which is a self oscillator and the *klystron*, which is an amplifier.

Displays

The receiver detects and amplifies the received pulses without undue distortion of their shape and it embodies a display system to present both the range and directional information available. The timing of the interval between transmitted and received pulses can be effected in several ways. The most common means uses a cathode ray tube similar to that used in a TV set. The cathode ray beam traverses the tube face horizontally at a steady rate. Where the beam strikes the tube face a bright spot is produced which, as the beam moves across, traces out a bright line.

The start of this line coincides with the moment of emission of the transmitter pulse. When an echo is received the spot is momentarily deflected transversely back to the original point, producing a trace. The length of this trace is a measure of the time interval or *delay time* of the echo pulse. When the spot reaches the extreme right hand end of its travel it 'flies back' to the left ready to commence the cycle over again when the next pulse is emitted. This was one of the earliest forms of display used in early warning radars and is still used for certain purposes.

In an alternative arrangement, the cathode ray beam is adjusted so that in the absence of any received signal it produces only a very faint trace on the tube face but is intensified to give a bright spot at the point where an echo is received. The beginning of the trace coincides with the centre of the tube face and the line rotates in synchronism with the scanning aerial. The tube face presents a map-like picture of the space around the radar, bright spots appearing at positions corresponding to the range and bearing of any targets. This is the display known as the *plan position indicator* or PPI and is commonly used in many radars.

Doppler radar

Another familiar acoustic phenomenon is the doppler effect, in which the sound heard by an observer is raised or lowered in pitch if the sound source is moving towards or away from him. the same effect occurs with radio waves, so that the radio frequency of an echo signal will be above or below the frequency of the emitted pulse if the target is approaching or receding. 81

This principle can be put to use in many ways. In a search radar, for example, since objects like buildings, trees or hills are stationary their echoes show no Doppler frequency shift and this may enable them to be cancelled out on the display, only moving targets such as aircraft being presented. Moreover, an aircraft can use radar to measure its ground speed by noting the frequency shift of echoes from the ground below and ahead of it. These principles are also put to considerable military use, in missile guidance systems for example.

Range and wavelengths

Radar waves, like light waves, travel more or less in straight lines when in free space. In the Earth's atmosphere, however, a small amount of bending takes place because the atmosphere decreases in density with height, so radar can see marginally beyond the horizon, but in designing a radar set this atmospheric bending can be ignored for all practical purposes. The range of a search radar is thus fundamentally limited by the curvature of the Earth, a serious matter so far as the detection of low targets is concerned. Raising the radar extends the horizon but to obtain a worthwhile extension, for example to detect very low level aircraft, it is necessary to carry the radar aloft in an aircraft. This arrangement is known as an *Airborne Early Warning* or AEW system.

All objects are capable of reflecting radio waves to some extent. The reflecting power, often called the *scattering coefficient*, depends on the shape and size of the object and the wavelength used. Large objects like ships and aircraft are good reflectors at all wavelengths

Below: the parabolic aerial shows the waveguide feed-receptor with its opening at the focal point of the reflector.

Above left and right: two different types of tropospheric scatter stations. Long distance microwave transmissions must rely on tropospheric scatter to reach receivers over the horizon. Atmospheric conditions in the troposphere have a considerable effect on the scattering of microwaves, and transmissions are usually restricted to distances less than 500 km (about 300 miles). The curved tubular structure (foreground, left) is a large waveguide.

up to ten metres or more in length (the first British early warning radars used a wavelength of between 10 and 15 m). Smaller objects are more easily detected, in general, at shorter wavelengths in the centimetric or microwave region. Most radars now use wavelengths in the range 3 to 25 cm.

Secondary radar

The form of radar thus far described, which relies on the passive reflection of radio waves, is now called *primary* radar to distinguish it from a more complex form known as *secondary* radar or sometimes *secondary surveillance radar* (SSR). In this the target (usually an aircraft) carries a small device which is both a receiver and transmitter, called a *transponder*. This receives the pulses from the ground radar and retransmits them to ground on a slightly different wavelength. At the same time it adds to the retransmitted signal a few additional pulses which are coded to convey such information as the identity (call-sign) and height of the target. The basic radar functions of measurement of range and direction are thus carried out, while in addition the identity of the target and possibly its height are ob-

tained. This is of great value in Air Traffic Control (ATC) and it is now mandatory for aircraft in certain categories flying in particular regions of the sky known as *controlled air space* to carry appropriate transponders. The system also forms the basis of the military identification system known as IFF (identification, friend or foe). ATC is described on page 85.

Applications

Some important applications of radar such as long-range early warning for defence and the longer range aspects of ATC have already been mentioned. Both defence and ATC also make use of medium-range search radars (100-150 mile range), the former for the control of defence weapons such as fighter aircraft and anti-aircraft missiles, and the latter for the *airfield approach* and *terminal control* phases of ATC. Still smaller radars may be used for local *airfield control* purposes, that is, management of traffic within a few miles of the field.

Search radar is used on ships for both air defence purposes and for navigation in poor visibility. Its use by merchant ships for the latter purpose is now very extensive. Tracking radars are primarily of value in such operations as the control and guidance of anti-aircraft weapons and for space exploration.

Radar carried in aircraft has many uses. It can be used by fighter aircraft to locate and intercept enemy aircraft. A form of surveillance radar can be used to produce a 'map' of the ground over which the aircraft is flying so that it can locate targets on the ground which it is seeking. Another similar type of radar known as

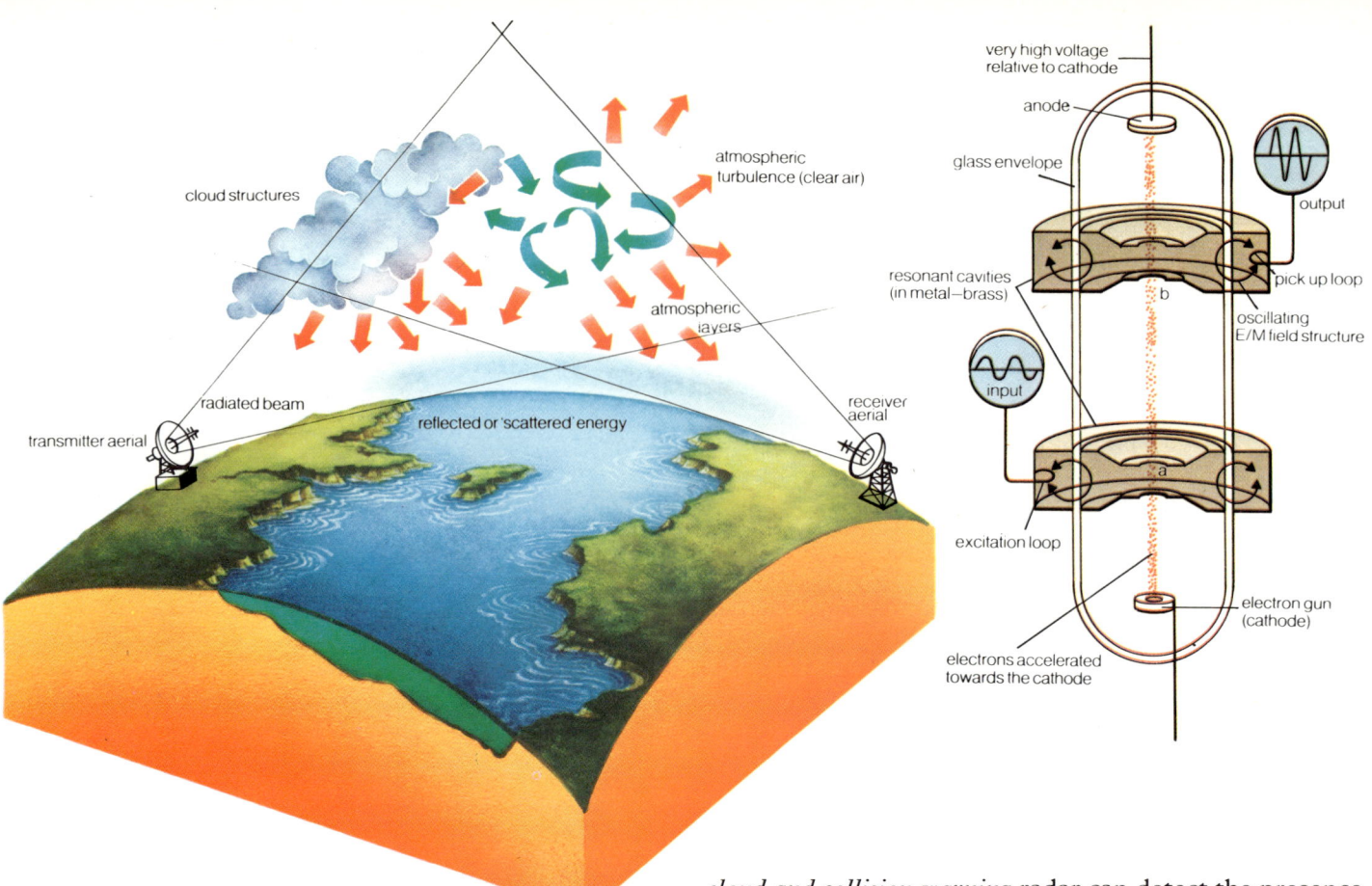

cloud structures

atmospheric turbulence (clear air)

atmospheric layers

radiated beam

transmitter aerial

reflected or 'scattered' energy

receiver aerial

very high voltage relative to cathode

anode

glass envelope

output

resonant cavities (in metal–brass)

pick up loop

oscillating E/M field structure

input

excitation loop

electron gun (cathode)

electrons accelerated towards the cathode

Above left: microwaves are 'scattered' (reflected and refracted) by the troposphere (the first 13km, 8 miles, of the atmosphere). Clouds, air turbulence, water vapour and constituent gases all affect this scattering. Above right: a double cavity klystron is used to amplify the microwave signals—at these high frequencies it replaces the valve. The electrons are accelerated and retarded by an alternating field in the first cavity (a). When electrons reach (b) they are 'bunched' and induce a large field in the second cavity.

cloud and collision warning radar can detect the presence of high ground or intense rain storms ahead of the aircraft and thus improve air safety.

Portable radars are used by ground troops to locate moving vehicles and even men up to ranges of a mile or two. To distinguish moving objects from the large number of stationary objects that tend to confuse the radar picture, the Doppler principle is usually employed. One such form of radar is also used by the police in 'speed traps' to detect speeding motorists. It may also be used as a perimeter defence to detect illegal entry into, or exit from, a defended area such as a prison.

Radar has applications in surveying, particularly in terrain where access is difficult. A device known as a *radar tellurometer* is in fact a type of distance measuring instrument. One use of radar in meteorology is the location of rain storms. This is important, particularly, in providing warning of the occurrence and movements of tropical storms. The use of tracking radar to follow meteorological atmospheric sounding balloons and thus enable upper atmospheric wind to be measured is another important use.

Safety

Living tissue can absorb radio waves to a certain extent and this results in some rise in temperature which may have harmful effects. The intensity of signals required to produce such effects is, however very great. Only the most powerful radars such as those used to detect intercontinental missiles at long range are really dangerous, and even so only within comparatively short distances of the radar. All radars for more normal applications are, to all intents and purposes, harmless unless the living tissues are placed directly in the aerial beam and very close to it (within a few feet).

AIR TRAFFIC CONTROL

Air traffic control, ATC, is one of the most vital factors in air safety. It is a system for preventing collisions between aircraft in congested areas, particularly in the neighbourhood of airports, where the air is full of aircraft of different sizes travelling in various directions at various speeds and heights. ATC also keeps air traffic flowing smoothly.

On those parts of long distance routes which are uncongested, the pilot uses the built in navigational aids of his aircraft, and sometimes electronic aids on the ground, to make his own way and avoid collisions without help. But as soon as he approaches a much flown over area, or nears an airport, he enters a control zone, where he is obliged to follow a course at a given speed and height, all prescribed to him by the air traffic controller.

The air traffic controller is the decision maker. It is he alone who has complete information on all aircraft movements within his control zone. He must exercize powers of discretion on the minimum safe spacing between aircraft, both vertically and horizontally, and determine priority in take-off and landing within the framework of flight schedules.

The minimum information required by a controller is the current height and position of all aircraft under his control, the intentions of all aircraft under, or soon to be under, control, and the identity of each aircraft. He gets this information from a *flight progress board* which tells him intention, identification, vertical position and timing, and from a *plan position radar* which gives the exact position and distance of all aircraft within his control zone.

The controller's work involves continuous updating of information as new situations develop and earlier ones pass from his control. He receives advance information of traffic about to enter his control zone from adjacent zones and informs adjacent zones of traffic leaving his zone. He also monitors and controls all traffic within his zone.

The controller communicates with the aircraft normally by VHF (very high frequency) radio telephone with a range of up to 200 miles (300 km) when the aircraft is at high altitude although the range decreases as the aircraft descends. A *radio direction finder* (RDF) system is frequently employed with the VHF radio link to supply compass bearing of any call received.

Wind speed and direction, visibility, cloud base, air temperature and barometric pressure data is fed to the controller from local sources and from meteorological centres. Runway visibility can now be accurately measured by electronic means rather than by someone's personal estimate, as is still usual today.

Flight plans

With certain exceptions, each flight requires a *flight plan* which includes aircraft identification, airport of departure and destination, route plan, desired cruising level, departure time and estimated time of arrival. The data is transmitted, generally by land line rather than radio, to the ATC control centre from airports within the controller's zone or from adjacent zones. The information is always to a standard format.

Radar control systems

The basic radar system gives a continuous plan, as seen from above, of all aircraft within radar range. The *plan position indicator* (PPI) radar display shows an aircraft 'target' as a bright spot with the range (distance) of the aircraft indicated by its distance from the centre of the screen and its bearing by the angle to the centre. An electronic means known as video mapping makes it possible to permanently superimpose fixed features such as defined airways on the screen. It is also possible to eliminate all unwanted permanent radar echoes from stationary objects and display only those which are actually moving (moving target indicators).

In yet another refinement the radar echo from a particular aircraft can be 'tagged' with its identity or other information as a code of letters and numbers, the identity tag slowly moving across the screen in synchronization with the movement of the aircraft.

PPI type radars are in three broad categories: long range surveillance, airfield control and airfield surface movement. *Long range surveillance* radars have typically up to 300 nautical miles (550 km) range from power of the order of two megawatts peak power. *Airfield control*

Left: inside the central tower at Chicago's O'Hare airport, one of the largest, busiest and most modern airports in the world. The sheer number of aircraft on the ground and in the air, and the amount of data about them that has to be taken in, combine to make the air traffic controller's job uniquely demanding.

radars operating at less power have typically 50 to 150 nautical miles (95 to 280 km) range. *Airfield surface movement* radars are designed for very high definition, and range is normally confined to runways, taxi-ways and aprons of the immediate airfield. Modern surface movement radars have sufficient picture resolution to identify individual aircraft types by their shape and size.

These radars are all of the 'primary' type ,which obtain information from a reflection of the radar beam from the aircraft or other 'targets', and require no co-operation from the aircraft. Another important type of radar system is known as *secondary surveillance radar* (see page 83). The transponder generates an automatic reply, which generally includes a coded message giving identity of the aircraft and present altitude, both of which can be integrated into the main PPI display and 'tagged' to the appropriate aircraft on the display.

Instrument landing system

The controller normally controls aircraft up to the final approach to the airfield when the pilots can lock on to the *instrument landing system* (ILS). This system provides a fixed radio beam so that an aircraft can align itself with the runway and adopt the correct descent path. The equipment comprises two ground transmitters, one emitting a beam to guide the aircraft in *azimuth* or compass bearing, the other a beam to guide the aircraft in altitude. The beams are known respectively as the *localizer* and *glidepath*. Both beams are modulated with tones at audio frequency (at a pitch which enables them to be heard) which are used to activate instruments in the aircraft flight deck (or indicate audibly to the pilot) whether he is deviating to the left or right of the centre line and above or below the glidepath.

Along the approach centre line are three vertically transmitted fan shaped beams known as the outer, middle, and inner *marker beacons*. Once brought to the position for final approach, the marker beacons indicate the distance to go, and the ILS system proper shows any deviation from the centre line and glidepath. If he keeps to the centre line and glidepath the pilot is brought accurately to the threshold of the runway at about 200 ft (60 m) altitude and can then complete the landing visually. The controller directs the aircraft to the appropriate runway exit for parking and discharge of passengers.

Radar altimeter

An ordinary aircraft altimeter uses a type of aneroid barometer which measures the changes of air pressure at different heights. Changes in pressure due to the weather can affect its readings. But because radio waves travel at a constant speed—about 186,000 mile/s (300,000 m/s)—radar altimeters can provide an absolute measurement of an aircraft's height above ground regardless of atmospheric conditions.

By pointing a radar aerial downwards, emitting a pulse of radio waves, and then seeing how long it takes for that pulse to be reflected by the earth and return to the radar's receiving aerial on the aircraft, a measure of the distance travelled by that pulse—and hence the aircraft's height—can be found.

The distance the pulse has travelled can be estimated from a display on a cathode ray tube or can be measured electronically. In either case it is only really accurate at high altitudes. As the aircraft descends nearer the earth, the time taken for the pulse to return to the aircraft becomes difficult to measure. At 1 mile (1.6 km) above the earth, for instance, the pulse would travel the return journey in about 10 millionths of a second. A pulse would thus have to be very short in duration to differentiate between the sent and received pulses. At an altitude of 100 feet, the time between sent and received pulses would be only about 0.2 millionths of a second so pulse durations would have to be unrealistically short.

Yet it is at such heights that altitude measurement

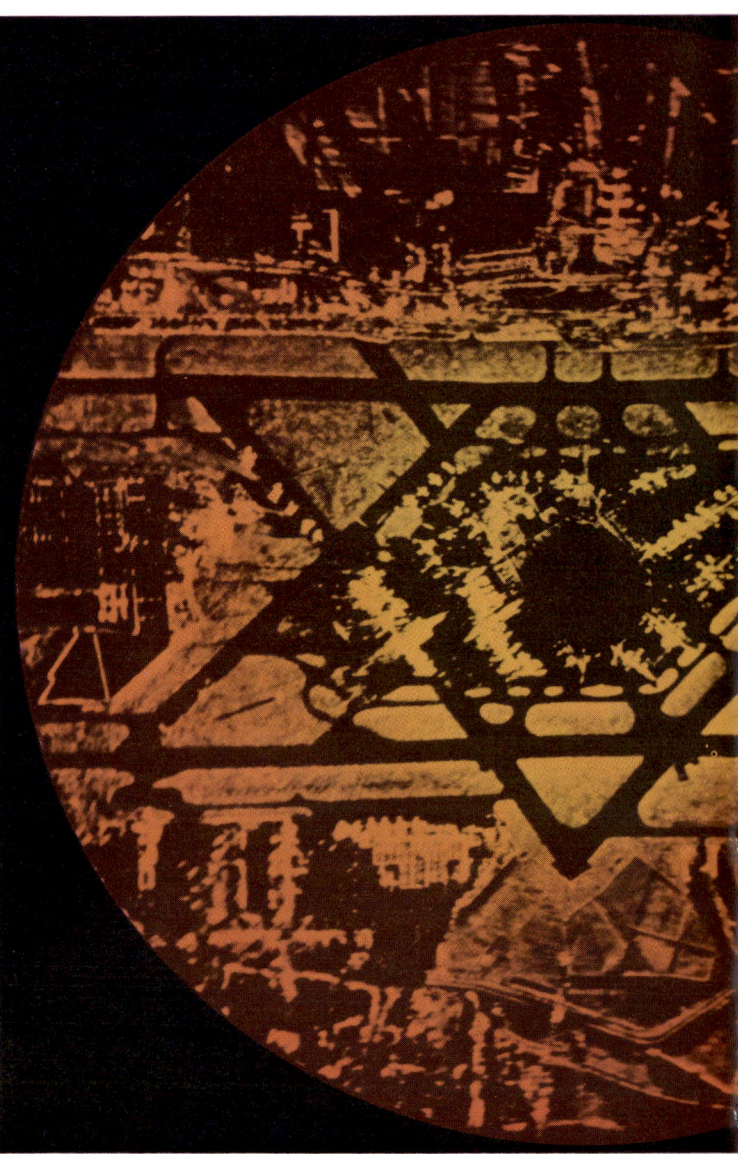

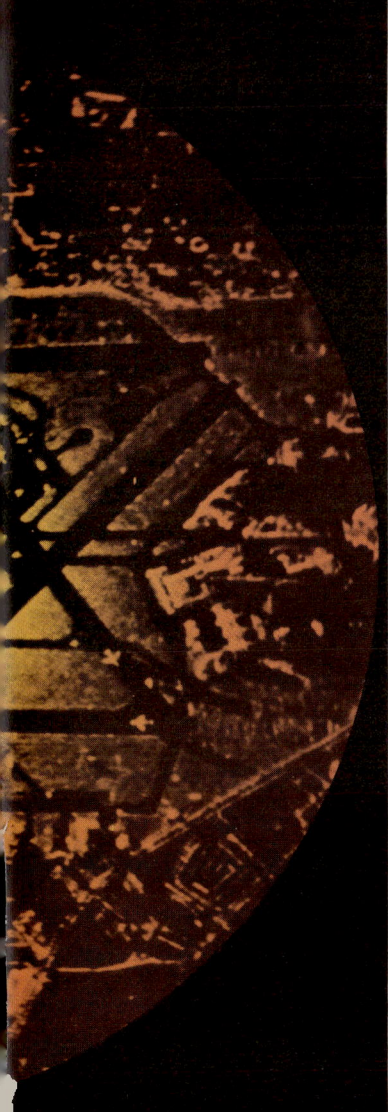

Chicago's O'Hare airport as it appears to the air traffic controller. Although he is backed up by radar and computer, in the final analysis it is his judgement that ensures the safety of every aircraft. Far left: London's Heathrow airport shown by the airfield surface movement radar. Individual aircraft are clearly visible, their long 'shadows' radiating outwards from the central aeriel on the control tower. Left: A modern radar display screen for Air Traffic Control.

becomes critical, and so a more complicated system known as an FM CW (frequency modulated, continuous wave) radar or radio altimeter has been developed. As in the simple pulse system, signals are emitted from a radar aerial, bounced off the ground and received back at the aircraft, but here the signal is continuous, centred around some high frequency such as 4200 MHz.

This signal is arranged to increase to another frequency 200 MHz higher at a steady rate before dropping back to the original frequency.

If a pulse is sent out at the beginning of this 'sweep', by the time it is returned the transmitter will be emitting a higher frequency. The difference depends on how long the pulse has taken to do the return journey. When these two frequencies are mixed electronically a new frequency—the difference between the two emerges. The value of this new frequency is measured by electronic circuits. It is directly proportional to the distance travelled by the original pulse, so it can be used to give the actual height.

In practice a typical FM radar today would sweep 120 times a second. Its range would be up to 10,000 feet (3000 m) over land and up to 20,000 feet (6000 m) over water, since reflections from water are clearer. Accuracy would be within 5 feet (1.5 m) for the higher ranges but would be better close to the ground—within 2 feet (0.6 m).

The high cost of radar-type altimeters has prevented their use in many commercial aircraft, though the decreasing cost of electronics should make them competitive with barometric types before very long. Where low level accuracy is needed—as in blind landings—their use is virtually compulsory.

Blind landing has been achieved thousands of times in commercial practice but always in acceptable visibility as part of the proving trials. The pilot has the system engaged but monitors the landing throughout and is ready to take manual control at any instant. Completely blind landing will become a reality only when the equipment is fully proved.

A parallel development is the provision of blind guidance for surface vehicles such as fire appliances and ambulances in case of accident in zero visibility conditions.

Stacking

At times of great congestion it is necessary for aircraft to queue, awaiting instructions to land. The controller directs aircraft to a holding or stacking area where aircraft fly round and round one above the other but separated by a safe vertical distance of about 1000 ft (300 m). The lowest aircraft is called off first after which the remaining aircraft descend one stage lower according to the safe stacking separation height. Aircraft arriving at a stacking area take the uppermost position. This is why aircraft arriving at a busy airport often have to circle for a considerable time before they get ATC clearance to land.

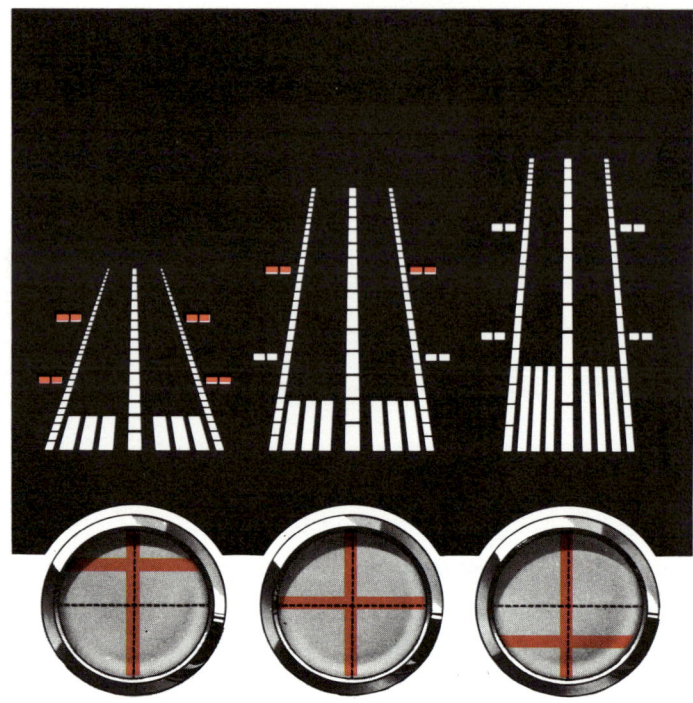

Top: VASI (visual approach slope indicator) is a simple but effective means of keeping an incoming pilot on the right glidepath as he nears the runway. It consists of two sets of lights fitted with reflectors and slats so that they send out red light over a very narrow angle and white light over an equally narrow, but higher, angle. A pilot approaching at the correct angle will see the lights as shown in the centre diagram. Above: the screen of a PPI (plan position indicator) radar used to survey aircraft movements near an airfield.

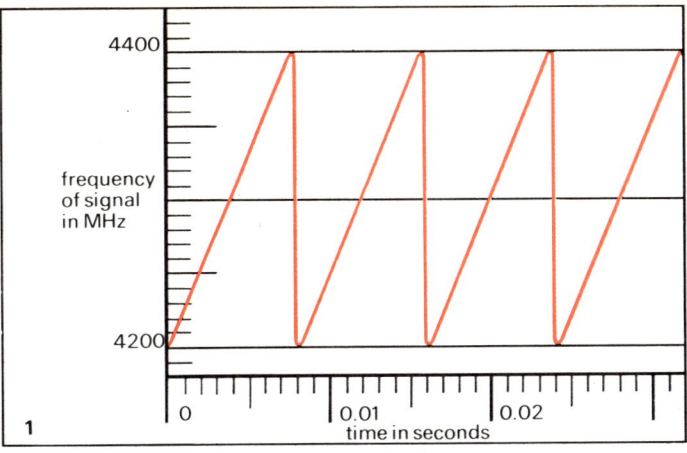

1

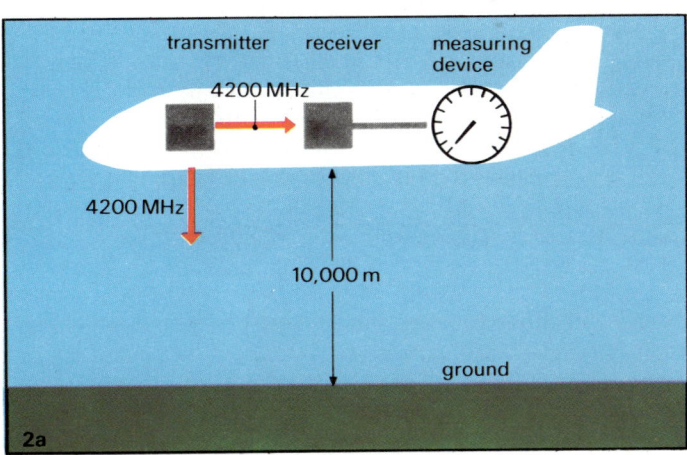

2a

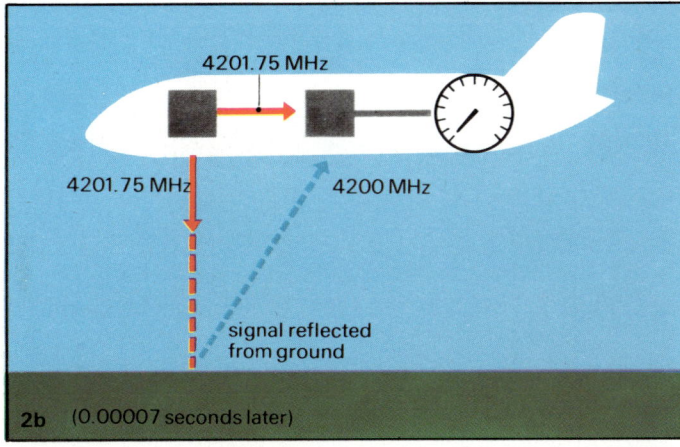

2b (0.00007 seconds later)

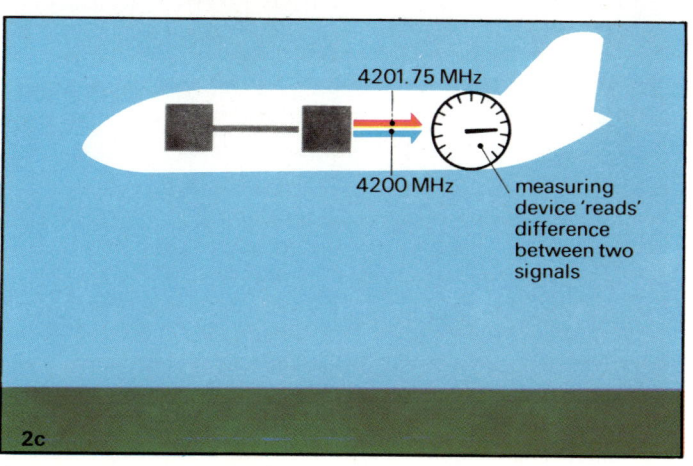

2c

Modern aids

The electronic computer now plays a central role in ATC information processing and storage and supplying data to individual controllers in a large complex. Its main function is to reduce the work load on controllers so that they can concentrate on supervision of aircraft movements and decision making.

The Eurocontrol Maastricht Automatic Data Processing system (MADAP) is a good example of a modern ATC system as it is multinational in the equipment used, the ATC officers who work in it, the countries that support it and the aircraft which fly through its area of operation.

MADAP controls the upper air space of a region covering Belgium, Luxembourg, the Netherlands and the northern part of the Federal Republic of Germany. Its design incorporates all the features outlined above with the exception of ILS and other ground aids which do not apply to upper air space.

The ATC centre will receive data from four radar centres and a continuous stream of flight data from airports and adjoining areas. All inputs, including radar data, are to be processed through high power computers to provide controllers with the information they want as soon as it is needed. For example, incoming flight plans will be held in the computer store until the aircraft concerned are entering the area. The MADAP installation has eight computers, more than 80 operating and training positions for controllers and some 140 radar and data display units. It is designed to deal simultaneously with 200 flight plans and 250 aircraft tracks. The computer complex also performs such tasks as printing out events such as an aircraft passing over a reporting area as they occur, and predicts conflict conditions. But automation is kept firmly in place. The equipment is only there to aid the controller, who is still the final decision maker.

Left: a modern radar altimeter works by sending out a radio signal of the shape shown in picture 1, with a constantly rising and falling frequency. A signal that has travelled to the ground and back will be at a different frequency from the signal that is going out when it returns. The difference depends on the distance to the ground, and can be 'read' by electronic means to give the height of the aircraft.

TELEMETRY

Telemetry, or telemetering, is the measurement of a physical quantity such as a voltage, pressure or temperature, and the transmission of the measured quantity (or *measurand*) over a distance to receiving apparatus, which displays or records the measured quantity. The link between the primary detector and the receiver may be a direct cable connection or a radio or microwave link.

The first telemetry systems were used by electricity supply undertakings for monitoring the voltages and currents throughout their supply networks, by direct landline connections (*pilot wires*) or, after World War 1, signals superimposed on the power lines themselves. One of the earliest known patents for telemetry was issued in the USA in 1885.

The basic telemetry system consists of the primary detector or pick-up, a transmission system, a receiving system, and an output device for the display or recording of the data.

Electrical telemetry

Electrical telemetry, such as that used for the supervision of power supply networks, in its simplest form consists of a remote metering system. In a substation, voltage transformers and current transformers are used to drive voltmeters and ammeters, and by using pilot wires to connect these to instruments in a central control room, duplicate readings can be obtained. This system works well over short distances where the number of individual sets of readings is small. As each set of information requires its own circuit or channel, it become expensive and impractical to provide a large number of channels over any great distance.

A variation of this system uses instruments which produce electrical pulses at a rate proportional to the value of the quantity they are measuring, and these pulses are transmitted to the receiving instruments which translate them back into voltages, currents or power levels. This is known as *pulse rate telemetry*. In *pulse length telemetry*, the lengths of the pulses, and not the rates at which they are transmitted, are proportional to the measured values.

Multiplex telemetry

To enable telemeter links to be transmitted over a single channel, some means of keeping them separated from each other must be provided. This is done by using various forms of *multiplexing*, such as *time division multiplexing* (see page 99). The time division multiplexing (TDM) system 'scans' each transmitting element in turn and transmits the signal pulses in sequence to the receiving station. The receiver scans the incoming signals and directs each set of pulses to its respective indicating or recording instrument. The transmitting and receiving ends of the system are kept in synchronization by means of a synchronizing pulse transmitted at the beginning of each 'frame' or scanning cycle. Time division multiplexing may use either a pulse rate system or a pulse length system (also called a *pulse width* or *pulse duration* system).

Radio telemetry

Radio telemetry, where the transmission of data between the two stations is by means of a radio link, employs a radio signal which is *modulated* by a *subcarrier* signal carrying the data. The subcarrier may contain a single data channel, or may itself be time division multiplexed (*commutated*). Frequency modulation is the main form of modulation used, and the carrier signal may be modulated by a group of subcarriers, each of a different frequency.

Phase modulation is often used instead of frequency modulation, and in this case the transmitted signal is represented by changes in the *phase angle* of the carrier wave as opposed to frequency or amplitude modulation.

The different types of multiplexing methods and the various forms of modulation are combined in several ways to produce telemetry links best suited to particular requirements. Many missile control systems use FM-FM telemetry, in which the carrier wave is frequency modulated by a group of subcarriers, which are themselves frequency modulated by the data signals they carry. FM-PM is similar to FM-FM, but the carrier is phase modulated by frequency modulated subcarriers.

Below: colour images of the planet Jupiter which were transmitted back to Earth, a distance of over 500 million miles (800 million kilometres) by the NASA space probe "Pioneer 10". This raw data is processed to remove faults and reconstruct a full colour picture from Jupiter's known colouring.

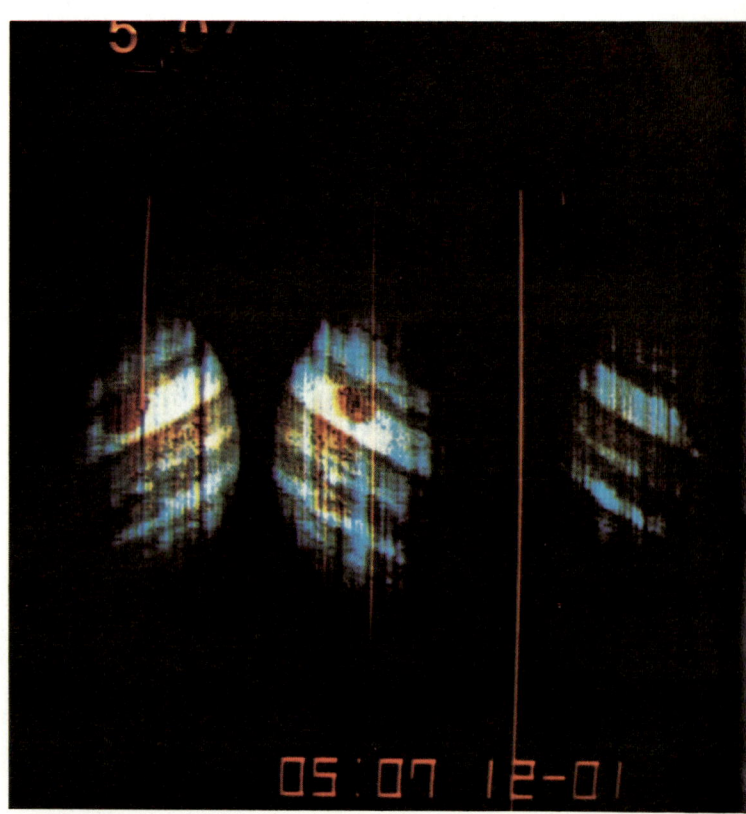

PDM-FM uses a pulse duration modulated subcarrier to frequency modulate the carrier wave, and PDM-PM uses a similar subcarrier to phase modulate the carrier. Where a large amount of data is to be transmitted, PDM-FM-FM is used. This system has a carrier wave frequency modulated by several subcarrier waves, each of which is frequency modulated by PDM.

Uses

In addition to its usefulness in electricity supply networks, telemetry has many applications in other distribution systems such as gas, oil or water pipelines. It enables the flow rates and pressures along a pipeline to be continuously monitored from a small number of control stations.

One of the most important uses of telemetry is the transmission of data to and from satellites, space probes, and manned space vehicles (see page 115). The telemetry systems used by manned space vehicles handle data concerning the course, position and engineering systems of the vehicle, and also physiological data such as the respiration and pulse rates of the astronauts.

Satellites and unmanned vehicles transmit data covering a wide range of subjects, depending on the particular application of the vehicle concerned. Apart from the sensors which monitor the on-board systems of the vehicle, such as its power systems, satellites and probes carry instruments which collect data, for example, on cosmic radiation, magnetic fields, and Earth resources, and all this data is transmitted back over radio telemetry links to tracking stations on the ground or to tracking ships at sea.

Above: A Philadelphia Electric Company control room in which system data is presented on colour cathode tube displays.

AUDIO-VISUAL AIDS IN EDUCATION

Audio-visual aids are used at all levels of education from the classroom through to industrial training, and enable the communication of ideas to be made more effectively. A wide variety of equipment is now available for this, which permits new forms of expression and instruction, with and without a teacher or demonstrator being present.

The simplest of audio-visual aids is also one of the oldest—a blackboard and a teacher. Modern educational pressures, however, demand increasing efficiency in presenting information. Writing on a blackboard requires time, slows the learning process and, for effective communication, requires a fair degree of skill on the part of the teacher. Many instructors still continue to use the blackboard, however, and would not be without it—others rely to a greater and greater extent upon the overhead projector.

The overhead projector

This is a simple device, consisting of a box which contains a powerful light source, with a transparent top surface or *platen*. Prepared semi-transparent drawings or models are placed on the platen. Alternatively, a continuous roll of transparent foil such as acetate sheet, which is arranged to be passed across the illuminated area from one roller to another, may be used. Information is written on this foil with a suitable pen. An image of the platen area is projected by means of a lens assembly and mirror, on to a screen placed behind the projector. The mirror and lens unit is usually supported on a vertical pillar at one corner of the box; it can be adjusted for sharp focusing.

The advantage of this form of aid is that the teacher faces the audience and the picture is thrown over his or her shoulder on to a screen behind. With hand drawn material the theme of a subject may be developed at the instructor's own pace. Professionally prepared material is also available in a wide variety of subjects. In some instances, a basic transparency (accurately located on

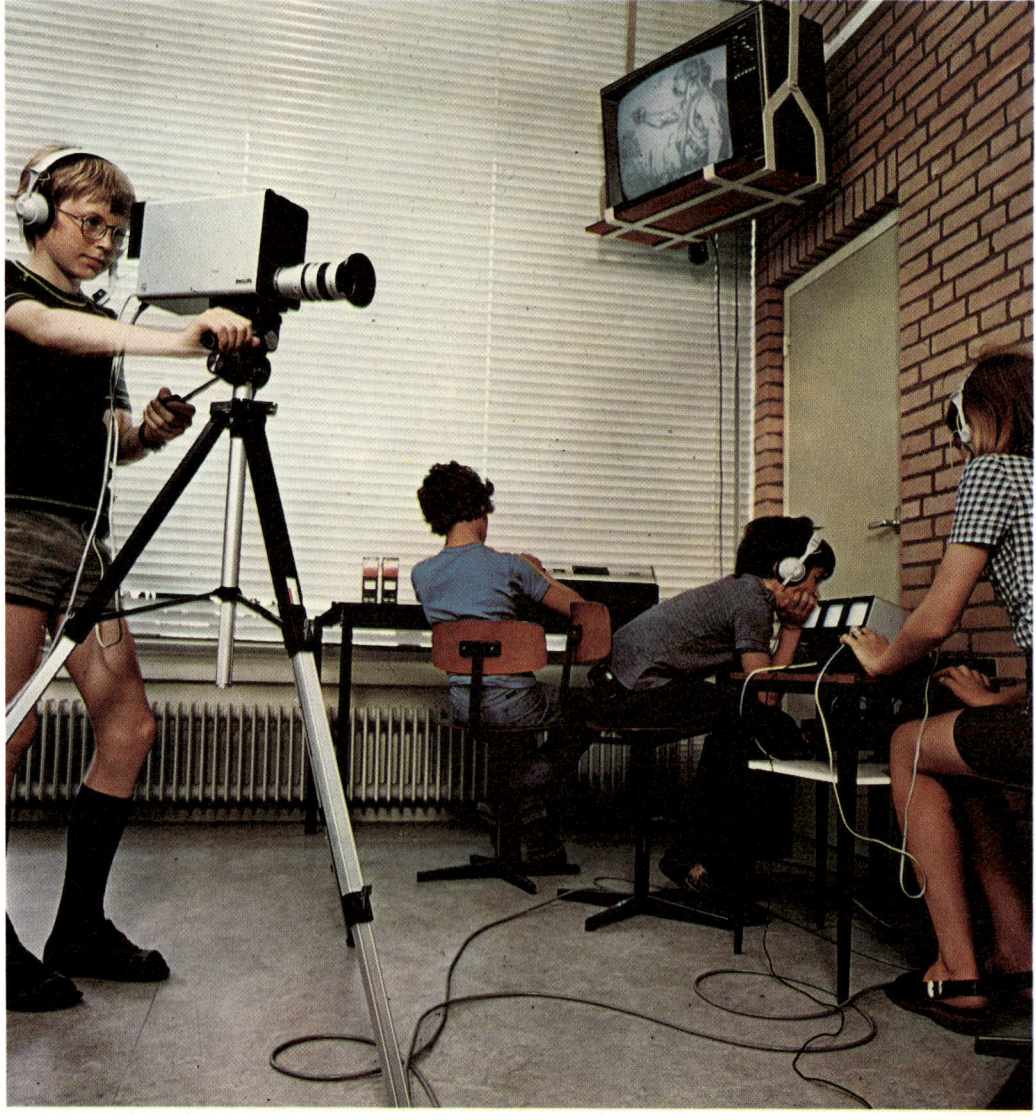

Right: Closed circuit television is becoming a popular educational aid in schools, even at elementary level.

the platen) is supplemented with added overlays that are flipped into position in sequence.

Working models, consisting of thin flat components (often cut from transparent or translucent plastic sheet) add interest to a presentation. Typical examples are mechanisms showing the function of a car engine, meshing gear wheels and so on.

Movie projectors

Although the overhead projector is now widely used, the movie projector has actually been established longer in many schools and training establishments. The commonest gauge of film is 16 mm but a narrow gauge, standard 8 mm and more recently, the improvedSuper 8 is now finding increasing favour, In general, the 8 mm gauge is less expensive than 16 mm, and the equipment is lighter and more compact. Although there are still many silent films available, the tendency now is towards sound.

The commonest form of machine is mounted firmly upon a stand and projects its image in a darkened room, with the loudspeaker contained within the projector, or alternatively, placed close to the screen, in front of the audience. For individual or small group instruction, compact projectors are available. These are usually self contained, suitcase type units and have a small translucent screen on to which the film image is back-projected.

For the larger type of projector the film is supplied on reels or spools, but for the compact types the film is more often supplied in cassettes. These are sealed plastic boxes which protect the film from mishandling, finger marks and dust. They slide easily into the projector and do not require any manipulative skill on the part of the user. Recent introductions in this field include 8 mm film which contains both still and motion picture material, linked with magnetic tape tracks which provide audio information and control the film speed.

Still projectors

The filmstrip or slide projector shows individual pictures in sequence. Filmstrips may be produced on 35 or 16 mm width material. They have the advantages of being light, strong and inexpensive, with a picture sequence which cannot be disarranged. Slides are generally made to the international 2 × 2 inch (50mm square) standard outline containing a picture area of 24 × 36 mm, either horizontal or upright, placed centrally in the slide. Other bigger sizes of slide are available for professional use in large scale presentations. Filmstrips and slides in colour are now superseding those in black and white.

Filmstrips, slides and motion picture materials are now nationally and internationally standardized through the British Standards Institution, the American National Standards Institute and the International Organization for Standardization so that they are globally interchangeable.

It is a common practice to link both filmstrips and

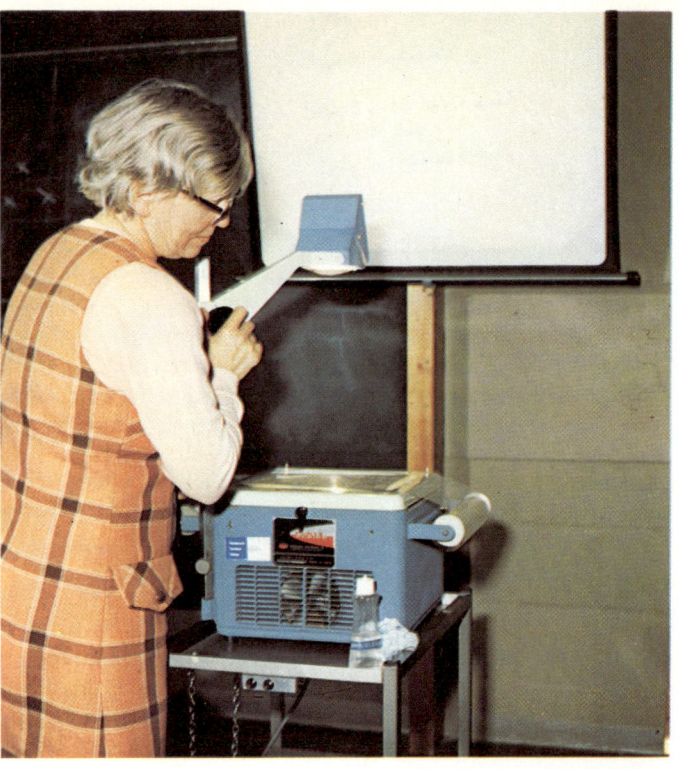

Top: the overhead projector is often preferred to blackboard and chalk, particularly where large amounts of information have to be written out, or diagrams prepared. Writing is less laborious, and the transparent rolls can be kept for future showing. Above: these children are watching a programme of slides with commentary provided by a cassette machine. The four track tape is used in one direction only: two tracks carry the sound, one is unused, and one carries 'bleeps' about a quarter of a second long which trigger the slide change.

slides with a sound accompaniment. The sound is usually recorded on magnetic tape, frequently in cassette form. This type of sound cassette contains a narrow width tape having two separate tracks. One of these carries the commentary, music and effects, while the second track carries the magnetic instructions which control the picture change. In advanced forms, two projectors may be linked together so that a picture from one of them appears to dissolve into the picture from the other. The rate of change is controlled by the information encoded on the second track.

Having established a basic principle of dual projectors, sound accompaniment and a control track, it is a logical step forward to a number of pairs of projectors. Such assemblies are often used in multi-screen or multi-image presentations of considerable complexity in which the audience is wholly involved, since both images and sound can be designed to provide a display of continuing interest.

Television and video tape recording
Television techniques have provided one of the more important advances in the audio visual field. TV is used for example, in schools, universities and in industry, in the form of closed circuit television (CCTV). This is a much more localized system than is used in normal broadcasting, because the camera and receiver (the set or monitor) are directly connected by a cable and no transmissions over the air take place. CCTV has the advantage over movie film that the results are seen immediately—the images do not have to be processed.

The television camera, providing either black and white or colour pictures, is small, compact and easy to operate. The real skill lies in the actual production of the programme.

It is common practice to link close circuit television with a videotape recorder (see page 65) so that the images seen by the television camera are recorded on magnetic tape in the same way that sound is stored on a conventional tape recorder. In professional broadcasting, 2 inch (50 mm) wide tape is used. In education is is more common to use 1 inch (25 mm) or 0.5 inch (12.5 mm) wide tape, which give a lower, but still acceptable picture quality. Later developments have shown that it is possible to record both picture and sound on tape as narrow as 0.25 inch (6 mm)—the width used on standard home tape recorders.

The combination of closed circuit television and VTR has proved to be a powerful audio-visual aid. Immediate playback of a training session, for example, allows students to study their own behaviour. In demonstrations and lectures, the camera can show to a large audience experiments or events which could otherwise only have been seen by a few people.

University lectures, even if they do not involve practical demonstration, benefit greatly by being pre-recorded since the lecturer can produce a much more polished presentation. The same tape can be played any

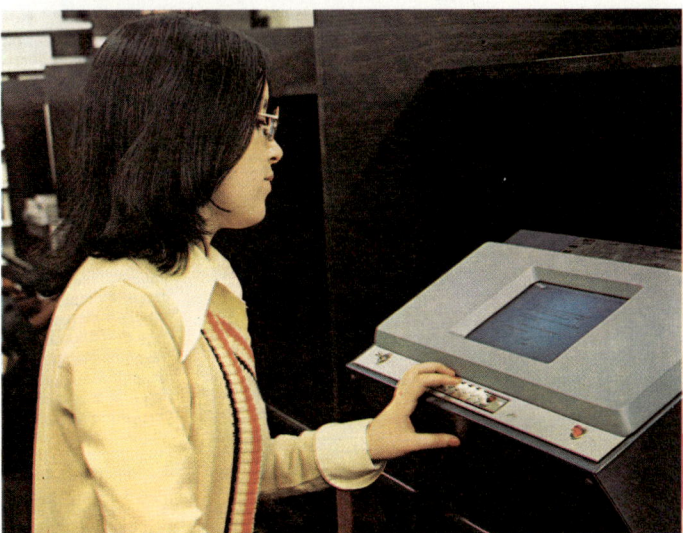

Top: part of a college audio-visual department. A range of videotapes prepared by the academic staff can be played back at any time, using machines as simple to operate as a home tape recorder. The student can stop on a single picture, or replay part of the tape at will. Centre: this teaching machine provides push-button question-and-answer monitoring. Bottom: video cassettes can store programmes for re-use.

number of times, so that the academic is freed from the tedium of delivering the same information to different classes.

Many countries now use over-the-air broadcasting for educational programmes, which are taken as part of school timetables. Apart from the obvious point that pupils might prefer to watch TV rather than listen to their teacher, this brings a wide range of visual resources into the classroom—language classes can effectively be presented from the foreign country, for example. In Britain, it is now possible to study for a university degree through programmes broadcast on the national radio and television networks.

A recent development, though one which is already becoming widespread, is the use of video cassettes. Using 0.5 or 0.75 inch (12.5 or 18 mm) tape in booksized cassettes, they can give up to an hour's playing time in black and white or colour. Recordings can be made almost as easily as with a sound-only tape recorder, and a player unit will replay the cassette over an ordinary television set. These cassettes have many applications in industry, particularly as sales aids and as a means of communication.

There is no doubt that communications technology will continue to expand in this field, not only in schools but in the growth of concepts like Britain's Open University and third world education by television.

Top: the language laboratory is now widely used in schools and adult classes. The students repeat phrases from a tape and the teacher can connect in to any student to check and correct pronunciation. Above: a development which allows a 35mm slide to be mounted with a thin rotating magnetic disc, thus combining each individual picture with up to 35 seconds of commentary, plus a slide change signal.

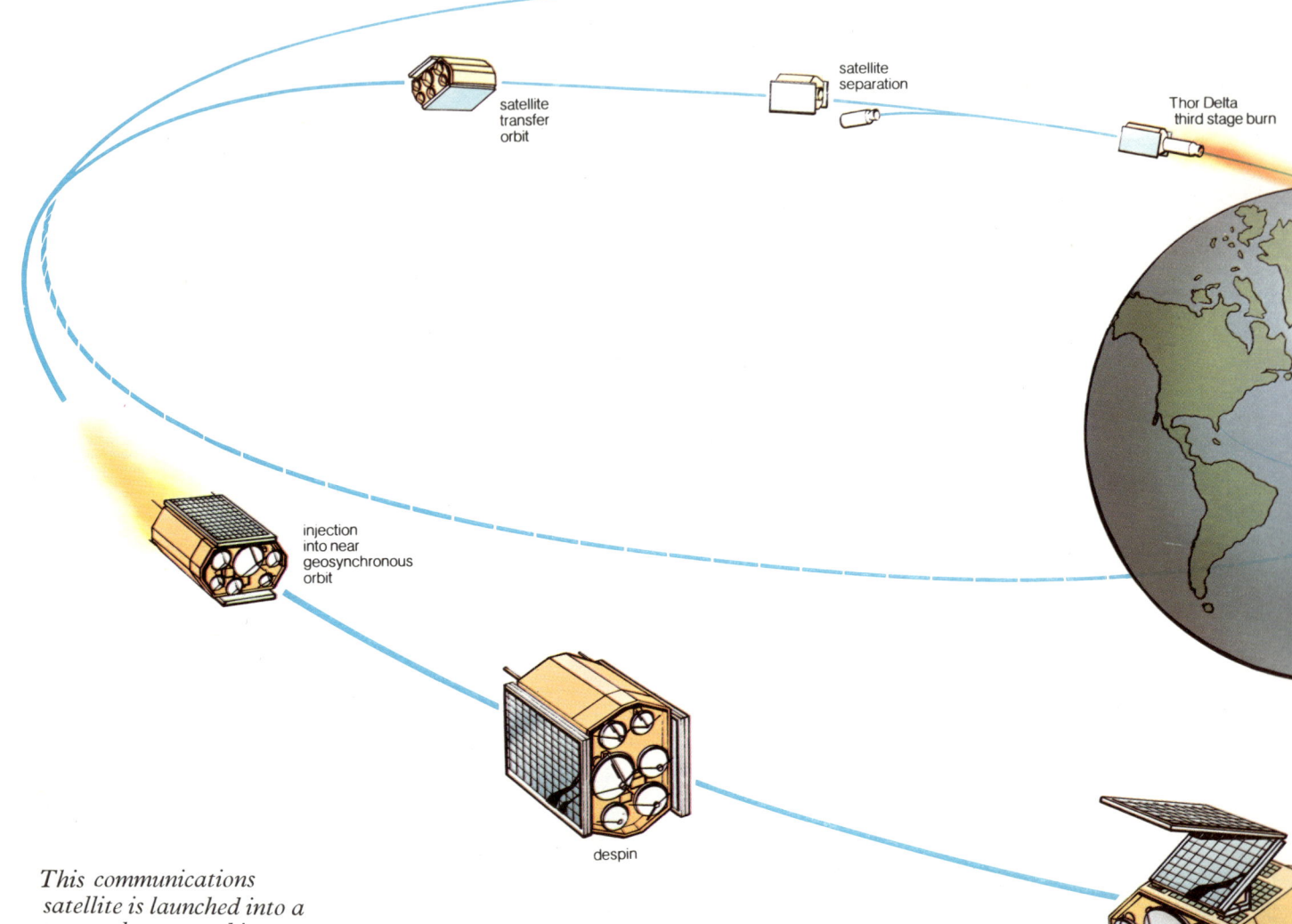

satellite
transfer
orbit

satellite
separation

Thor Delta
third stage burn

injection
into near
geosynchronous
orbit

despin

sun acquisition
& deploy arrays

This communications satellite is launched into a geosynchronous orbit at an altitude of 22,300 miles (35,880 km), at which it orbits at the same speed as the Earth's rotation to keep it above the same spot over the equator. It is launched by a three stage rocket, but uses a rocket motor of its own to acquire the correct station. Three axis stabilization allows it to keep its antenna dishes pointing accurately at the ground while the solar arrays turn once a day to follow the Sun.

NEW FRONTIERS

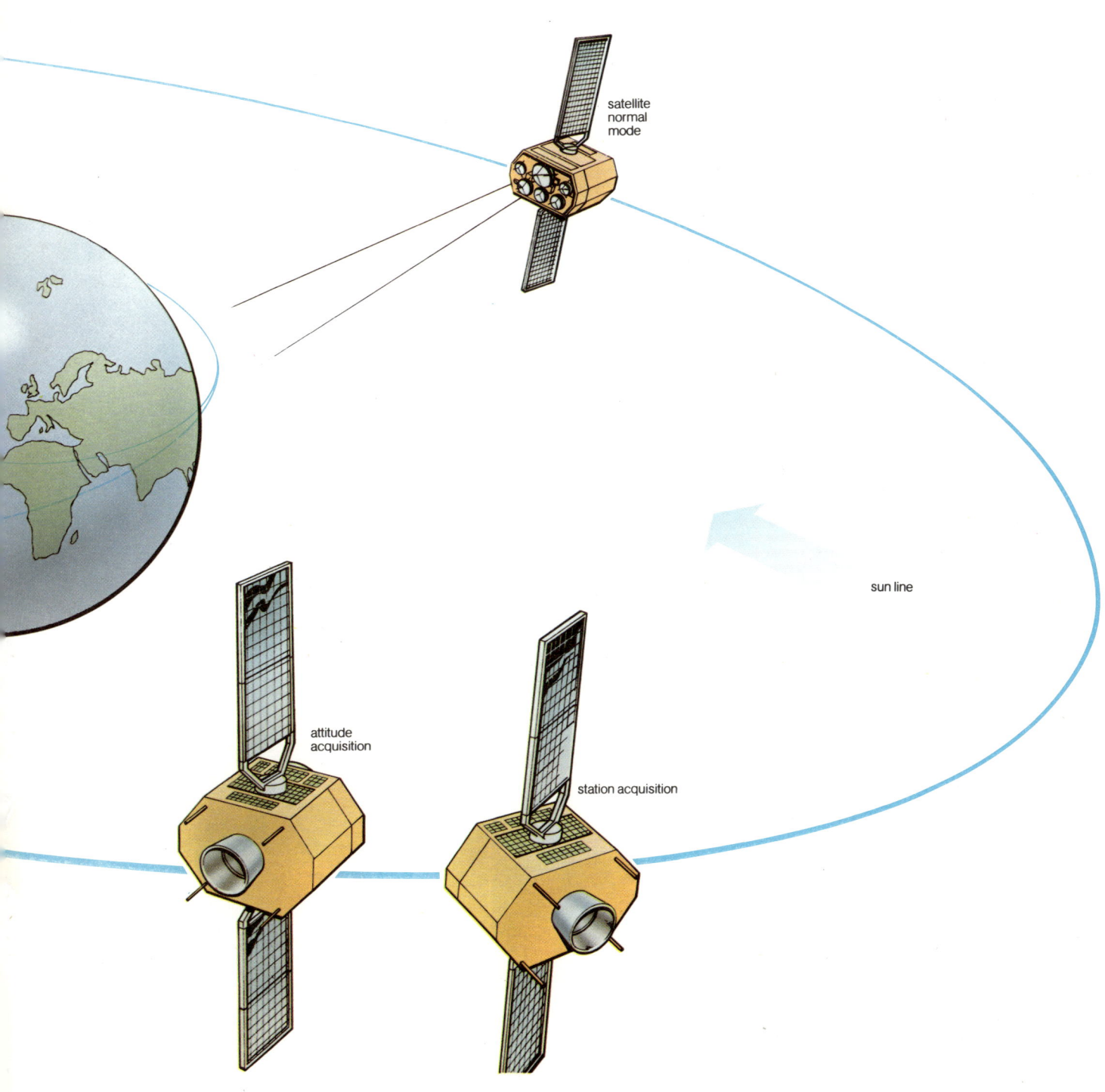

satellite
normal
mode

sun line

attitude
acquisition

station acquisition

PULSE CODE MODULATION

Pulse code modulation (PCM), which can be compared with amplitude modulation and frequency modulation, was invented in 1938. By the late 1960s engineers viewed it as the saviour of audio (sound) and video (picture) transmission, in a world suffering badly from a so-called communication explosion.

PCM is a prime example of a digital system. It involves the transmission of information not as a smoothly varying analogue signal (such as in amplitude modulation, or frequency modulation), but as a series of separate pulses, The amplitude, length, position and presence of a pulse form the code and this code represents the signal to be transmitted, such as speech or a picture. Relative to the more conventional types of modulation, PCM signals are particularly free from noise (that is, unwanted signals superimposed on the wanted signal), they suffer little interference and may be regenerated in repeater stations (which make up for 'fading') without distortion. Also, many separate signals may be passed through a given channel by the method of *multiplexing* (interleaving of the signals).

Analogue and digital systems

Any physical quantity may be measured, transmitted and displayed in either an analogue or a digital form. For example, clocks can be made to display time in either form: the analogue form is hands sweeping around the face with an (almost) continuous motion; in digital form, time can be represented as a series of numbers. This latter system is called a digital readout device.

In a similar way the familiar pointer-and-scale of such instruments as voltmeters and thermometers is rapidly being replaced by digital displays in many situations.

In electronic systems, valves [vacuum tubes] and transistors must faithfully amplify analogue signals, that is, they must follow the incoming signal exactly. With digital systems, however, these same devices need only behave as switches in an on-off fashion. For example, if a signal is present this turns the transistor 'on' and when no signal is present it is in the 'off' state. With the introduction of reliable transistors and integrated circuits, electronics engineers have found that digital systems are simpler and more reliable than their analogue counterparts.

The technique of PCM

An analogue signal (such as a voltage representing speech) can be changed into digital form with a pulse code *modulator*. To do this, the signal must be inspected or *sampled* at regular intervals and the amplitude of the signal at these sampling points transformed into a digital signal. This is usually a binary numerical form where the amplitude is represented as a series of 'on' or 'off', 'yes' or 'no', '0' or '1' states that can be easily handled by a switching transistor. The binary system is a different system for representing numbers. Whereas the decimal system has ten symbols (0 to 9) binary employs only two symbols (0 to 1) and it is for this reason that digital (switching) systems use binary.

The more frequently the samples are taken, the more

Below: PCM uses a binary code to represent the magnitude of the signal at regular intervals (samples). The table gives the 4 digit binary equivalents to numbers from 1 to 15.

number	binary code	number	binary code
0	0000	8	1000
1	0001	9	1001
2	0010	10	1010
3	0011	11	1011
4	0100	12	1100
5	0101	13	1101
6	0110	14	1110
7	0111	15	1111

table of 4 digit binary code

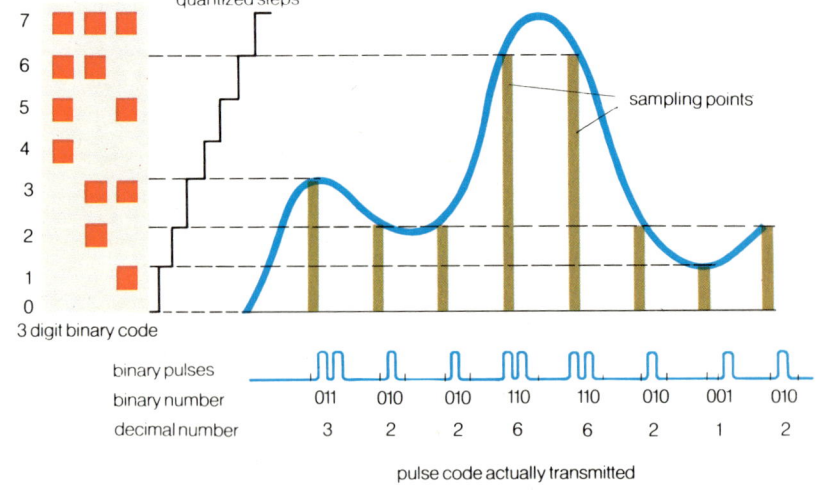

conversion of signal into 3 digit binary code

quantized steps

sampling points

3 digit binary code

binary pulses								
binary number	011	010	010	110	110	010	001	010
decimal number	3	2	2	6	6	2	1	2

pulse code actually transmitted

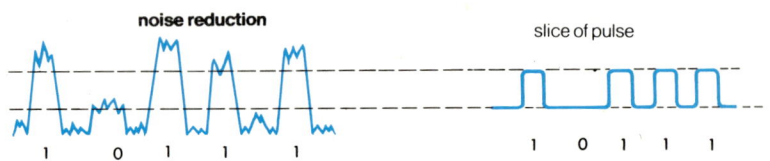

noise reduction

1   0   1   1   1

slice of pulse

1   0   1   1   1

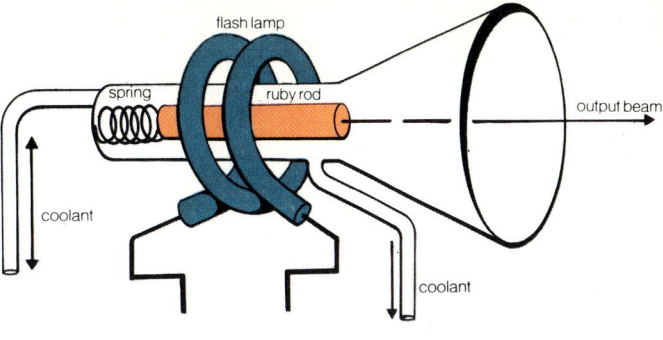

ingle wavelength nature, radiation from a laser resembles that from a radio transmitter. If the same techniques are evolved for impressing signals on laser beams s are used for radio waves (such as amplitude modulation) then lasers can be used for communication. The mount of information that can be carried by a wave of electromagnetic radiation increases as the frequency increases. The frequency of a laser beam is so much higher han radio frequencies that it is possible in principle to carry many million radio transmissions on a single laser beam. Also the greater directionality of a laser beam as compared with conventional radio transmission means that less power would be required to communicate between two stations.

The notion of all the world's broadcasting requirements being satisfied by using a single laser beam is an exciting one, but several problems remain to be solved before this becomes a practical reality. The most serious of these problems is the fact that laser light, like any other form of light, is stopped by fog and cloud. In outer space this obviously creates no problems but for terrestrial communications it will be necessary to send the beam along tubes or pipes to overcome the atmospheric difficulties. Use of glass fibres to carry the laser beam is envisaged but at present there is great difficulty in manufacturing glass fibres sufficiently perfect to enable them to be used over long distances.

Holography

Another technique which utilizes the coherence of laser sources is holography, by which means it is possible to produce images of objects and scenes in absolutely perfect three dimensional realism.

Holography was conceived and predicted in 1947 by the British scientist, Dennis Gabor, but the practical demonstration of the technique had to await the invention of the laser. Because a laser beam is highly ordered, that is, monochromatic and coherent, details of the depth of a scene illuminated by such a beam are contained in the phase relationships of the waves arriving at the holographic recording plate. A wave arriving from a more distant part of the scene will 'lag' behind waves from closer points and it is this information about lagging and leading waves which is recorded in a hologram.

To record this information a *reference beam* is required with which to compare the phase relationships of the *object team*. This is achieved by splitting the laser beam into two parts: one is directed at the scene from which the reflected (object) beam is derived and the other part is aimed directly at the recording plate (this is the reference beam). Where the object and reference beams meet at the plate they will interact or *interfere*. Interference is a phenomenon associated with coherent light.

When the crests of two waves coincide an enhancement of light intensity or amplitude occurs through the wave energies adding together. This process is called *constructive interference*. When the crest of one wave

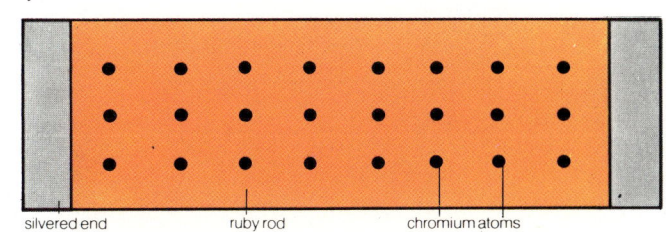

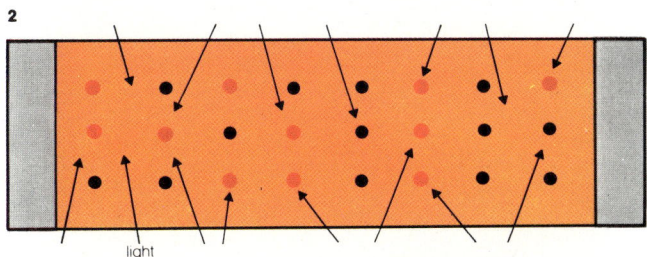

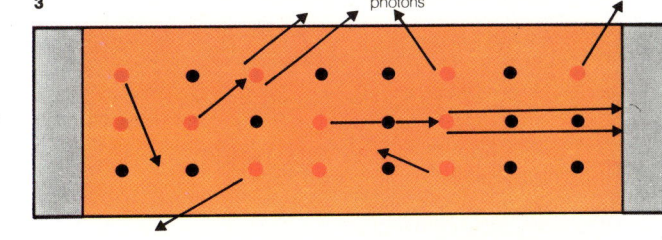

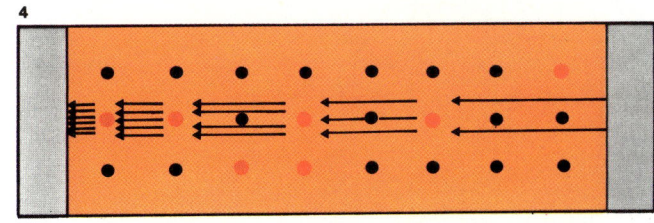

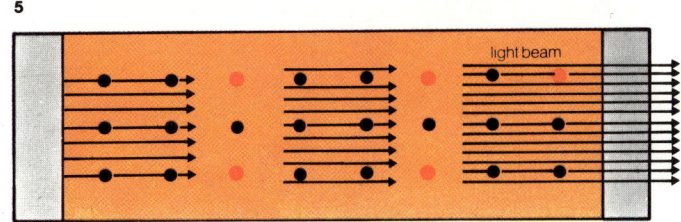

Top: ruby laser with helical flash lamp. Above: chromium atoms in the ground state (1) are excited by light from the flash tube (2); some of them emit photons which stimulate further photon release (3). These are reflected back and forth between the silvered ends as shown in (4) and (5), and finally emitted as a powerful beam.

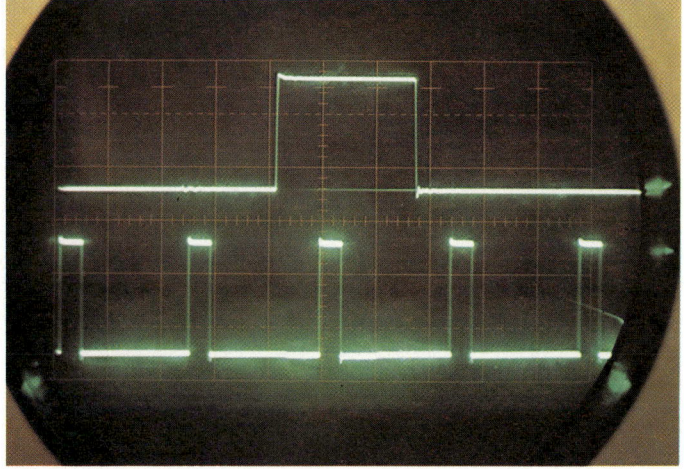

accurately the signal can be represented, but this ultimately depends on the fastest rates of change encountered in the signal. Telephone systems, for example, provide an essentially low quality communication with an upper frequency limit in the region of 4000 Hz. But to transmit even this low quality signal 'faithfully' requires a sampling of 8000 Hz (that is, 8000 samples per second—or twice the maximum frequency to be transmitted).

As each sample is converted into a binary form using an analogue-to-digital converter (digitizer) it is fed to a device called a shift register. From here, the binary code leaves as a series of pulses which can be readily transmitted to the receiver. In the receiver is a *demodulator* which consists of another shift register and a digital-to-analogue converter, which together perform the opposite operation to the pulse code modulator. The train of pulses enters the shift register from which the binary number can be extracted and converted into an equivalent voltage using the digital-to-analogue converter.

Apart from the sampling rate, the other important factor in determining the quality of a PCM signal is the number of *quantization levels* into which the signal amplitude can be classified. Quantizing turns the smooth waveform into steps—fewer steps means poorer quality. With telephone signals, 128 quantization levels are sufficient but for high fidelity more are required. With 128 quantization levels, a 7 bit binary code is re-

quired ($2^7=128$). The total number of levels used must cover the maximum range of possible signal values.

Time division multiplexing

Where several signals are to be transmitted along one channel, time division multiplexing (TDM) is used. As in the single case, each signal is converted into a binary form and fed to its own shift register. The shift registers are shifted in sequence so that sample one of signal one is followed by sample one of signal two and so on through to the last signal then back to sample two of signal one, and the cycle is repeated. At the beginning of each cycle a framing signal (indexing pulse) is transmitted so that the receiver equipment can be synchronized, thus allowing the various signals to be separated.

Repeaters

However a signal is transmitted there will be some loss of energy en route. This is true even of very efficient methods such as those using laser beams and microwave frequency waveguides. Because of its resistance, the conventional cable is particularly 'lossy'. Furthermore, random background hisses and crackles increase with distance.

Even with a noisy channel, however, a positive pulse can be readily detected. In the repeaters, required at distances of a kilometre or so in transmission cables, each detected pulse causes another to be produced at full strength, while background noise may even be reduced. Thus, the original signal is easily regenerated in the repeater and this can be done as often as necessary. Conventional (analogue) repeaters amplify everything that they receive including distortion and noise and so the quality is poor over long distances.

Applications

The use of PCM has been outlined in the case of audio transmissions. Here the advantages of low cost, low noise, low distortion and the technique of multiplexing make this system most valuable in comparison with other forms of cable or broadcast transmissions.

Research already indicates that future developments will be just as beneficial. In particular, communication by microwaves and light beams is possible—the much higher frequencies allow a far greater density of information to be carried. Microwave systems have been tested already that can carry hundreds of thousands of telephone conversions or hundreds of colour television programmes simultaneously in a wave-guide a few centimetres in diameter. And, although the technology has not yet been adequately developed, a laser beam could easily carry all the telecommunications traffic of the world.

In a very different context, the fact that PCM is insensitive to noise is of great value when communicating across the huge distances to space probes. Radio transmitters of only a few watts of power send back to Earth the high quality television pictures of planetary surfaces with which we are now so familiar. A form of PCM coding is used in these systems and in other forms of telemetry, (see page 90).

LASERS AND HOLOGRAPHY

Lasers and masers are devices for producing intensified electromagnetic radiation by a process involving energy states within the atoms of materials.

The word *maser* is derived from the initial letters of the phrase 'Microwave Amplification by the Stimulated Emission of Radiation', and it is the process of stimulated emission, first predicted theoretically by Albert Einstein in 1917, that accounts for certain unique characteristics of the radiation produced.

We have seen that gamma rays, visible light and radio waves are all forms of electromagnetic radiation differing only in respect of *wavelength*, which is the distance between successive maxima on the wave profile. Radio waves range from 10,000 metres to 1 metre wavelength and the range occupied by visible light and infra-red radiation is of the order 0.1 cm to 0.0001 cm. The range from 1 metre to 0.1 cm in the electromagnetic *spectrum* (wavelength range) is the microwave region.

The development of the maser in the late 1950s made possible for the first time the generation and amplification of single wavelength radiations in the microwave region and the range was extended in 1960 with the invention of the optical maser to produce single wavelength radiations in the visible region of the electromagnetic spectrum. The optical maser is generally referred to as a laser from the expression 'Light Amplification by the Stimulated Emission of Radiation'.

Applications of lasers

The remarkable properties of lasers—the high intensity and single wavelength nature of the emitted light—have already led to a large number of applications in a number of fields of activity, and many other applications are envisaged.

For example, an optical lens can be used to focus a laser beam on to a very small area, and this technique has been used in several industrial applications. Holes have been produced in very hard substances including steel and diamonds, and as such a tool the laser has the advantage that no physical contact with the material is required, very small holes may be produced without affecting the surrounding material and the process is very rapid. These advantages have also influenced the use of laser beams in welding operations.

In the field of medicine, lasers have been used successfully in the treatment of detached retinas and show promise of being useful in the treatment of cancer. The condition of detached retina occurs in the eye when the fluid within the eyeball seeps through a hole in the retina. The retina can eventually become detached from the back of the eyeball, causing blindness. Flaws in the retina have in the past been treated by surgery but can now be welded by a flash of light lasting for about a thousandth of a second. The light can be precisely aimed and it rarely requires more than a single pulse to attain action in the correct location.

However, it is in the field of communication that the laser has its most exciting potential. In its coherent,

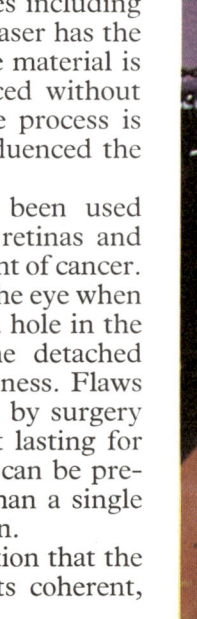

Right: a laser beam spreads out so little in thousands of miles of travel that it can be reflected off the Moon to measure accurately the distance from the Earth.

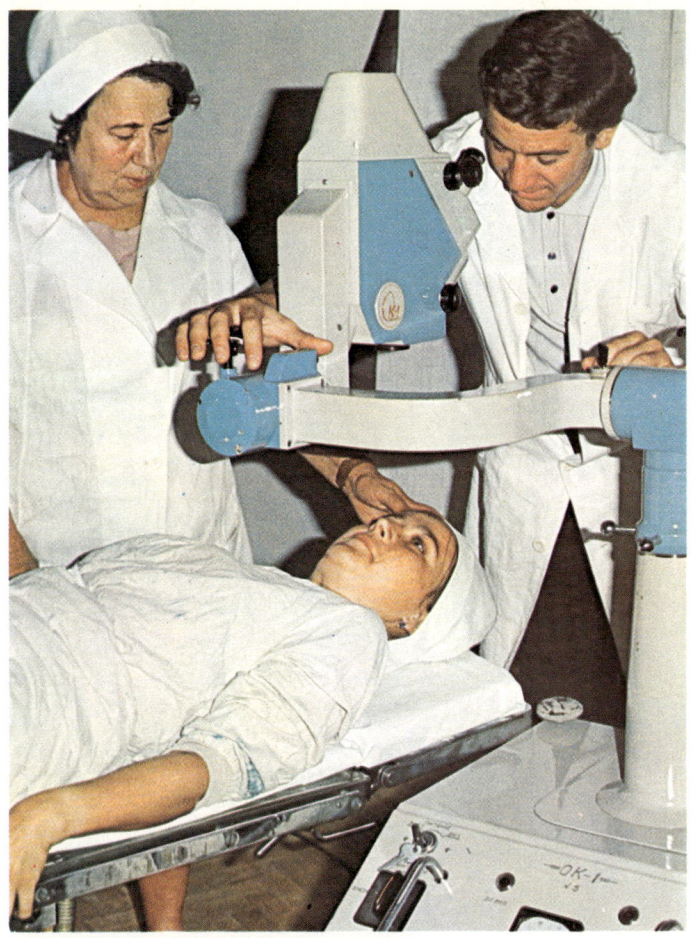

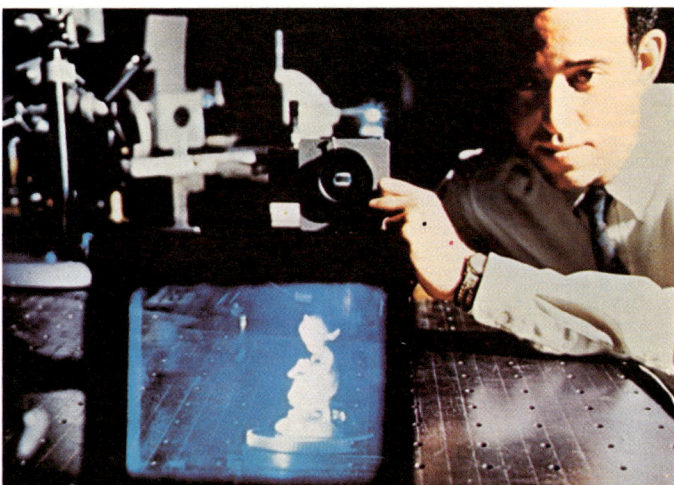

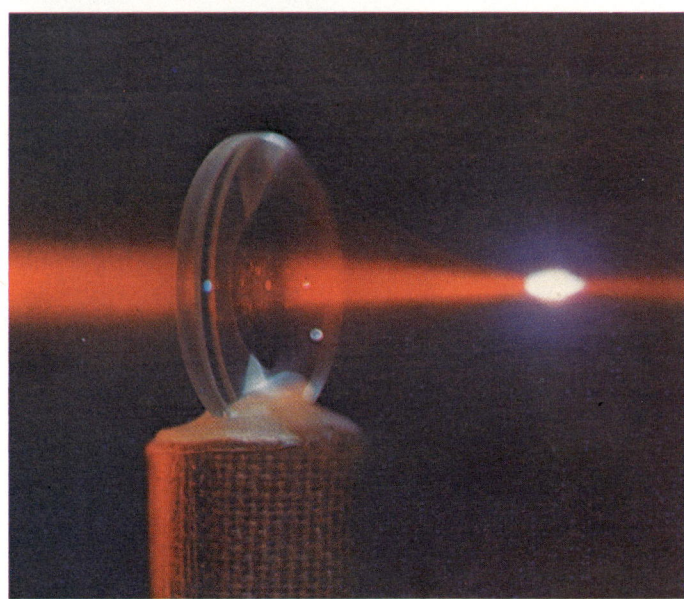

Above, top: laser beam apparatus in use at the Filatov Hospital, Odessa in the Ukraine. This is used for the treatment of detached retinas. Above: this laser beam is used in the motor industry for welding. The beam, focused through the lens, heats the air at the focal point. Above, right: the object that can be seen in the bluish screen is a truly three-dimensional image produced by the interaction of a blue laser beam with the hologram (the screen). The image appears to the observer to be situated behind the hologram, and the holographic plate itself looks like a simple glass screen. Holography may one day give us three-dimensional television.

coincides with a minimum position, or trough, of a second wave, a reduced intensity is obtained—*destructive interference*. Constructive interference occurs when the two waves arrive at a point *in phase* with each other. Destructive interference occurs when the waves arrive *out of phase*—that is, when one crest coincides with a trough—a phase difference of half a wavelength.

The resulting amplitudes at the holograph plate do not change with time, although the impinging waves are time varying. This means that *standing wave patterns* are established and it is these standing waves which are recorded on the light sensitive film or plate. Furthermore, this recorded pattern contains both amplitude and phase information about the object beams. A conventional photograph records only the amplitudes of the light arriving at the film.

The hologram

The developed holographic film, or hologram, looks nothing like the recorded scene. If the object being recorded is a simple flat reflecting surface, the resulting interference patterns show a series of light and dark bands, whereas the pattern produced by light reflected from a single point on an object consists of a series of concentric rings. A practical hologram of an object or scene is a highly complex pattern of superimposed circles from the many points on the object that reflect light.

Reconstructing the original scene

Normally the hologram is developed as a transparency, although there are other ways of recording a holographic scene. To construct an image of the original scene this transparency must be illuminated with a beam of coherent light similar to that used as the reference beam in recording. Viewed from the other side, a complete reconstruction of the original object is obtained.

In detail, the reconstructing laser beam is modulated (changed) in amplitude and phase as it passes through the hologram transparency in such a way that it resembles the original object beam. This produces a *virtual image* of the object which, to the observer,

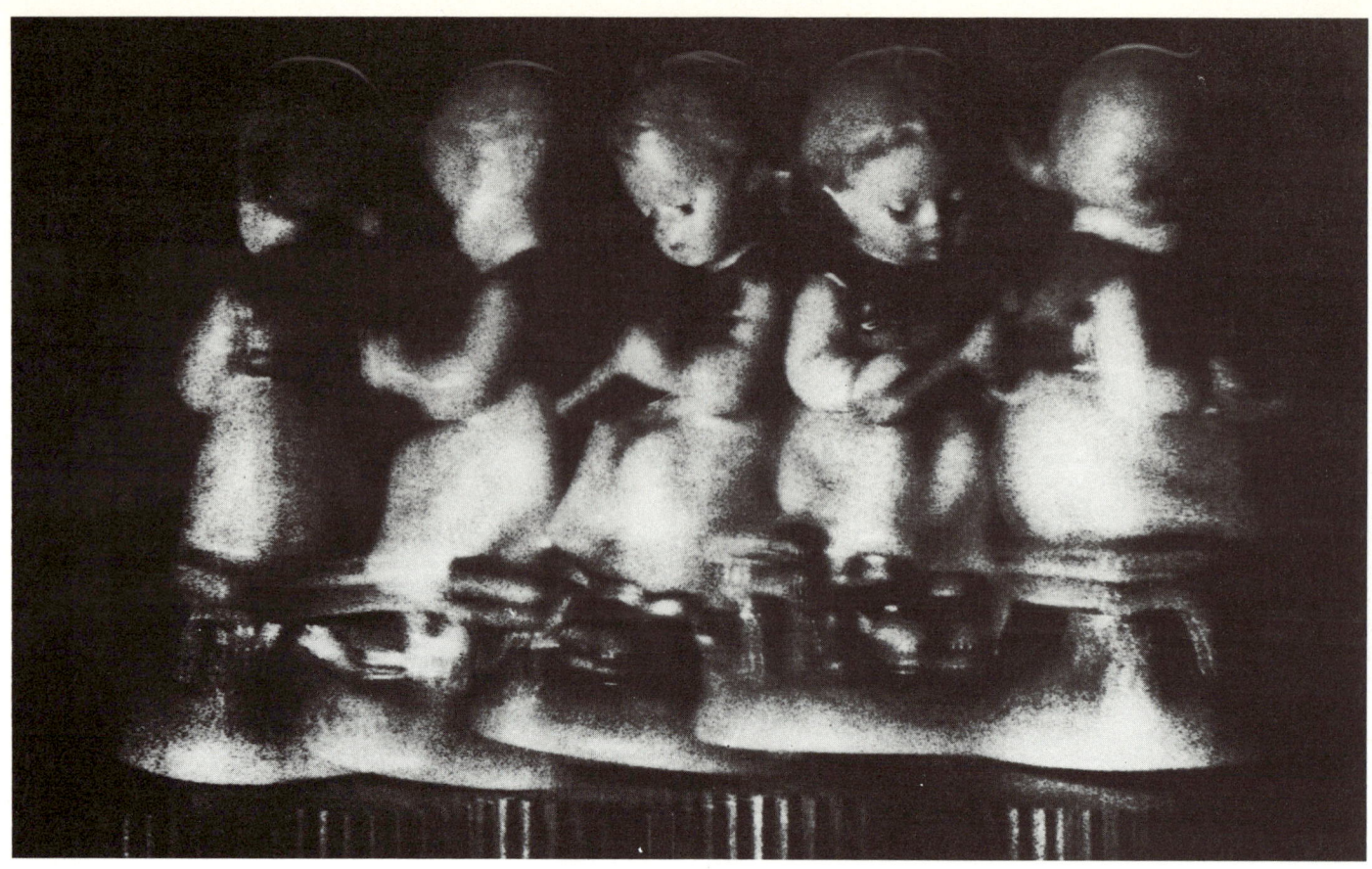

Above: Five superimposed views of the same image from one hologram. Holograms have the advantage that a large number can be stored on a single photographic place, and different images will be reconstructed according to the angle of laser beam illuminating the plate.

appears to be behind the hologram. It is this image which can be seen by the eye. There is also a *real image* formed on the same side as the observer. This cannot be seen as it is a *focused* image, but with a screen placed in the focal area the image can be viewed on the screen. Shifting the screen backwards and forwards will bring different parts of the real image into focus.

Since colour is dependent on frequency, any hologram produced using a single laser beam will give a monochrome (single colour) reconstruction of the object. It is possible, however, by choosing three laser beams giving different frequency beams (corresponding to the three primary colours—red, green and blue) to record and reconstruct a scene in full colour.

Applications of holography

Several properties of holograms render them of great importance for technological and engineering applications. One such feature is that many holograms may be stored in a single photographic plate. This is possible provided the direction of the reference beam relative to the plate is changed between exposures so that the superimposed interference patterns are not confused. In this way a large amount of information can be stored on a single plate and retrieved simply by illuminating at an appropriate angle, making it an important technique in data storage.

Holography is a relatively recent discovery and new applications are continually being developed. For instance, the technique has been applied to the problem of producing sharp images of objects travelling at very high velocities. More significant in the field of communications is the prospect of truly three dimensional images in the field of television and cinema. Interest in lasers is certainly widespread and many exciting new developments can be expected.

COMMUNICATIONS SATELLITES

Long-distance telecommunications depended until the 1960s on either cables or on the reflection of radio signals off ionized (electrically charged) layers in the atmosphere. Cables have only a limited number of lines available, and ionospheric reflections are subject to fading and are of rather poor quality.

As long ago as 1945 it was suggested that satellites above the Earth would offer many advantages in communications. A satellite is in view from a considerable part of the Earth at any one time—more so the higher it is—and therefore offers a distortion free path between many stations, instead of just two as in the case of a cable. The techniques of launching communication satellites are exactly the same as those used for other types. The satellite is first fired into a low circular orbit, then boosted into a higher elliptical orbit. At a carefully chosen moment, an *apogee motor* is fired to make the orbit circular.

Types of satellite

The first large communications satellite to be orbited was Echo 1, in 1960. This was a *passive* satellite—it had no electronics on board, but simply reflected signals. It, and Echo 2 launched in 1964, was a 100 ft (32 m) aluminium-coated Mylar balloon in an orbit 1000 miles (1610 km) above the Earth's surface. Just as a steel or glass ball gives a wide angle reflected view of the scene around, Echo reflected any signal beamed at it, but at greatly reduced power. Despite its simplicity, the power problem and the fact that space particles eventually punctured and distorted it made the passive satellite of limited value, and none are now used.

Active satellites, on the other hand, are 'booster' or repeater stations—they receive signals from ground stations, amplify them, and retransmit them to other ground stations. This system offers much greater efficiency, and only with satellites of this type is it possible to handle television broadcasts.

Orbits

Satellites are governed by Kepler's laws of planetary motion. Briefly the higher the satellite is, the slower it moves. A satellite like Echo 1 in a low circular orbit, 1075 miles (1271 km) above the Earth, will orbit in exactly two hours, and will move quite rapidly across the sky. This means that the antennas tracking the satellites have to move as well, and run the risk of losing it. At an altitude of 22,300 miles (36,000 km), however, the orbital period is 23 hours 56 minutes. If the satellite is above the equator, it will keep track exactly with the Earth's surface—the four minute discrepancy is due to the Earth's rotation around the Sun, which makes it fall four minutes behind every day with respect to the stars.

This *geostationary* or *synchronous* orbit is used by the majority of communication satellites, since it offers several operating advantages. The ground stations can point at almost the same spot in the sky continuously—there is usually a slight movement of the satellite—and the antennas on the spacecraft can be made highly directional. With an equatorial orbit, coverage between latitudes 60° north and south is possible, taking in most

Left: one of the Molniya 1 series of satellites which form the Soviet communications satellite system. The two antenna assemblies, one of which is shown here, are capable of independent movement so that they can be aligned with the Earth at all times.

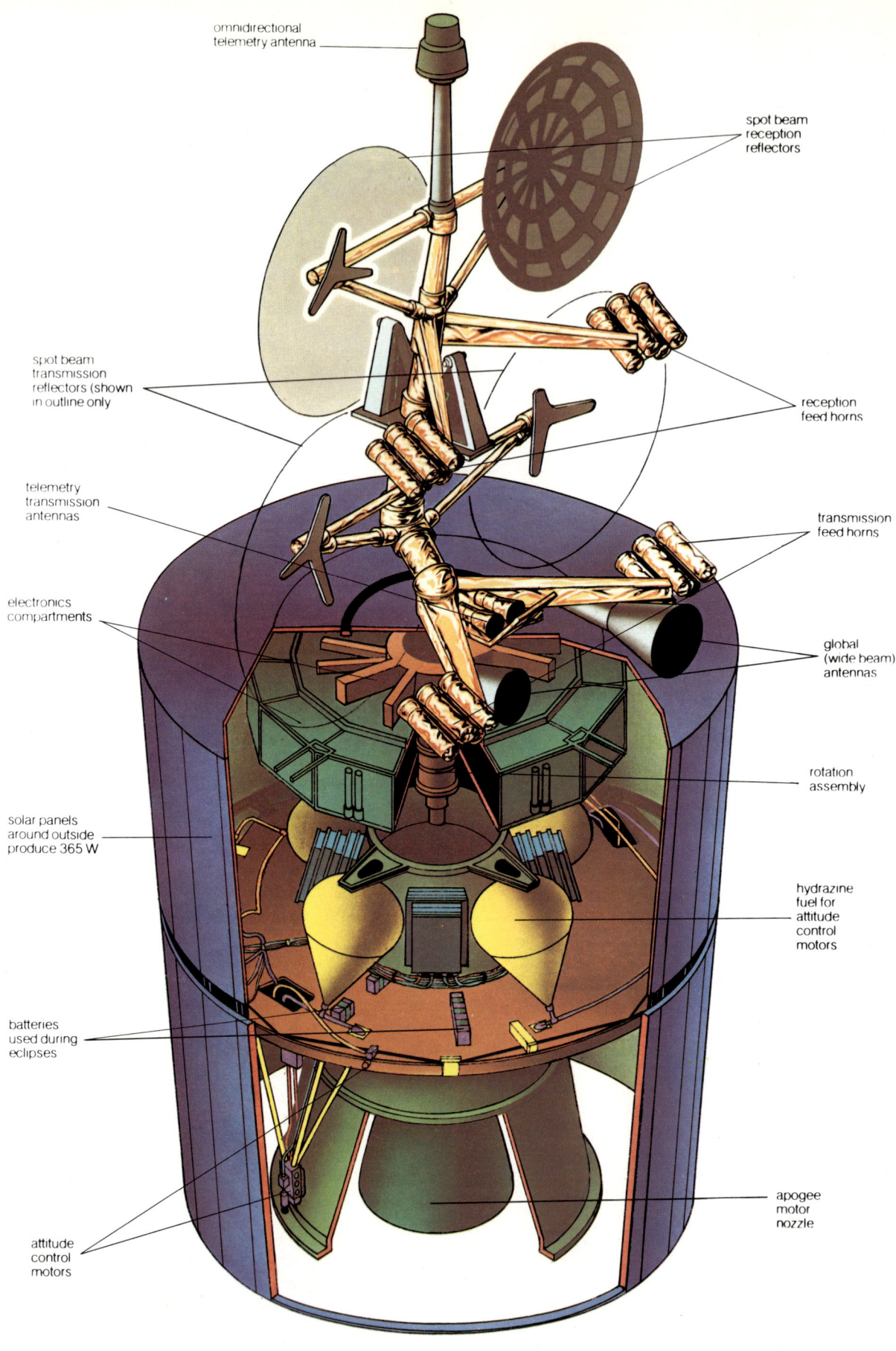

omnidirectional
telemetry antenna

spot beam
reception
reflectors

spot beam
transmission
reflectors (shown
in outline only)

reception
feed horns

telemetry
transmission
antennas

transmission
feed horns

electronics
compartments

global
(wide beam)
antennas

rotation
assembly

solar panels
around outside
produce 365 W

hydrazine
fuel for
attitude
control
motors

batteries
used during
eclipses

attitude
control
motors

apogee
motor
nozzle

of the inhabited parts of the world. A high orbit will take the spacecraft into the Earth's shadow less frequently than a low one, so the solar cells which provide power can be used almost continuously. Furthermore low orbits decay fairly rapidly—the drag caused by the Earth's thin upper atmosphere at heights below 1000 miles (1610 km) causes the satellite to lose orbital energy and eventually burn up.

Two drawbacks of synchronous orbits are that the signals have to travel further, so more power is needed, and the delay time in transmissions. Radio waves travel at 186,000 miles per second (300,000 km s), so there is a delay of about 120 milli-seconds on each journey between Earth and satellite. This gives a delay of 0.5 of a second between a remark and its reply, once thought to rule out telephone conversations via satellite but in practice scarcely noticeable. But a double hop, using two satellites—say between Britain and the Pacific—would introduce a delay of a second, which might be objectionable.

All currently operating commercial communications satellites are of the synchronous type. The Soviet Union, however, has its own Molniya ('Lightning') network, which uses satellites in highly elliptical orbits. These have their low points, or *perigees*, only 310 miles (500 km) above the Earth, though the high points, or *apogees*, are at 24,800 miles (40,000 km). This gives an orbital period of exactly 12 hours. Instead of being in an equatorial orbit, the orbit is inclined so that the apogee is above the Soviet Union. In this way, the satellite spends about 8 hours high over Siberia, impossible with a geostationary orbit, and then speeds rapidly through perigee over the South Pacific.

Satellite technology

So that the antennas of the satellite can be pointed accurately at the Earth, the craft must be stabilized in some way. One common way is by *spin stabilization*: the main body of the satellite is spun at about one revolution per second. Like a gyroscope, it will remain pointing in the same direction in space, chosen to be parallel to the Earth's axis. The communications gear and antennas are mounted on a platform at the top which is counter-rotated by a motor so as to remain stationary with respect to the Earth.

Another method, which is coming into use, is *three-axis stabilization*. In this system, the main body of the satellite, including the antennas and amplifiers, is maintained pointing towards the Earth with one axis of the craft parallel with the Earth's. This is usually done using gas control jets, supplied with enough fuel to last several years, the lifetime of a satellite. This gives much more accurate pointing capabilities, with no problems of keeping a platform continuously turning. The cells are mounted on large paddles, which have to be kept continuously pointing towards the Sun.

The interior of a satellite should be at a constant temperature because of the sensitive electronics and the requirements of moving parts. Specific heaters are provided where necessary, but passive control is often used—the outside of the craft is arranged to absorb a fraction of the Sun's heat, by virtue of its colouring.

Satellites normally have separate antennas for receiving and transmission. Transmission antennas may give global coverage—about a 20° beam—or they may have parabolic dishes to give spot beams of a few degrees, producing higher power coverage of a selected station. The antennas can usually be directed at a particular area on command from the ground.

The satellite has to amplify the incoming signal some ten thousand million times for rebroadcasting. Because of this incoming and broadcast frequencies are different, so there is no chance of them interfering. Microwaves are used: they are not affected by the ionized layers in the atmosphere, which reflect most other signals. In most satellites, the incoming frequency is about 6 GHz, and the rebroadcast frequency about 4 GHz. Other bands, at 7 and 8 GHz, and 11 and 14 GHz, are coming into use.

These high frequencies are somewhat beyond the capabilities of transistor or semiconductor circuits, so they are normally handled at an exact fraction of the frequency, then multiplied again for transmission. The transmitter used is usually a thermionic device called a *travelling wave tube*. Powers of between 10 and 20 watts are common.

This satellite is powered by solar energy, derived from photoelectric cells. A typical output is 350 watts DC. Batteries provide for when the Sun is eclipsed by the Earth.

Ground stations

The number of ground stations is increasing rapidly, with 90 in operation around the world by 1974. Most are of the 'dish' type, usually 98 feet (30 m) in diameter. Some, however, are of the 'horn' variety—these are less susceptible to external signals, but have to be protected by a 'radome' building.

The antennas beam the radio signal, acting like a radio telescope in reverse. The beam is usually less than a degree in size, so power is not wasted.

Most antennas are movable, but they may be almost completely fixed, with just a small degree of movement, for the sake of cheapness where just one satellite is to be used.

Since the transmitted and received signals are on quite different frequencies, the same antennas can be used simultaneously for both. The transmitted power can vary from less than a hundred watts, in small transmitters dealing with telephone calls only, to several kilowatts in the case of the largest stations handling colour television channels and several thousand telephone lines.

Uses

Although popularly associated with TV coverage of international events, communications satellites are otherwise fully occupied with telephone traffic and data transmission. Cables are still being laid across oceans to provide communications between main centres (see page 27), but satellites are linking cities and nations which would otherwise have had to wait years for a cable. This is particularly important in the case of small and developing nations—many African countries are now in full communication with the rest of the world, at the cost of a single ground station.

Satellites are now becoming increasingly useful for providing 'regional' services, handling continental rather than intercontinental traffic. Satellites providing separate coverage of the USA, Canada and Europe are planned, and cable companies in the USA who formerly objected to expenditure on satellites are now setting up their own, to avoid having to pay to use a rival company's lines.

Direct broadcasting from satellites to sky-pointing antennas on homes is being discussed, and would be particularly valuable in providing TV services to developing nations. The high power requirements on board such satellites have not yet been achieved, however, though experimental systems are being planned.

One of the three antennas at Goonhilly in Cornwall, near the spot from which Marconi made the first transatlantic radio broadcast.

THE RADIO TELESCOPE

Inevitably, the development of radio technology has not been limited to terrestrial communications. Should mankind one day establish contact with intelligent life elsewhere in the universe, it is more likely to be via radio astronomy than through our present limited programs of space exploration. Radio telescopes have meanwhile added a great deal to our knowledge of the galaxies, since the minute radiation received from stars can be used to plot 'radiation maps' of the universe. Astronomical objects produce not only the visible light that we usually associate with the stars and other celestial bodies, but also all the other wavelengths of electromagnetic radiation, from gamma rays to radio waves. Of these, only optical and radio waves can reach the Earth's surface, as longer waves than radio are reflected back into space by the ionosphere, an upper layer of the atmosphere, while the other wavelengths are absorbed by the lower layers of the Earth's atmosphere. At the ground there are therefore two wavelength 'windows' for astronomical observations, optical telescopes utilizing one, and radio telescopes the other.

Right: five of the eight 42 foot (13m) dishes which comprise the three mile (5km) interferometer at Cambridge. Below: how aperture synthesis effectively builds a large dish out of two smaller ones, utilizing the earth's rotation. The telescopes are shown as if viewed from the object they are observing over a period of twelve hours.

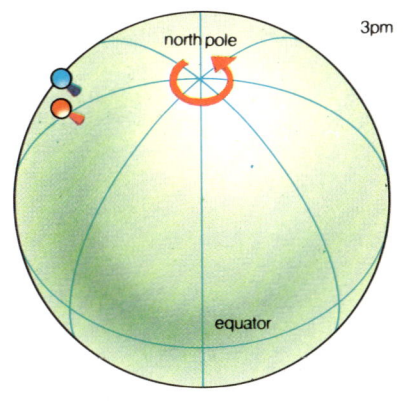

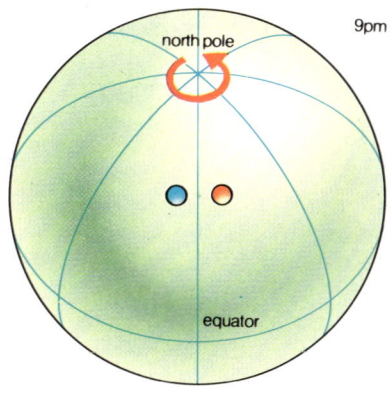

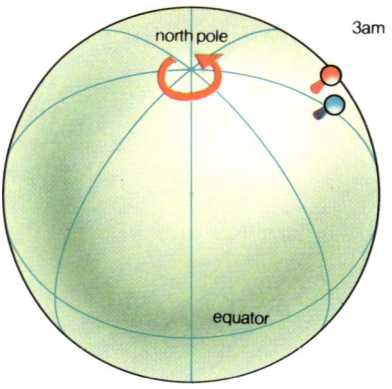

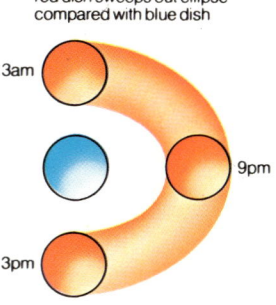

red dish sweeps out ellipse compared with blue dish

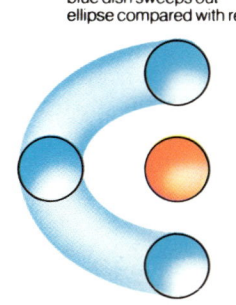

blue dish sweeps out ellipse compared with red

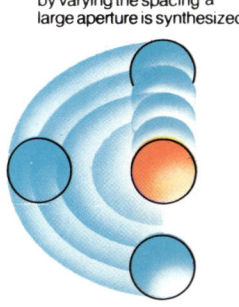

by varying the spacing a large aperture is synthesized

The energy received from space as radio waves is extremely small, the total amount collected by all radio telescopes since the beginning of radio astronomy being much less than the energy needed to light a flashlight bulb for a millionth of a second. To prevent interference from broadcasting stations, certain radio frequencies have been allocated by international agreement for the sole use of radio astronomy.

History

Extra-terrestrial radio waves were first discovered accidentally in 1932 when Karl Jansky in New Jersey was investigating the direction of arrival of radiation from thunderstorms. He found a source of interference ('static') which was at a fixed position relative to the stars, and so appeared to move as the Earth rotates. The source of radiation was near the constellation of Saggitarius, where the centre of our Galaxy (the Milky Way) lies, and further work by another American, Grote Reber, showed that the whole of the Milky Way emits radiation at wavelengths of a few metres. Reber published contour maps to display the intensity of radiation from different parts of the sky (similar to ordinary maps, but with peaks of intensity instead of mountains), and such maps are still used to present radio astronomy results.

When news of Reber's research reached Holland it inspired Hendrick van de Hulst to predict that neutral hydrogen, H I, (the hydrogen of interstellar space exists in two forms, H I, which is neutral, and H II, which is ionized) would emit radiation at just one particular wavelength (21.1 cm). If this 'H I line' is observed to be at a slightly different wavelength it means that the hydrogen cloud emitting the radiation is moving towards or away from the Earth. This is because the wavelength is changed by the doppler effect, the same effect which, when applied to sound waves, causes the pitch of a rapidly moving whistle to fall as it passes the listener. The change in wavelength gives directly the velocity of the hydrogen cloud, and so *H I spectrometry* is a very valuable branch of radio astronomy, quite distinct from the *continuum* (all frequency) type of radiation first investigated by Jansky and Reber. Both branches of radio astronomy, however, have advanced only through the continual improvement in the radio telescopes used as detectors.

Basically any radio telescope consists of three parts. First, the *antenna* (or aerial) which actually receives the radio waves and converts them into an electrical output; then an amplifier to increase the very weak signal from the antenna to a large enough power to drive the *output device* which displays the result or stores it on magnetic or paper tape for later analysis.

Antennae

The antenna of a radio telescope can take many forms, the simplest being just a large number of simple dipole aerials (like a television aerial) spread over an area of ground and wired together. The most familiar type, however is the 'big dish', where the radio waves are reflected to the focus of a concave metal bowl and are there detected by one simple dipole. The largest fully steerable dish in the world (100 m, 328 ft, in diameter) is at Effelsberg in West Germany, although there is a fixed dish of 300 m (1000 ft) diameter built in a depression in the ground at Arecibo (Puerto Rico) which only detects sources which pass nearly overhead.

There are two reasons for making an antenna with as large a collecting area as possible, the first being that a large antenna collects more of the power from the

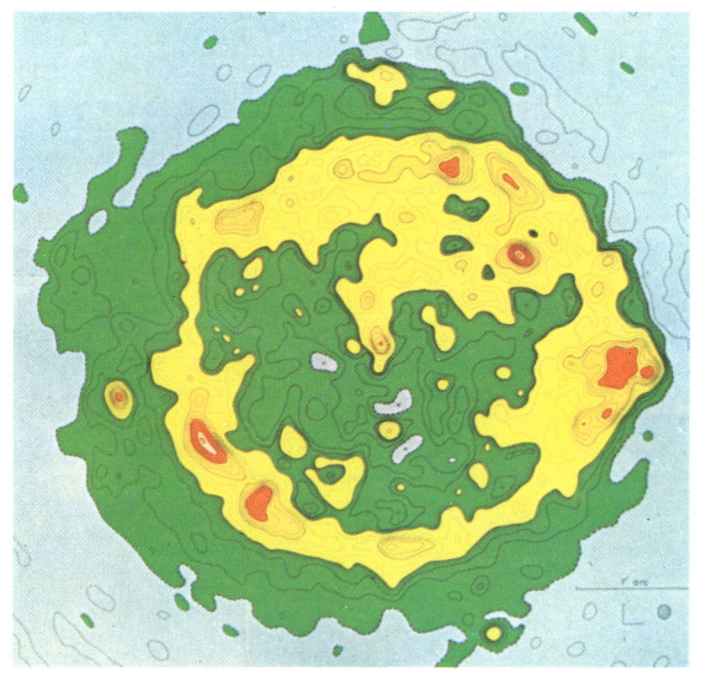

Far left: an aerial view of the 1000 ft (3000 m) Arecibo dish. The dish is constructed of wire mesh and serves as a reflector for radio waves longer than the size of the mesh. The antenna itself is in the cage suspended over the centre of the dish. It can be circled around so that the dish effectively points to different parts of the sky within a few degrees of the zenith. Above left: a contour map of the remains of an exploded star, with strongest emission coloured red. Above: a 'cuts map' of the same object. Left: giant radio telescopes like this use radio waves emanating from outer space just as optical telescopes use light waves.

source, and so is more sensitive. The second reason is that the *resolving power* (smallest detail that can be detected) of any kind of telescope depends on the wavelength of the radiation divided by the diameter of the telescope. Radio waves are so much longer than light waves that a radio telescope which could resolve as much detail as a large optical telescope would need to be several miles in diameter. Such a dish would be impossible to build in practice, but the effect of a large dish can be *synthesized* by combining electrically the outputs from a number of smaller aerials which cover an area equal to the size of the (fictional) large dish. The simplest arrangement of dishes for this purpose is on an east-west line, so that the rotation of the Earth causes the dishes effectively to rotate about each other in ellipses, as seen from a point outside the Earth. The

Above: the 328ft (100m) fully steerable Effelsberg dish, here shown pointing directly overhead.

largest Earth-rotation-synthesis instrument is the Five Kilometre telescope at Cambridge, which, when working at a wavelength of a few centimetres, can resolve as much detail as an optical telescope.

Amplifiers

Radio telescopes often work at the highest possible frequency (shortest wavelength) because this gives the best resolving power for a particular sized aerial, and the progress of radio astronomy has depended closely on the development of electronic amplifiers to work efficiently at these very high frequencies (up to several GHz—thousand million cycles per second). A number of specialized types of amplifier have been developed (some of which use a *maser*), and one of these is generally placed at the focus of the antenna so as to *pre-amplify* the very weak signal before it passes down a cable to the main amplifier which may be several hundred metres away. The pre-amplifier also converts the signal to a lower frequency, because this is less attenuated by the cable, and also so that it can be amplified by a conventional transistor amplifier at the other end.

Output devices

The output device may simply be a chart recorder in which the deflection of the pen shows the strength of radiation from different parts of the source as the telescope scans over it. An Earth-rotation-synthesis telescope, on the other hand, requires continuous observing for twelve hours before a map can be made of the source and so the signals must be recorded as they come in. At the end of twelve hours they are processed to produce a map which can be drawn by a contour map plotter.

In the case of a telescope which is observing the neutral hydrogen line at 21.1 cm, the output is split up into different frequencies by an electronic circuit known as a *spectrometer*, and the output at each frequency, corresponding to HI clouds at different velocities, can be displayed in either of the above ways. Alternatively for just one position in the sky, a graph of the radio power at different frequencies will distinguish between HI clouds which lie at different distances along the same line of sight, each having a slightly different velocity.

A more recent development in radio astronomy is very long baseline interferometry (VLBI), in which two radio telescopes on different continents, several thousand miles apart, observe the same source at the same time, the output from each being recorded. The two recordings are later combined electronically to give the *interference pattern* of the source, and from this some details of the source can be deduced down to a resolution a thousand times better than even that of an optical telescope. The distances between the telescopes can also be measured by this technique to an accuracy of less than a metre, and in a few years it will be possible to test whether the Earth's continents are drifting apart, and by exactly how much, simply by measuring the change in distance between two radio telescopes.

SPACE PROBES

Space probes are some of the most complicated robots devised, since they have to replace the abilities of man on long journeys through space to the Moon and planets and, on arriving at their destination, have to act as eyes and senses to detect what is there. An Earth satellite sends back measurements and sometimes photographs of the terrain below it, but a space probe must often carry out precise manoeuvres when at a vast distance from Earth. Probes have been sent to the Moon, Mars, Venus, Mercury, Jupiter and Saturn; they have orbited the Sun to investigate conditions in space on the far side of Earth's orbit, so keeping the whole Sun under surveillance; and they have given simultaneous measurements of space particles at several points widely distributed through the solar system.

Design

The design of any space probe depends basically upon its destination and what it has to do. Almost all space probes and satellites have a fairly elementary framework around which can be added the various experiments and systems, and all probes of a particular class, such as the Mariners which were sent to Mercury, Venus and Mars, have basic similarities.

Near the Sun there are few problems of power supply; panels of solar cells will provide adequate supplies of electricity for several years. In the case of probes intended for Mars and beyond, however, the solar intensity is much lower and power from solar panels is limited.

In the case of the Pioneer craft destined for Jupiter and Saturn, no solar panels at all were used, since the solar intensity near Saturn is almost one hundredth of that near the Earth. Instead, four thermonuclear generators, producing heat from the radioactive decay of plutonium-238 isotope, were used to provide 130 watts of power. This output deteriorates with time, and it seems likely that only about 80 watts will be available when Pioneer 11 encounters Saturn in 1979.

To protect the scientific instruments from radiation from these generators, the power units are located on booms pointing away from the instrument packages. Booms are often used on spacecraft where some particular instruments for collecting data, such as a magnetometer, may be affected by the others.

Another dominant feature of a space probe's design is the telemetry antennae. The transmitter power is usually very low, of the order of a few watts, so to make the best use of it the signals must be beamed back to Earth by a parabolic dish reflector, which gives a narrow beam. In the case of Pioneer 10 and 11, this dish dominates the whole craft, being nine feet (2.7 m) in diameter. A low-gain 'spike' antenna is also provided for transmission at a low rate if the main beam is not exactly aligned with Earth. Very large parabolic dishes on Earth, such as NASA's Deep Space Network of dishes up to 210 feet (64 m) diameter, are needed to detect the very weak signals.

In order that the craft can point its antennae and experiments in the chosen direction, it must be *stabilized* in some way. The two methods available for any space vehicle are *spin stabilization* and *three axis stabilization*. In the former, the craft is set spinning by a platform on the launch vehicle just before it is sent on its way into space. Like a gyroscope, it will tend to stay spinning in the same direction in space. Where rapid pictures are to be taken and where a number of experiments have to be pointed in different directions, this is unsuitable. For most space probes, therefore, three axis stabilization is used in which the craft is kept in a particular orientation by means of attitude correctors. This means that the orientation of the craft must be known, and for this Sun and star *sensors* are employed

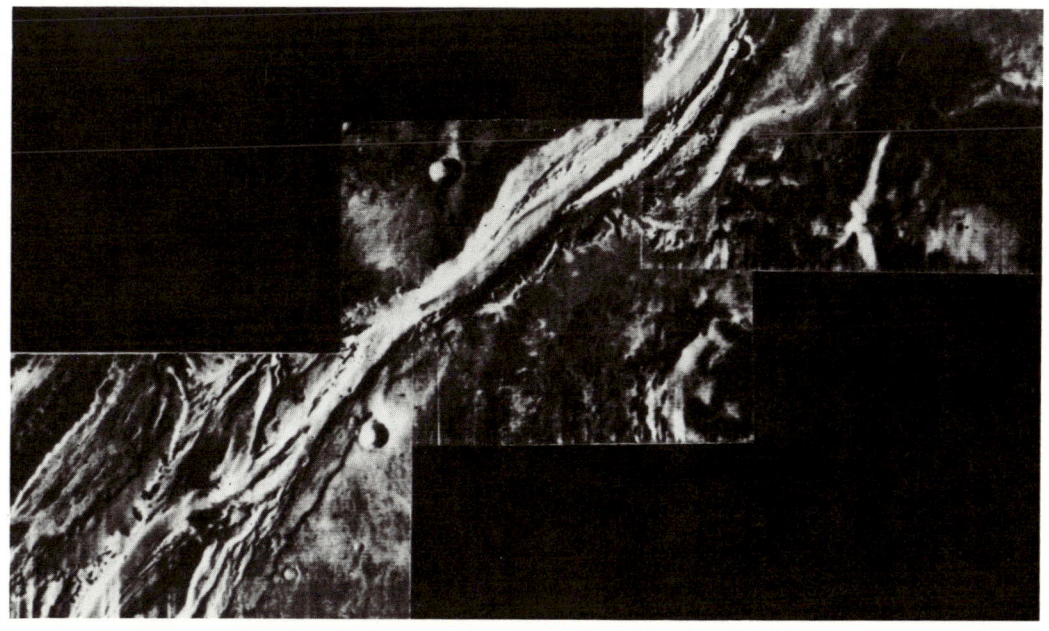

Left: Pictures of the surface of Mars taken by Mariner 9's 1972 orbital flight. Pictures such as this raised hopes that water once flowed, though landing probes have since provided no conclusive evidence of life.

*The Surveyor 3 soft-landed
on the moon in April 1967.
In November 1969 the
Apollo 12 astronauts
Charles Conrad and Alan
Bean brought their lander
Intrepid (in the background)
down within 200 meters of
Surveyor 3 and removed the
television camera.*

Below: Pioneer 6, launched in 1965, is one of a series of probes designed to measure field strengths and particles in interplanetary space, giving information about the activity of the Sun.

to detect the direction of their chosen object. The Sun is easy to find as the brightest object in the sky, and one star only is needed to fix the orientation of the craft. The star Canopus, the second brightest in the sky, is generally used because of its brightness and its large angle from the Sun.

Minor effects, such as the gravitational pulls of the planets, may disturb the attitude. In this case, the attitude is corrected by means of small gas (usually nitrogen) jets. Another method, with the advantage that it does not deplete gas supplies, is to arrange a set of *reaction wheels* inside the spacecraft. By spinning one of these, the probe can be made to turn in the opposite direction at a rather slow rate.

The Pioneer probes, unlike most others, are spin stabilized. These craft are designed for long lifetimes: Pioneer 6, which became operational in 1965, has given many years service, and Pioneer 11, launched in 1973, is intended to encounter Saturn in 1979. The gas used in three axis stabilization could be used up on lengthy missions.

As well as correcting the attitude of craft, their orbits or paths through space have to be corrected from time to time. A probe in space will follow an ellipse round the Sun as predicted by Kepler's Laws, unless its rocket is fired. This changes the orbit, and as soon as

the rocket stops, the probe will continue along a new orbit, slightly different. These course correction manoeuvres are carefully calculated when the orbit of the probe is known, and if carried out accurately only one correction will be needed per mission. The craft is commanded to fire its rocket for a precise length of time at a certain instant. In this way extreme precision of aiming can be carried out.

Landers

A number of space probes are designed not simply to travel past (*fly by*) a planet or to go into orbit around the planet, but have to land on the planet or on the Moon. Some of the earlier probes made little or no attempt to slow their velocity before striking the surface, and were known as *hard landers*. Some, such as the Ranger series, made no attempt to brake their progress and hit the Moon, taking television pictures as they went. Others, such as Luna 9 and Luna 13, had more of a 'rough landing' since their retro-rockets fired until they were very close to the lunar surface, then cut off leaving the device to drop. The instruments were protected by being inside a ball-shaped capsule which was ejected from the main craft before impact to bounce and roll across the surface, coming to rest some distance away from the rocket. Four petals then opened out after an interval in such a way that the probe was forced upright and the instruments were revealed.

An improved technique was used by the Surveyor craft, five of which landed on the Moon in 1966 and 1967. These were equipped with controlled *vernier rockets* to keep the spacecraft attitude correct while the main retro-rocket slowed the craft down. This was then ejected and the vernier rockets took the spacecraft down to a soft landing. An essential feature of this

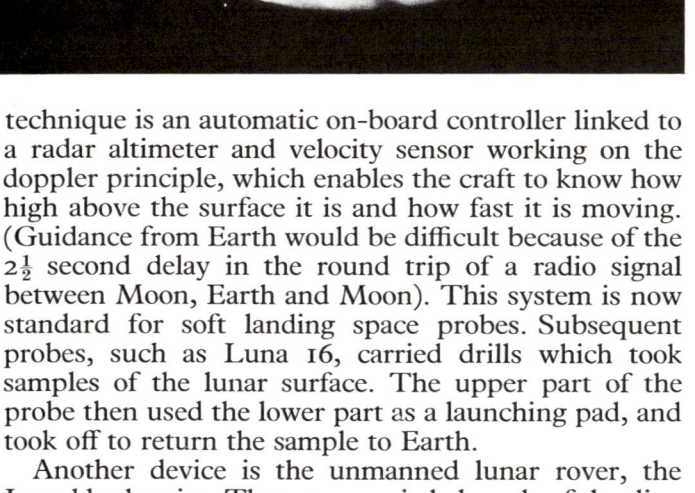

Left: both these pictures were taken by Mariner 10. Far left is Mercury, never previously seen as anything but a disc with vague shadings because its proximity to the sun makes it difficult to observe.

The atmospheric circulation zones of Venus, left, were photographed in ultraviolet light, since Venus is completely cloud covered. Below: Mariner 10 with its solar panels folded prior to launch.

technique is an automatic on-board controller linked to a radar altimeter and velocity sensor working on the doppler principle, which enables the craft to know how high above the surface it is and how fast it is moving. (Guidance from Earth would be difficult because of the $2\frac{1}{2}$ second delay in the round trip of a radio signal between Moon, Earth and Moon). This system is now standard for soft landing space probes. Subsequent probes, such as Luna 16, carried drills which took samples of the lunar surface. The upper part of the probe then used the lower part as a launching pad, and took off to return the sample to Earth.

Another device is the unmanned lunar rover, the Lunokhod series. These are carried aboard soft landing craft, and move about the Moon's surface under the control of a driver on Earth. The vehicles are equipped with such instruments as X-ray spectrometers for soil analysis, X-ray telescopes and television cameras which can show the driver where the rover is going and also return higher resolution pictures.

The Moon has no appreciable atmosphere, but the planets Mars and Venus have thin and thick atmospheres respectively. By using the atmospheres to slow down the craft, less fuel is needed for the descent. The Viking craft which landed on Mars in 1976, for example, descended on a parachute after preliminary rocket braking, and then carried out a powered landing using rockets with a large number of nozzles to spread the exhaust in an attempt to reduce soil erosion—of importance since the probe was designed to examine the Martian soil for possible traces of life.

The very thick atmosphere of Venus presents particular problems and no completely successful landing has so far been carried out. The atmospheric pressure at the surface of Venus is about 90 times that on Earth, the temperature is about 475°C (887°F) and there appear to be very strong convection currents. Succeeding craft have been made to withstand greater and greater pressures as previous craft failed before reaching the surface; Venera 7 apparently reached the surface after a very rough parachute ride, and transmitted very faint signals for some 23 minutes. No rocket braking was used, and the craft seems to have struck the surface rather hard in the grip of a thermal current.

Instruments

The point of sending space probes to the planets is to obtain details of conditions on the way and on arrival. The photographs sent back are the most spectacular results from probes, but scientific measurements of temperature, atmospheric pressure and composition, soil composition, magnetic field and particle densities are also made and sent back to Earth in the form of telemetry.

*Above: On 20 July 1969
Neil Armstrong stepped out
of the Apollo II lunar
module and became the first
man to set foot on the Moon.
It was a moment the whole
world watched. The
excitement of this historic
event was, for many people,
mingled with disappoint-
ment at the sight of that
barren and lifeless land-
scape. Yet intelligent life
elsewhere in the Universe
must exist—and one day
communications technology
will establish links beyond
our solar system, thus
turning another piece of
science fiction into reality.*

The cameras used for photography are not simple television cameras. The Moon probes Ranger and Surveyor had television cameras of special design, though neither returned the sort of continuous signals that normal broadcasting stations send out. Instead each picture took a short while to 'read' from the face of the camera tube. One reason for this is the *band-width* of the telemetry channel used: not enough information could be sent in the time needed.

The problems of insufficient bandwidth, coupled with the distance of the probe from Earth and low power supplies, have led to a variety of methods being used. The highest quality pictures ever sent back from space were from the Lunar Orbiter craft which orbited the Moon prior to the manned Apollo landings. True photographs were taken by a pair of cameras, and the film was then processed on board the spacecraft by bringing it into contact with a chemical-impregnated film. The pictures were then read out by a 'flying spot' of light, produced on the face of a cathode ray tube which allowed the area of the photograph to be scanned as with a TV tube. The varying amount of light passing through the various parts of the film was picked up by a photomultiplier tube and turned into an electrical signal for return to Earth. The resulting photographs, when reconstituted, were sharp enough to reveal the grain structure of the original emulsion, and almost the whole lunar surface was mapped this way to a high resolution.

The Mariner craft sent to Mars, Venus and Mercury were equipped with tape recorders to record the camera output for later transmission at a slow rate. Mariner 9, for example, sent back a total of 7329 pictures of Mars over a period of a year from orbit. Two cameras, effectively small astronomical telescopes, were used with a variety of filters to measure colour and polarization of the surface. In addition, an infra-red *radiometer* or detector was aimed in the same direction as the cameras to measure the surface temperature. Similarly, a *spectrometer* observed the infra-red absorption resulting from carbon dioxide, the main component of the thin Martian atmosphere. Areas where greatest carbon dioxide was observed and hence where the atmosphere was deepest, could therefore be linked with the photographs taken to decide the height of the surface at each particular point.

In the case of the spin-stabilized Pioneers 10 and 11, sent to Jupiter, the spinning of the spacecraft would have made normal photography difficult. Instead, an imaging device was set to view a mirror which slowly turned, reflecting the scene around the craft into the detector. As the probe spun on its axis, so a complete picture was built up in lines, like a TV picture. No cathode ray tubes or other television equipment were used, however. Each picture took between 25 and 110 minutes to build up, but in view of the great distance over which signals had to be sent, it would not have been possible to transmit pictures more rapidly anyway.

INDEX